Jane's

WARSHIP

RECOGNITION
GUIDE

Keith Faulkner

HarperCollins*Publishers*

Design: Rod Teasdale

HarperCollinsPublishers
PO Box, Glasgow G4 0NB

First published 1996

Reprint   5 7 9 10 8 6 4

© Jane's Information Group 1996

ISBN 0 00 4709810

Printed in Italy by Amadeus S.p.A.

Contents

Contents

Contents

Contents

Contents

Acknowledgements:

Many people are involved in the production of a book of this nature, and it is impossible to thank them all. However, I would like to give special thanks to the following.

Captain Richard Sharpe RN, whose kind advice and patience has been invaluable. Ian Sturton for the excellent line drawings. Lieutenant Pirie RN, Joint Services Photographic Interpretation. The Flag Institute of Chester. Kevin Borras, Jeff Pye, Anita Slade, Kevin Box, Nina Covell and Sulann Staniford for their hard work in the editorial and production process; and finally, Ian Drury for his help in the production of this second edition.

FOREWORD

Warship identification has progressed a long way since Admiral Nelson put his telescope to his blind eye and said "I see no ships". As well as the traditional visual recognition, we now have thermal imagery, acoustic signatures, electronic emission analysis, magnetic anomalies and even wake detection devices.

In spite of this march of technology, the classification criteria which must be met before a weapon can be released at an intended target remain difficult to achieve. The sequence of detection, classification, localisation and attack (or surveillance) demands an unambiguous recognition of the target at some stage during this process. The trouble with technological solutions is that they are seldom absolutely reliable and are vulnerable to deception and jamming. Often there is no absolute certainty that you have the right target, or even any target at all. Usually only accurate visual recognition can resolve the problem.

Examples of false target analysis are particularly prevalent in anti-submarine warfare, precisely because visual recognition is rarely possible. The result is weapon or decoy expenditure on false alarms, with expensive torpedoes chasing banks of krill or exploding harmlessley against prominent objects on the bottom.

Surface ship classification by non-visual means ought to be easier, and sometimes is, if the target is in calm, deep, open waters, transmitting on identifiable electronic equipment and well away from other activities. Much more likely is that weather conditions are foul, transmission policies have been planned to generate deception and the whole area is alive with merchant and fishing vessels navigating around complex archipelagoes.

Another problem is that many modern anti-ship weapons have ranges far in excess of the firing platform's ability to make its own classification, so some form of third party targeting may be needed to take advantage of these extended ranges. This brings in all the uncertainties of data transfer which always looks easy in the manufacturer's brochures, but requires skilled management and equipment reliability if mistakes are to be avoided. Whether you fire as a result of your own sensor information or on data provided by others, it is always a great comfort to know the classification has at some stage involved visual recognition.

So, in most cases, certain target identification by sighting is just as important as it always has been, not only to avoid needless waste of costly and limited ammunition, but also to prevent the 'friendly fire' incidents in which allies hit each other or harmless civilians going about their lawful business.

Ship recognition may look easy to the desk-bound warrior. In the fog of war it remains one of the most difficult and decisive ingredients of the successful prosecution of a target.

Richard Sharpe – 1996

INTRODUCTION

Jane's Fighting Ships Recognition Guide has been produced primarily to be a tool to help the reader identify any of the ships featured, to provide information on the physical characteristics of the ships and the main weapons and systems and to indicate which helicopters and fixed-wing aircraft are carried. The book has been designed to appeal to a wide range of users, for example the professionals such as naval, airborne and coastguard personnel; the knowledgeable enthusiasts, whether service or civilian; and finally those who have a genuine interest in warships and want to be able to identify the different types and classes and to further their knowledge of the weapons fits and capabilities.

The most important feature of recognition is the visual impact of, for example, hulls, masts, radar aerials, funnels and major gun and missile mountings. To assist the reader with the task of identifying a particular ship three different types of visual aid have been included. Firstly, each entry has a photograph occupying the right-hand page which has been selected for its clarity and the detail it shows. Secondly, each entry has a detailed line diagram on the left hand page which when used in conjunction with the photograph will help to identify the position of all major weapons systems and give an impression of the overall outline of the ship. Thirdly, at the top of every page is a silhouette which can be used in the traditional way to help with horizon or sun-backed views.

Composite diagrams of a theoretical warship and submarine are to be found at the front of the book which are designed to assist the less experienced reader to identify the relevant parts of ships and to become familiar with the terminology used in the text.

To enable the reader to identify the country of operation of a particular ship the Flags and Ensigns of nations are included, in full colour at the front of the book.

Despite the sophistication of modern electronic sensors the subject of visual ship recognition remains as important now as it has ever been and is still taught to members of armed forces in most countries around the world. This book is intended to be a lead-in to the subject of recognition for the student and is not a comprehensive volume of ship types with full data on equipments and systems. Jane's publishes a series of yearbooks and binders covering ships and their associated equipments in great detail. Examples of these are *Jane's*

Fighting Ships, Jane's Naval Weapon Systems, Jane's Underwater Warfare Systems, Jane's Radar and EW Systems and *Jane's C4I Systems*. In addition to these titles *Jane's High-Speed Marine Craft* covers civilian applications of high-speed craft.

Three hundred warship classesa of the world are represented in the book. Ships classes have been selected for reasons ranging from those ships which may be the most numerous, the most heavily armed, the most tactically important or which are most likely to be seen away from their country's territorial waters. All of these rules do not necessarily apply in all cases, for example many smaller patrol craft and mine warfare vessels are rarely seen away from home shores.

The book has been structured to make its use as easy as possible. There are nine sections which cover the nine major types of warships, namely - *Aircraft Carriers, Cruisers, Destroyers, Frigates, Corvettes, Patrol Forces, Amphibious Forces, Mine Warfare Forces* and *Submarines*. The book is ordered with the larger surface warships, *Aircraft Carriers*, down to *Patrol Forces* in descending displacement. The exceptions to this are *Amphibious Forces, Mine Warfare Forces* and *Submarines* which can be found towards the back of the book. There is no significance of a ships' strategic or tactical importance by its position in the book. Each section is presented in alphabetical order of country, and where more than one ship class is operated by a country, the class names run alphabetically. The exception to this is *Submarines* which are presented in alphabetical country order and within each country appear in type order SS, SSN, SSBN etc and then follow alphabetically by class name.

Where applicable and available, information is included under the following headings which conform to the format used in *Jane's Fighting Ships*.

Country - (where the ship is operated, not necessarily where built).

Ship type - (submarine, destroyer, corvette etc).

Class - (class name used by that country).

Numbers active, building or ordered - (numbers in a class either in active service, in the process of being built or that have had a firm order placed). There are a few instances where the term 'proposed' is used which indicates that an interest in purchase has been shown, but no firm order placed.

Name (Pennant Number) - (names and pennant numbers within a class).

Recognition Features - (this section includes features which have significance for recognition, therefore not all equipments will be mentioned; in the majority of classes the features are taken in order from the forward end of the ship working aft).

Displacement - (full load displacement of the ship, in tons).

Length - (overall maximum length of the ship in feet and metres).

Beam - (overall maximum width of the ship in feet and metres).

Draught - (depth of ship from waterline to keel unless otherwise indicated).

Flight deck length - (overall maximum length of flight deck in feet and metres).

Flight deck width - (overall maximum width of flight deck in feet and metres).

Speed - (ship's maximum speed in knots).

Range - (ship's range in miles, usually indicating economical cruising speed in knots).

Missiles - (surface-to-air and surface-to-surface missiles, indicating numbers and types of launchers where possible).

Guns - (numbers, calibres, types and manufacturers of fitted guns).

Mines - (numbers and types carried).

A/S mortars - (numbers and types fitted).

Decoys - (numbers, manufacturers and types fitted).

Radars - (types of radars fitted: air search, navigation etc; numbers fitted, manufacturer and model of types).

Sonars - (numbers fitted and types).

Fixed wing aircraft - (numbers and types carried).

Helicopters - (numbers and types carried).

General Notes:

a. In the **Name (Pennant Number)** section the names and pennant numbers of the relevant ships will only be included where applicable. Some countries do not use pennant numbers, or change them so frequently that the information would soon be of little value, and indeed could be misleading.

b. In the **Recognition Features** section the term **mounting** on its own always refers to a **gun mounting**, for example **5 in mounting (A position)**. If the weapons mounting in question is a **missile or A/S mounting** sited in A, B, X or Y **gun mounting** positions, an example of the term used would be **SAM launcher (A mounting position)**.

c. In the **Recognition Features** section the terms SAM, SSM etc, are generally used, but if a ship has **more than one SAM or SSM** then the specific system is named.

d. There are some cases where the same ships fall into the **Patrol Forces** category with one country and are designated as **Corvettes** by another country and vice versa. This can also apply in some instances to **Frigates** and **Corvettes**. To avoid confusion this has been pointed out in the text.

e. There are a few instances where a line diagram may not display exactly the same weapons fit as the photograph. This is where there are different versions of that class within a navy.

GLOSSARY

AAW	Anti-air warfare
ACDS	Advanced combat direction system
ACV	Air cushion vehicle
AEW	Airborne early warning
ANV	Advanced naval vehicle
ARM	Anti-radiation vehicle
A/S, ASW	Anti-submarine (warfare)
ASM	Air-to-surface missile
ASROC/SUBROC	Rocket-assisted torpedo, part of whose range is in the air
BPDMS	Base point defence missile system
Cal	Calibre - the diameter of a gun barrel; also used for measuring the length of the barrel
CIWS	Close-in-weapons system
cp	Controllable pitch propellers
DP	Depth charge
DCT	Depth charge thrower
Displacement	The weight of water displaced by a ship's hull when floating
DSRV	Deep submergence recovery vehicle
ECM	Electronic countermeasures
ECCM	Electronic counter-countermeasures
EHF	Extremely high frequency
ELF	Extremely low frequency
ELINT	Electronic intelligence
ESM	Electronic support measures
EW	Electronic warfare
FAC	Fast attack craft
FLIR	Forward looking infra-red radar
FRAM	Fleet rehabilitation and modernisation programme
GFCS	Gun fire control system
GMLS	Guided missile launch system
GPS	Geographical positioning system
GWS	Guided weapons system
HF	High frequency
IFF	Identification friend/foe
LAMPS	Light airborne multi-purpose system
LF	Low frequency
LMCR	Liquid metal cooled reactor
LRMP	Long-range maritime patrol
MAD	Magnetic anomaly detector
MCMV	Mine countermeasures vessel
MDF	Maritime defence force
MF	Medium frequency
MFCS	Missile fire control system
MG	Machine gun
MIRV	Multiple, independently targetable re-entry vehicle
MRV	Multiple re-entry vehicle
MSA	Maritime Safety Agency
MSC	US Military Sealift Command
MSC	Coastal minesweeper
MSH	Minehunter
MW	Megawatt
NBC	Nuclear, biological and chemical warfare
nm	Nautical miles
NTDS	Naval tactical direction system
NTU	New threat upgrade
oa	Overall length
PDMS	Point defence missile system
PWR	Pressurised water reactor
RAM	Radar absorbent material
RAS	Replenishment at sea
RBU	Anti-submarine rocket launcher
Ro-ro	Roll-on/roll-off
ROV	Remote operated vehicle
SAM	Surface-to-air missile
SAR	Search and rescue
SATCOM	Satellite communications

SES	Surface effect ships	**TACAN**	Tactical air navigation system
SHF	Super high frequency	**TACTASS**	Tactical Towed Acoustic Sensor System
SINS	Ship's inertial navigation system	**TAS**	Target Acquisition System
SLBM	Submarine-launched ballistic missile	**TASS**	Towed Array Surveillance System
SLCM	Ship-launched cruise missile	**UHF**	Ultra-high frequency
SLEP	Service Life Extension Programme	**VDS**	Variable depth sonar
SRBOC	Super rapid blooming offboard chaff	**Vertrep**	Vertical replenishment
SSDE	Submerged signal and decoy ejector	**VLF**	Very low frequency
SSM	Surface-to-surface missile	**VLS**	Vertical launch system
STIR	Surveillance Target Indicator Radar	**VSTOL**	Vertical or short take-off/landing
SURTASS	Surface Towed Array Surveillance System	**VTOL**	Vertical take-off/landing
SUWN-1	Surface-to-underwater missile launcher	**WIG**	Wing-in-ground effect
SWATH	Small waterplane area twin hull	**wl**	Water line

NATO STANAG DESIGNATORS FOR SHIPS IN THIS PUBLICATION

DESIGNATOR	REPORTING TITLE	DESCRIPTION
AA	Auxiliary type ship, general	General designator for all naval auxiliary type ships
AH	Hospital ship	Ship 40 m or more providing hospital services
AP	Personnel transport	Ship of 120 m or over to transport troops and their supplies
CA	Cruiser, gun	A cruiser with 6 in guns or larger as main armament and carries no missiles
CC	Cruiser, general	Cruisers of 150 m and over
CG	Cruiser, guided missile	Cruiser having guided missiles as main armament
CGN	Cruiser, guided missile, nuclear	As CG but with nuclear propulsion
CV	Aircraft carrier	Designator for aircraft carriers and multi-role aircraft carriers
CVG	Aircraft carrier, guided missile	Aircraft carrier fitted with surface-to-air guided missiles
CVH	Aircraft carrier, VSTOL/helicopter	Carrier not fitted with arrest gear/catapult, operating VSTOL and/or helicopters which is not an amphibious or minewarfare vessel
CVN	Aircraft carrier, nuclear	As CV but with nuclear propulsion
CVS	Aircraft carrier, ASW	Carrier capable of operating VSTOL and/or helicopters in sustained ASW operations
DD	Destroyer, general	General designator for destroyer type ships in range of circa 95 to 140 m.
DDG	Destroyer, guided missile	Destroyer fitted with surface-to-air guided missiles
FF	Frigate/corvette general	General designator for frigate. Ship of 75 to 150 m. Generally lighter surface armament than DD
FFG	Frigate, guided missile	Frigate fitted with surface-to-air guided missiles
FFH	Frigate, helicopter	Frigate carrying helicopters
FFT	Frigate	Frigate which can be used as a training platform
FS	Corvette	Small escort of 60 to 100 m
LCC	Amphibious command ship	Command ship for amphibious taskforce and landing assault operations
LCM	Landing craft, mechanised	Landing craft of 15 to 25 m capable of carrying one tank or 50-200 troops. Must have landing ramp
LCP	Landing craft, personnel	Landing craft of 7.5 to 30 m suitable for only personnel
LCU	Landing craft, utility	All purpose landing craft of 25 to 55 m capable of handling 2-3 tanks or 300-450 troops. Must have landing ramp
LCVP	Landing craft, vehicle, personnel	Similar to LCP but capable of carrying light vehicle in place of troops
LHA	Amphibious general assault ship	Large general purpose amphibious assault ship for landing an assault force from helicopters or landing craft. Must have internal stowage, ramp and flooded well
LHD	Amphibious assault ship, multi-purpose	Large multi-purpose amphibious ship for landing an assault force from helicopters, landing craft or amphibious vehicles. Can also conduct missions with VSTOL aircraft and ASW helicopters
LL	Amphibious vessel, general	General designator for amphibious vessels
LPA	Amphibious transport, personnel	Ship capable of carrying 1300-1500 troops and landing them in its own landing craft

LPD	Amphibious transport, dock	Capable of carrying 1000 troops, up to 9 LCM. Must have helicopter platform
LPH	Amphibious assault ship	Large helicopter carrier for landing circa 1800 troops with its own aircraft
LSD	Landing ship, dock	Primarily tank and vehicle carrier, also capable of carrying 150-400 troops
LSM	Landing ship, medium	Of 45 to 85 m capable of beaching to land troops and tanks
LST	Landing ship, tank	Of 85 to 160 m to transport troops, vehicles and tanks for amphibious assault. Must have bow doors and/or ramps
MM	Minewarfare vessels, general	General designator for minewarfare vessels
MCM	Mine countermeasures vessel	Minehunter with mechanical and influence sweep capability
MH	Minehunter, general	Fitted with equipment to hunt mines
MHC	Minehunter, coastal	Ship of 25 to 60 m with enhanced minehunting capability. May also carry sweep gear and mine clearance divers
MHS	Minehunter and sweeper, general	Minehunter with influence and mechanical sweep capability
MS	Minesweeper, general	Ship designed to sweep mines
MSC	Minesweeper, coastal	Of 40 to 60 m
MSO	Minesweeper, ocean	Of 46 m or more
PP	Patrol vessel, general	General designator for patrol vessels
PG	Patrol ship, general	Of 45 to 85 m not designed to operate in open ocean. Must have at least 76 mm armament
PHM	Patrol combatant, guided missile	High speed (hydrofoil) craft with SSM capability
PT	Patrol/torpedo boat	High speed (35 kts) of 20 to 30 m. Anti-surface ship torpedo equipped
SS	Submarine, general	General designator for submarines
SSA	Submarine, missile	Submarines fitted with underwater-to-surface guided missiles
SSBN	Submarine, ballistic missile, nuclear	Primary strategic nuclear submarine armed with ballistic missiles
SSGN	Submarine, attack, surface missile, nuclear	Nuclear submarine fitted with underwater or surface to surface missiles
SSK	Submarine, patrol	Non-nuclear long range patrol submarine may have anti-surface or anti-submarine role
SSN	Submarine, attack, nuclear	Nuclear attack submarine with both anti-submarine and anti-surface capability

Note: It should be noted that not all countries conform to the NATO STANAG codings for their ships. There are a number of ships in this publication whose designations will not be found in the above list (see France).

Composite Warship

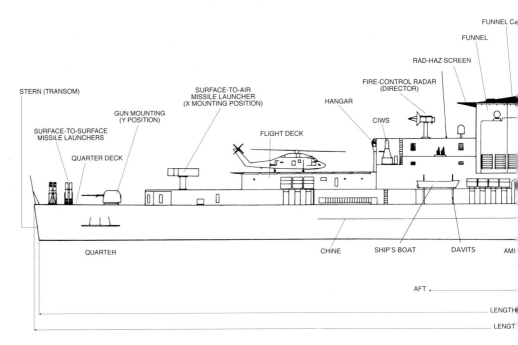

STARBOARD SIDE

R|

FUNNEL C/

FUNNEL

RAD-HAZ SCREEN

FIRE-CONTROL RADAR
(DIRECTOR)

STERN (TRANSOM)

SURFACE-TO-AIR
MISSILE LAUNCHER
(X MOUNTING POSITION)

HANGAR

CIWS

GUN MOUNTING
(Y POSITION)

FLIGHT DECK

SURFACE-TO-SURFACE
MISSILE LAUNCHERS

QUARTER DECK

QUARTER

CHINE

SHIP'S BOAT

DAVITS

AMI

AFT

LENGTH

LENGT

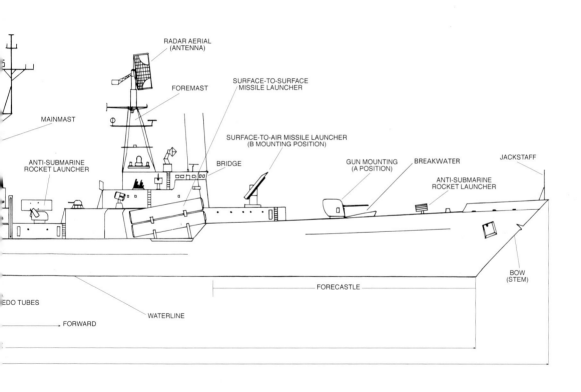

RADAR AERIAL
(ANTENNA)

SURFACE-TO-SURFACE
MISSILE LAUNCHER

FOREMAST

SURFACE-TO-AIR MISSILE LAUNCHER
(B MOUNTING POSITION)

MAINMAST

GUN MOUNTING
(A POSITION)

BREAKWATER

JACKSTAFF

BRIDGE

ANTI-SUBMARINE
ROCKET LAUNCHER

ANTI-SUBMARINE
ROCKET LAUNCHER

BOW
(STEM)

EDO TUBES

FORECASTLE

WATERLINE

FORWARD

Types of Warship Masts

AFT ⟶ FWD AFT ⟶ FWD AFT ⟶ FWD

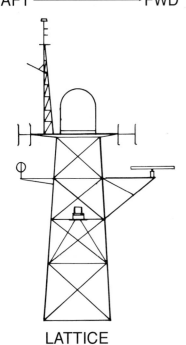

LATTICE

TRIPOD

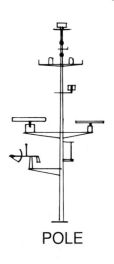

POLE

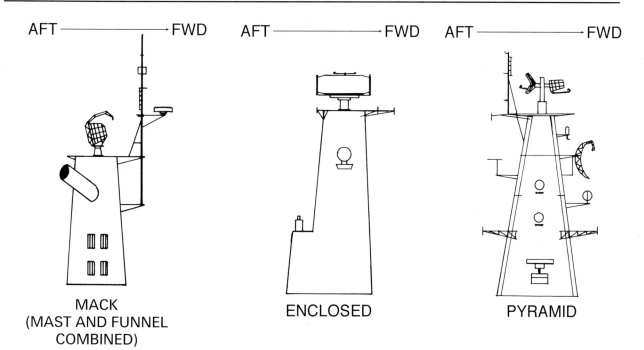

AFT ⟶ FWD

AFT ⟶ FWD

AFT ⟶ FWD

MACK
(MAST AND FUNNEL
COMBINED)

ENCLOSED

PYRAMID

Composite Warship

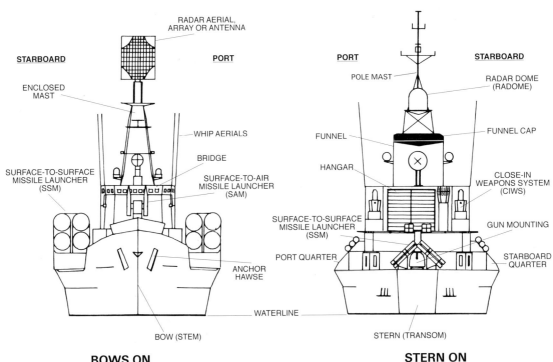

RADAR AERIAL,
ARRAY OR ANTENNA

STARBOARD

PORT

ENCLOSED
MAST

WHIP AERIALS

BRIDGE

SURFACE-TO-SURFACE
MISSILE LAUNCHER
(SSM)

SURFACE-TO-AIR
MISSILE LAUNCHER
(SAM)

ANCHOR
HAWSE

BOW (STEM)

BOWS ON

PORT

STARBOARD

POLE MAST

RADAR DOME
(RADOME)

FUNNEL

FUNNEL CAP

HANGAR

CLOSE-IN
WEAPONS SYSTEM
(CIWS)

SURFACE-TO-SURFACE
MISSILE LAUNCHER
(SSM)

GUN MOUNTING

PORT QUARTER

STARBOARD
QUARTER

WATERLINE

STERN (TRANSOM)

STERN ON

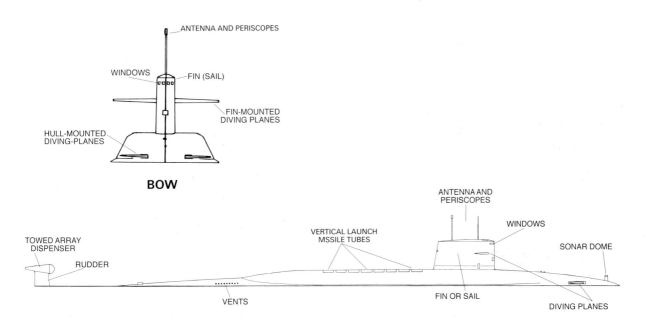

ANTENNA AND PERISCOPES

WINDOWS — FIN (SAIL)

FIN-MOUNTED DIVING PLANES

HULL-MOUNTED DIVING-PLANES

BOW

TOWED ARRAY DISPENSER

RUDDER

VERTICAL LAUNCH MSSILE TUBES

ANTENNA AND PERISCOPES

WINDOWS

SONAR DOME

VENTS

FIN OR SAIL

DIVING PLANES

Ensigns and Flags of the World's Navies

The following pictorial representations show each country's ensign where it has one or its national flag.
In cases where countries do not have ensigns their warships normally fly the national flag.

Albania
National Flag

Algeria
Ensign

Angola
National Flag

Anguilla
Ensign

Antigua
National Flag

Argentina
National Flag and Ensign

Australia
Ensign

Austria
Ensign

Azerbaijan
National Flag

Bahamas
Ensign

Bahrain
National Flag

Bangladesh
National Flag

Barbados
Ensign

Belgium
Ensign

Belize
National Flag

Benin
National Flag

Bermuda
National Flag

Bolivia
Ensign

Brazil
National Flag

Brunei
Ensign

Bulgaria
Ensign

Burma
National Flag

Cambodia
National Flag

Cameroon
National Flag

Canada
National Flag and Ensign

Cape Verde
National Flag

Chile
National Flag and Ensign

China, People's Republic
Ensign

Colombia
Ensign

Comoro Islands
National Flag

Congo
National Flag

Cook Islands
National Flag

Costa Rica
Ensign and Government Flag

Croatia
National Flag

Cuba
National Flag and Ensign

Cyprus, Republic
National Flag

Cyprus, Turkish Republic
(Not recognised by United Nations)
National Flag

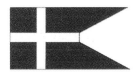

Denmark
Ensign

Djibouti
National Flag

Dominica
National Flag

Dominican Republic
Ensign

Ecuador
National Flag and Ensign

Egypt
Ensign

El Salvador
National Flag and Ensign

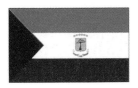

Equatorial Guinea
National Flag

Estonia
National Flag

Ethiopia
National Flag

Faroes
The Islands Flag

Falkland Islands
Falkland Islands Flag

Fiji
Ensign

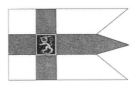

Finland
Ensign

France
Ensign

Gabon
National Flag

Gambia
National Flag

Georgia
National Flag

Germany
Ensign

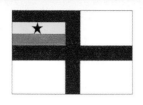

Ghana
Ensign

Greece
National Flag and Ensign

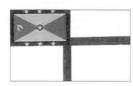

Grenada
Ensign

Guatemala
National Flag and Ensign

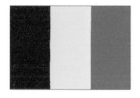

Guinea
National Flag

Guinea-Bissau
National Flag

Guyana
National Flag

Haiti
State Flag and Ensign

Honduras
Ensign

Hong Kong
Hong Kong Flag

Hungary
National Flag

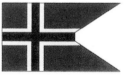

Iceland
Ensign

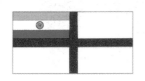

India
Ensign

Indonesia
National Flag and Ensign

Iran
National Flag

Iraq
National Flag

Ireland
National Flag and Ensign

Israel
Ensign

Italy
Ensign

Ivory Coast
National Flag

Jamaica
Ensign

Japan
Ensign

Jordan
Ensign

Kenya
Ensign

Korea, Democratic People's Republic (North)
National Flag

Korea, Republic (South)
Ensign

Kuwait
National Flag

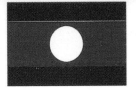

Laos
National Flag

Latvia
Ensign

Lebanon
National Flag

Liberia
National Flag and Ensign

Libya
National Flag

Lithuania
National Flag

Madagascar
National Flag

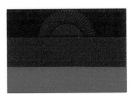

Malawi
National Flag

Malaysia
Ensign

Maldives
National Flag

Mali
National Flag

Malta
National Flag

Mauritania
National Flag

Mauritius
Ensign

Mexico
National Flag and Ensign

Monserrat
National Flag

Morocco
Ensign

Mozambique
National Flag

NATO
*Flag of the North Atlantic
Treaty Organization*

Netherlands
National Flag and Ensign

New Zealand
Ensign

Nicaragua
National Flag and Ensign

Nigeria
Ensign

Norway
Ensign

Oman
Ensign

Pakistan
Ensign

Panama
National Flag and Ensign

Papua New Guinea
Ensign

Paraguay
National Flag and Ensign

Paraguay
*National Flag and Ensign
(reverse)*

Peru
Ensign

Philippines
National Flag

Poland
Ensign

Portugal
National Flag and Ensign

Qatar
National Flag

Romania
National Flag and Ensign

Russia
Ensign

Russia
Border Guard Ensign

Russia & Ukraine
(Black Sea Fleet)
Ensign

St Kitts-Nevis
National Flag

St Lucia
National Flag

St Vincent
National Flag

Saudi Arabia
Ensign

Senegal
National Flag

Seychelles
National Flag

Sierre Leone
Ensign

Singapore
Ensign

Solomon Islands
National Flag

Somalia
National Flag

South Africa
Naval Ensign

Spain
National Flag and Ensign

Sri Lanka
Ensign

Sudan
National Flag

Surinam
National Flag

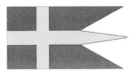

Sweden
Ensign and Jack

Switzerland
National Flag

Syria
National Flag

Taiwan
National Flag and Ensign

Tanzania
Ensign

Thailand
Ensign

Togo
National Flag

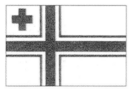

Tonga
Ensign

Trinidad and Tobago
Ensign

Tunisia
National Flag

Turkey
National Flag and Ensign

Turks and Caicos
National Flag

Uganda
National Flag

Ukraine
National Flag

Union of Soviet Socialist Republics (former)
Ensign

United Arab Emirates
National Flag

United Kingdom
Ensign

United States of America
National Flag and Ensign

Uruguay
National Flag and Ensign

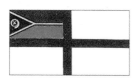

Vanuatu
Ensign

Venezuela
National Flag and Ensign

Vietnam
National Flag

Virgin Islands
National Flag

Western Samoa
National Flag

Yemen
National Flag

Yugoslavia
National Flag

Zaire
National Flag

Country: BRAZIL
Ship type: AIRCRAFT CARRIERS
Class: COLOSSUS
Active: 1

Name (Pennant Number): MINAS GERAIS (ex-HMS *Vengeance*) (A 11)

Recognition Features:
- Lattice catapult spur at bows.
- Island forward of midships, starboard side.
- Lattice mainmast immediately forward of funnel supporting large air search radar aerial on platform at half mast.
- Short tapered funnel atop island, sloping aft.
- 40 mm/56 mountings on platforms at forward and after ends of island.
- Angled flight deck.

Displacement full load, tons: 19,890.0
Length, feet (metres): 695.0 (211.8)
Beam, feet (metres): 80.0 (24.4)
Draught, feet (metres): 24.5 (7.5)
Flight deck length, feet (metres): 690 (210.3)
Flight deck width, feet (metres): 119.6 (36.4)
Speed, knots: 24.0
Range, miles: 12,000 at 14 kts

Guns: 10 Bofors 40 mm/56 (2 quad Mk 2, 1 twin Mk 1).
2 – 47 mm saluting guns.
Decoys: Plessey Shield launcher.
Radars:
Air search – Lockheed SPS 40B.
Air/surface search – Plessey AWS 4.
Navigation – Signaal ZW 06.
Fire control – 2 SPG 34.

Fixed wing aircraft: 6 Grumman S-2G Trackers.
Helicopters: 4-6 Agusta SH-3A Sea Kings.
2 Aerospatiale UH-13 Ecureuil II.
3 Aerospatiale UH-14 Super Puma.

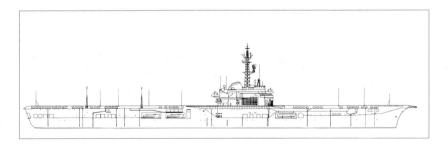

MINAS GERAIS

Country: FRANCE
Ship type: AIRCRAFT CARRIERS
Class: CLEMENCEAU (CV)
Active: 2

Name (Pennant Number): CLEMENCEAU (R 98), FOCH (R 99)

Recognition Features:
● SAM launchers forward of island (stbd) and port side aft.
● Large island just forward of midships, starboard side (three bridges, flag, command and aviation).
● Black-capped, raked funnel atop centre of island.
● Spherical landing approach control (NRBA 51) dome at after end of island.
● Single pole mainmast supporting air/surface search radar aerial forward and air search radar aerial aft.
● Note 1 – *Clemenceau* mainmast shorter than *Foch*.
● Note 2 – Flight deck letters, F – *Foch* and U – *Clemenceau*.

Displacement full load, tons: 32,780.0
Length, feet (metres): 869.4 (265.0)
Beam, feet (metres): 104.1 (31.7) (hull)
Draught, feet (metres): 28.2 (8.6)
Flight deck length, feet (metres): 543.0 (165.5)
Flight deck width, feet (metres): 96.8 (29.5)
Speed, knots: 32.0
Range, miles: 7500 at 18 kts

Missiles:
SAM – 2 Thomson-CSF Crotale EDIR launchers.
Guns: 4 DCN 3.9 in *(100 mm)*/55 Mod 53.
12.7 mm MGs.
Decoys: 2 CSEE Sagaie launchers.

Radars:
Air search – Thomson-CSF DRBV 23B.
Air/surface search – 2 DRBI 10, 1 DRBV 15.
Navigation – Racal Decca 1226.
Fire control – 2 Thomson-CSF DRBC 32B.
2 Crotale.
Landing approach control – NRBA 51.
Sonars: Westinghouse SQS 505; hull-mounted.

Fixed wing aircraft: 18 Super Etendard.
4 Etendard IVP.
8 Crusaders.
7 Alize.

Helicopters: 2 SA 365F Dauphin 2.

Clemenceau Class

FOCH

French Navy

Charles de Gaulle (CVN)

Country: FRANCE
Ship type: AIRCRAFT CARRIERS
Class: CHARLES DE GAULLE (CVN)
Active: 1

Name (Pennant Number): CHARLES DE GAULLE (R91)

Recognition Features:
- Sweeping bow with near vertical stern
- Very distinctive clean superstructure, angled surfaces for reduced radar signature
- Large angular island starboard side, well forward of midships
- Sturdy enclosed mainmast atop island, supporting tall pole mast
- Large spherical air-search radar dome atop after end of bridge roof
- Angled flight deck terminating port side just forward of island
- Two VLS SAM launchers outboard of flight deck sited amidships port side and just forward of island, starboard side

Displacement full load, tons: 39, 680 (36,600 standard)
Length, feet (metres): 857.7 (261.5)
Beam, feet (metres): 211.3 (64.4)
Draught, feet (metres): 27.8 (8.5)
Speed, knots: 27

Missiles:
   SSM - 4 EUROSAM VLS, Octupal launchers
   SAM - 2 Matra Sadral PDMS sextupal launchers
Guns: 8 Giat 20F2 20 mm
Decoys: 4 CSEE Sagaie launchers
Dassault LAD offboard decoys
Radars:
   Air search - Thomson-CSF DRBJ 11 D/E
                    Thomson-CSF DRBJ 26D
   Air/Surface search - Thomson-CSF DRBV 15C
   Navigation - Two Racal 1229
   Fire control - Arabel I/J band
Sonars: To include SLAT torpedo attack warning

Fixed wing aircraft: 30-40 including Rafale(M), Super Etendards, E-2C Hawkeye AEW
Helicopters: AS 565 Panther

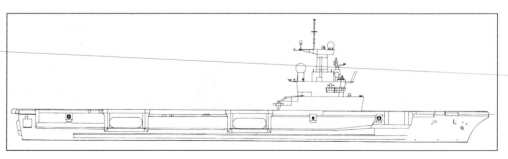

Charles de Gaulle (CVN)

CHARLES DE GAULLE

H M Steele

Country: FRANCE
Ship type: AIRCRAFT CARRIERS (HELICOPTERS)
Class: JEANNE D'ARC (CVH)
Active: 1

Name (Pennant Number): JEANNE D'ARC (ex-*La Résolue*) (R 97)

Recognition Features:
● Long forecastle.
● SSM launcher immediately forward of bridge.
● Main superstructure one third of ship's length from bow.
● Pole mainmast forward of funnel supporting air/surface search and air search radar aerials.
● Tall black-capped funnel at after end of bridge structure.
● Flight deck extending from bridge aft to break at short quarterdeck.
● Four 3.9 in mountings, two on flight deck level in line with forward edge of bridge, port and starboard; two on quarterdeck, port and starboard.

Displacement full load, tons: 13,270.0
Length, feet (metres): 597.1 (182.0)
Beam, feet (metres): 78.7 (24.0) (hull)
Draught, feet (metres): 24.0 (7.3)
Flight deck length, feet (metres): 203.4 (62.0)
Flight deck width, feet (metres): 68.9 (21.0)
Speed, knots: 26.5
Range, miles: 6000 at 15 kts

Missiles:
SSM – 6 Aerospatiale MM 38 Exocet.
Guns: 4 DCN 3.9 in *(100 mm)*/55 Mod 1964 CADAM.
Decoys: 2 CSEE/VSEL Syllex launchers (may not be fitted).

Radars:
Air search – Thomson-CSF DRBV 22D.
Air/surface search – DRBV 51.
Navigation – DRBN 32 (Decca 1226).
Fire control – 3 Thomson-CSF DRBC 32A.
Sonars: Thomson Sintra DUBV 24C; hull-mounted.

Helicopters: 4 Alouette III (to be replaced by Dauphin). War inventory includes 8 Super Puma and Lynx.

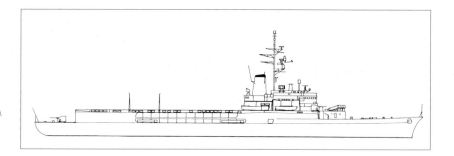

Jeanne D'Arc Class

JEANNE D'ARC

Hachiro Nakai

Aircraft Carriers – France

Country: INDIA
Ship type: AIRCRAFT CARRIERS
Class: HERMES
Active: 1

Name (Pennant Number): VIRAAT (Ex-British *Hermes* Class) (R 22)

Recognition Features:
- Fitted with 12° ski-ramp.
- Large midships island, starboard side.
- Medium height, enclosed mast at forward end of island with air search radar aerial atop.
- Short square profile funnel, mid-island.
- Tall lattice mainmast at after end of island supporting radar and communications aerials.
- Crane derrick immediately aft of island starboard side.
- Four LCVPs on after davits, two port two starboard.

Displacement full load, tons: 28,700.0
Length, feet (metres): 685.0 (208.8)
Beam, feet (metres): 90.0 (27.4)
Draught, feet (metres): 28.5 (8.7)
Speed, knots: 28.0

Missiles:
 SAM – 2 Shorts Seacat launchers.
Guns: Some 30 mm/65 ADGs may be fitted.
Decoys: 2 Knebworth Corvus launchers.
Radars:
 Air search – Marconi Type 996.
 Air/surface search – Plessey Type 994.
 Navigation – 2 Racal Decca 1006.
 Fire control – 2 Plessey Type 904.
Sonars: Graseby Type 184M; hull-mounted.

Fixed wing aircraft: 12 Sea Harriers FRS Mk 51 (capacity for 30).
Helicopters: 7 Sea King Mk 42B/C.
Ka-27 Helix.

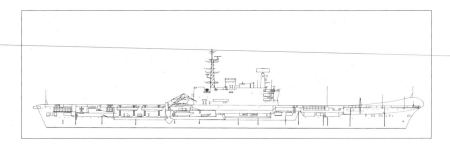

Hermes Class

VIRAAT

Indian Navy

Country: INDIA
Ship type: AIRCRAFT CARRIERS
Class: MAJESTIC
Active: 1

Name (Pennant Number): VIKRANT (ex-HMS *Hercules*) (R 11)

Recognition Features:
- No angled flight deck.
- 9.75° ski-ramp.
- Four 40 mm/70 mountings fitted forward of island, one port three starboard.
- Small island forward of midships, starboard side.
- Lattice mainmast and short vertical funnel atop central island.
- Crane gantry immediately aft of island (starboard side).
- Three 40 mm/70 mountings fitted aft of island, two port one starboard.

Displacement full load, tons: 19,500.0
Length, feet (metres): 700.0 (213.4)
Beam, feet (metres): 80.0 (24.4)
Draught, feet (metres): 24.0 (7.3)
Flight deck length, feet (metres): 690.0 (210.0)
Flight deck width, feet (metres): 112.0 (34.0)
Speed, knots: 24.5
Range, miles: 12,000 at 14 kts

Guns: 7 Bofors 40 mm/70; (some may have been replaced by 30 mm/65 ADGs).
Radars:
    Air search – Signaal LW 08.
    Air/surface search – Signaal DA 05.
    Navigation – Signaal ZW 06.
Sonars: Graseby 750; hull-mounted.

Fixed wing aircraft: 6 Sea Harriers FRS Mk 51.
Helicopters: 9 Sea Kings Mk 42 ASW/ASV.
1 Chetak SAR.

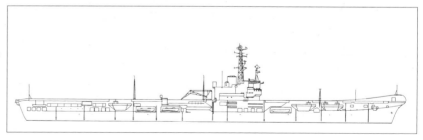

Majestic Class

VIKRANT

Country: ITALY
Ship type: AIRCRAFT CARRIERS
Class: GARIBALDI
Active: 1

Name (Pennant Number): GIUSEPPE GARIBALDI (C 551)

Recognition Features:
- 6.5° ski-ramp.
- Large midships island.
- Short mast forward of funnel supporting square profile, long range air search radar aerial.
- Air search radar aerial atop forward end of bridge.
- Integral, short, black-capped funnel after end of island.
- Two tall pole masts, after one supporting air/surface search radar aerial.
- SSM launchers, two port two starboard, below after end of flight deck.
- Three 40 mm/70 mountings, one port one starboard below flight deck just aft of ski-ramp, one centre-line aft quarterdeck.

Displacement full load, tons: 13,370.0
Length, feet (metres): 591.0 (180.0)
Beam, feet (metres): 110.2 (33.4)
Draught, feet (metres): 22.0 (6.7)
Flight deck length, feet (metres): 570.2 (173.8)
Flight deck width, feet (metres): 99.7 (30.4)
Speed, knots: 30.0
Range, miles: 7000 at 20 kts

Missiles:
    SSM – 4 OTO Melara Teseo Mk 2 (TG 2).
    SAM – 2 Selenia Elsag Albatros launchers.
Guns: 6 Breda 40 mm/70 (3 twin).
Torpedoes: 6 – 324 mm B-515 (2 triple) tubes. Honeywell Mk 46. To be replaced by A 290.

Decoys: AN/SLQ 25 Nixie; noisemaker.
2 Breda SCLAR 105 mm launchers.
Radars:
    Long range air search – Hughes SPS 52C, 3D.
    Air search – Selenia SPS 768 (RAN 3L).
              SMA SPN 728.
    Air/surface search – Selenia SPS 774 (RAN 10S).
    Surface search/target indication – SMA SPS 702 UPX; 718 beacon.
    Navigation – SMA SPN 749(V)2.
    Fire control – 3 Selenia SPG 75 (RTN 30X).
                3 Selenia SPG 74 (RTN 20X).
Sonars: Raytheon DE 1160 LF; bow-mounted.

Fixed wing aircraft: 16 AV-8B Harrier II.
Helicopters: 18 SH-3D Sea King helicopters (12 in hangar, 6 on deck). Capacity is either 16 Harriers or 18 Sea Kings.

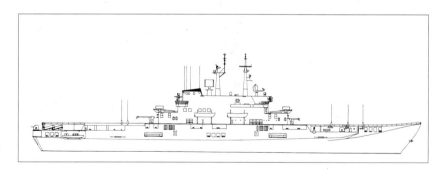

Garibaldi Class

GIUSEPPE GARIBALDI

Giorgio Arra

Country: RUSSIA AND ASSOCIATED STATES
Ship type: AIRCRAFT CARRIERS
Class: KUZNETSOV (TYPE 1143.5) (CV)
Active: 1
Building: 1

Name (Pennant Number): ADMIRAL KUZNETSOV (ex-*Tbilisi*, ex-*Leonid Brezhnev*), VARYAG (ex-*Riga*)

Recognition Features:
● Typical high, sweeping bow profile.
● 12° ski-ramp.
● Angled flight deck.
● SSM launchers forward end of flight deck with flush deck covers.
● High freeboard of 16.5 m.
● Large island aft of midships, starboard side.
● Distinctive cylindrical Tacan radar aerial housing forward of funnel atop island/bridge.
● Short, slightly raked funnel at after end of island structure.
● Square stern with clear flight deck overhang.

Displacement full load, tons: 67,500.0
Length, feet (metres): 918.6 (280.0) wl
Beam, feet (metres): 121.4 (37.0) wl
Draught, feet (metres): 34.4 (10.5)
Flight deck length, feet (metres): 999.0 (304.5)
Flight deck width, feet (metres): 229.7 (70.0)
Speed, knots: 30.0

Missiles:
SSM – 12 SS-N-19 Shipwreck launchers (flush mounted).
SAM – 4 SA-N-9 sextuple vertical launchers.

SAM/Guns – 8 CADS-N-1; each with twin 30 mm Gatling combined with 8 SA-N-11 and Hot Flash/Hot Spot fire control radar/optronic director.
Guns: 6-30 mm/65 AK 630; 6 barrels per mounting.
A/S mortars: 2 RBU 12000.
Decoys: chaff launchers.
Radars:
Air search – Sky Watch, 3D.
Air/surface search – Top Plate.
Surface search – 2 Strut Pair.
Navigation – 3 Palm Frond.
Fire control – 4 Cross Sword.
Aircraft control – Fly Trap B.
Sonars: Horse Jaw; hull-mounted.

Fixed wing aircraft: 20 Su-27K Flanker D.
4 Su-25 UTG Frogfoot.
Helicopters: 15 Ka-27 Helix.
3 Ka-29 Helix AEW.

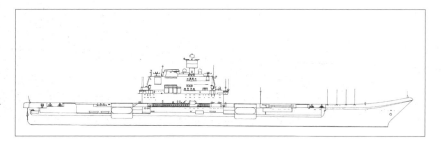

Kuznetsov Class

ADMIRAL KUZNETSOV

Country: RUSSIA AND ASSOCIATED STATES
Ship type: AIRCRAFT CARRIERS
Class: MODIFIED KIEV (TYPE 1143.4) (CVG)
Active: 1

Name (Pennant Number): ADMIRAL GORSHKOV (ex-*Baku*)

Recognition Features:
- Raked bow, square stern.
- Angled flight deck only.
- Two anti-submarine mortars in bows (on forward/aft line).
- Six SSM launchers arranged with four forward of two on centreline.
- Two 3.9 in mountings sited on raised sponsons (on forward/aft line) immediately forward of bridge.
- Large island just forward of midships, starboard side.
- Distinctive cylindrical Tacan radar aerial housing centrally sited atop island.
- Smaller cylindrical air search radar aerial housing at after end of island structure.

Displacement full load, tons: 44,500.0
Length, feet (metres): 899.0 (274.0) oa
Beam, feet (metres): 167.3 (51.0) oa
Draught, feet (metres): 32.8 (10.0) (screws)
Flight deck length, feet (metres): 640.0 (195.0)
Flight deck width, feet (metres): 68.0 (20.7)
Speed, knots: 32.0
Range, miles: 13,500 at 18 kts

Missiles:
    SSM – 12 SS-N-12 Sandbox (6 twin) launchers.
    SAM – 4 SA-N-9 Gauntlet sextuple vertical launchers.
Guns: 2 – 3.9 in *(100 mm)*/59.
    8 – 30 mm/65.
A/S mortars: 2 RBU 12000; 10 tubes per launcher.

Decoys: 2 twin chaff launchers.
Towed torpedo decoy.
Radars:
    Air search – Sky Watch; 4 Planar phased array, 3D.
    Air/surface search – Plate Steer.
    Surface search – 2 Strut Pair.
    Navigation – 3 Palm Frond.
    Fire control – Trap Door.
                Kite Screech.
                 4 Bass Tilt.
                 4 Cross Sword.
    Aircraft control – Fly Trap.
                 Cake Stand.
Sonars: Horse Jaw; hull-mounted.
Horse Tail; VDS.

Fixed wing aircraft: 12 VSTOL.
Helicopters: 19 Ka-27 Helix A.
3 Ka-25 Hormone B (OTHT).

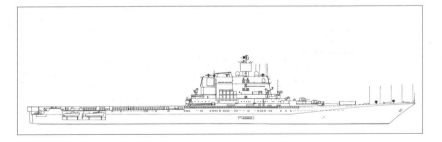

Modified Kiev Class

ADMIRAL GORSHKOV

Country: SPAIN
Ship type: AIRCRAFT CARRIERS
Class: PRINCIPE DE ASTURIAS
Active: 1

Name (Pennant Number): PRINCIPE DE ASTURIAS (ex-*Almirante Carrero Blanco*) (R 11)

Recognition Features:
- 12° ski-ramp fitted.
- Unusual, overhanging aircraft lift at after end of flight deck.
- Two 20 mm/120 mountings at flare of bows, port and starboard.
- Crane gantry forward of island, starboard side.
- Island much further aft of midships than usual, starboard side.
- Large lattice mainmast at forward end of island supporting square profile air search radar aerial.
- Raked funnel mid-island with four protruding individual exhausts at top.
- Aircraft control radar dome at after end of island structure.
- Two 20 mm/120 mountings right aft, port and starboard.

Displacement full load, tons: 17,188.0
Length, feet (metres): 642.7 (195.9) oa
Beam, feet (metres): 79.7 (24.3)
Draught, feet (metres): 30.8 (9.4)
Flight deck length, feet (metres): 575.1 (175.3)
Flight deck width, feet (metres): 95.1 (29.0)
Speed, knots: 26.0
Range, miles: 6500 at 20 kts

Guns: 4 Bazán Meroka 12-barrelled 20 mm/120.
2 Rheinmetall 37 mm saluting guns.
Decoys: 4 Loral Hycor SRBOC 6-barrelled Mk 36.
SLQ 25 Nixie; towed torpedo decoy.
US Prairie/Masker; hull noise/blade rate suppression.

Radars:
Air search – Hughes SPS 52 C/D, 3D.
Surface search – ISC Cardion SPS 55.
Fire control – 1 Selenia RAN 12L.
4 Sperry VPS 2.
1 RTN 11L/X.
Aircraft control – ITT SPN 35 A.

Fixed wing aircraft: 6-12 AV 8B Bravo.
Helicopters: 6-10 SH-3 Sea Kings.
2-4 AB 212ASW/EW.
2 SH-60B Seahawks.

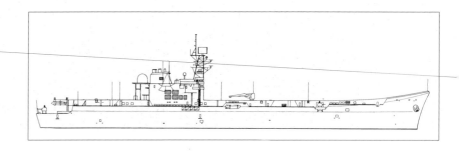

Principe de Asturias Class

PRINCIPE DE ASTURIAS

Invincible Class

Country: UNITED KINGDOM
Ship type: AIRCRAFT CARRIERS
Class: INVINCIBLE (CVG)
Active: 3

Name (Pennant Number): INVINCIBLE (R 05), ILLUSTRIOUS (R 06), ARK ROYAL (R 07)

Recognition Features:

● 12° ski-ramp fitted on offset, port side flight deck.
● SAM launcher situated outboard, midway along ski-ramp, starboard side.
● Very long island situated amidships, starboard side.
● Twin funnels, one immediately aft of bridge, one aft of mainmast; forward funnel taller. Both funnels have twin, black painted exhausts atop.
● Two fire control radar domes, one at each extreme of island (forward and aft).
● Central, enclosed mainmast supporting surface search radar aerial, 992R (R 07) or 996(2) (R 05 and R 06).
● CIWS mountings fitted at bows, port side aft and immediately forward of after funnel. Goalkeeper (R 05 and R 06); Vulcan Phalanx (R 07).
● Note – *Illustrious* has a new mainmast which is 'Waisted' at two thirds height and tapers at the top.

Displacement full load, tons: 20,600.0
Length, feet (metres): 685.8 (209.1) oa
Beam, feet (metres): 118.0 (36.0) oa
Draught, feet (metres): 26.0 (8.0)
Flight deck length, feet (metres): 550 (167.8)
Flight deck width, feet (metres): 44.3 (13.5)
Speed, knots: 28.0
Range, miles: 7000 at 19 kts

Missiles:

SAM – British Aerospace Sea Dart twin launcher.

Guns: 3 GE/GD 20 mm Mk 15 Vulcan Phalanx (R07).
3 Signaal/GE 30 mm 7-barrelled Gatling Goalkeeper (R05 and 06).
2 Oerlikon/BMARC 20 mm GAM-BO1.
Decoys: 8 Sea Gnat dispensers.
Prairie Masker noise suppression system.
Radars:
Air search – Marconi/Signaal Type 1022.
Surface search – Marconi Type 992R (R 07).
Plessey Type 996(2) (R 05 and 06).
Navigation – 2 Kelvin Hughes Type 1006 (R 05 and 07).
Type 1007 (R 06).
Fire control – 2 Marconi Type 909 or 909(1) (R 06).
Sonars: Plessey Type 2016; hull-mounted.

Fixed wing aircraft: 9 British Aerospace Sea Harrier FRS 1/2.
Helicopters: 9 Westland Sea King HAS 6 (maximum).
3 Westland Sea King AEW 2.

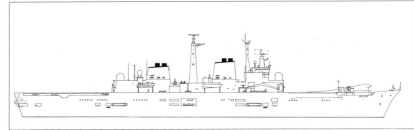

Invincible Class

INVINCIBLE

H M Steele

Country: UNITED STATES OF AMERICA
Ship type: AIRCRAFT CARRIERS
Class: ENTERPRISE (CVN)
Active: 1

Name (Pennant Number): ENTERPRISE (CVN 65)

Recognition Features:
- Angled flight deck.
- Island well aft of midships, starboard side.
- Island comprises unusual box shaped bridge supported on significantly narrower column structure.
- Square profile air search radar aerial mounted atop the bridge, forward.
- SAM launchers mounted port and starboard, outboard, at after end of flight deck. Third launcher situated starboard side forward, approximately quarter of ships length from bows.
- CIWS mountings situated right aft below flight deck overhang.

Displacement full load, tons: 93,970.0
Length, feet (metres): 1123.0 (342.3)
Beam, feet (metres): 133.0 (40.5)
Draught, feet (metres): 39.0 (11.9)
Flight deck length, feet (metres): 1088.0 (331.6)
Flight deck width, feet (metres): 252.0 (76.8)
Speed, knots: 33.0

Missiles:
SAM – 3 Raytheon GMLS Mk 29 launchers.
Guns: 3 GE/GD 20 mm Vulcan Phalanx Mk 15.
Decoys: 4 Loral Hycor SRBOC 6-barrelled Mk 36.
SSTDS.
SLQ-36 Nixie (Phase I).

Radars:
Air search – ITT SPS 48E, 3D.
Raytheon SPS 49(V)5.
Hughes Mk 23 TAS.
Surface search – Norden SPS 67.
Navigation – Raytheon SPS 64(V)9.
Furuno 900.
Fire control – 6 Mk 95.

Fixed wing aircraft: (Transitional air wing including)
20 F14 Tomcat.
20 F/A-18 Hornet.
4 EA-6B Prowler.
16 A-6E Intruders.
4 E-2C Hawkeye.
6 S-3A/B Viking.
Helicopters: 8 SH-3G/H Sea King or SH-60F Seahawk.

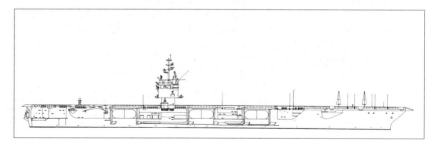

Enterprise Class

ENTERPRISE

Giorgio Arra

Kitty Hawk and John F Kennedy Class

Country: UNITED STATES OF AMERICA
Ship type: AIRCRAFT CARRIERS
Class: KITTY HAWK and JOHN F KENNEDY (CV)
Active: 4

Name (Pennant Number): KITTY HAWK (CV 63), CONSTELLATION (CV 64), AMERICA (CV 66), JOHN F KENNEDY (CV 67)

Recognition Features:
- Built to an improved *Forrestal* design. Can readily be recognised by the island structure being set further aft than in the *Forrestal* class.
- Angled flight deck.
- Complex pole mast central island, housing radar, WT and EW aerials.
- Funnel at rear of island structure, flush with top of bridge.
- Tall lattice mast immediately aft of bridge supporting square profile air search radar aerial.
- Crane derrick starboard aft, outboard of flight deck.
- CIWS mountings, one port side aft below flight deck overhang, one halfway up island structure starboard side and one port side forward sited on platform below round of angled flight deck.
- Two deck-edge lifts fitted forward of island superstructure, a third aft of the island, and a fourth port side quarter.

Displacement full load, tons: 81,123.0 (CV 63), 81,773 (CV 64), 79,724.0 (CV 66), 80,941.0 (CV 67)
Length, feet (metres): 1062.5 (323.6) (CV 63), 1072.5 (326.9) (CV 64), 1047.5 (319.3) (CV 66), 1052.0 (320.6) (CV 67)
Beam, feet (metres): 130.0 (39.6)
Draught, feet (metres): 37.4 (11.4)
Flight deck length, feet (metres): 1046.0 (318.8)
Flight deck width, feet (metres): 252.0 (76.8)
Speed, knots: 32.0
Range, miles: 12 000 at 20 kts

Missiles:
SAM – 3 Raytheon GMLS Mk 29 octuple launchers.
Guns: 3 GE/GD 20 mm Vulcan Phalanx Mk 15.
Decoys: 4 Loral Hycor SRBOC 6-barrelled Mk 36.
SSTDS.
SLQ-36 Nixie (Phase I).
Radars:
Air search – ITT SPS 48C/E, 3D.
Raytheon SPS 49(V)5.
Hughes Mk 23 TAS.
Surface search – Raytheon SPS 10F or Norden SPS 67.
Navigation – Raytheon SPN 64(V)9.
Furuno 900.
Fire control – 6 Mk 95.
Sonar: Fitted for SQS 23 (CV 66-67).

Fixed wing aircraft: (Transitional air wing including)
20 F14 Tomcat; 20 F/A-18 Hornet; 4 EA-6B Prowler; 16 A-6E Intruders; 4 E-2C Hawkeye; 6 S-3A/B Viking.
Power Projection Airwing substitutes 4 more Hornets for 4 Intruders and reduces Prowlers and Hawkeyes by one each.
Helicopters: 8 SH-3G/H Sea King or SH-60F Seahawk.

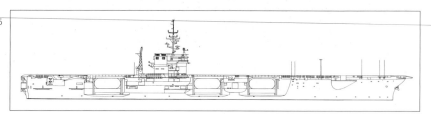

Kitty Hawk and John F Kennedy Class

AMERICA

H M Steele

Country: UNITED STATES OF AMERICA
Ship type: AIRCRAFT CARRIERS
Class: NIMITZ (CVN)
Active: 6
Building: 2
Projected: 1

Name (Pennant Number): NIMITZ (CVN 68), DWIGHT D EISENHOWER
(CVN 69), CARL VINSON (CVN 70), THEODORE ROOSEVELT (CVN 71), ABRAHAM LINCOLN
(CVN 72), GEORGE WASHINGTON (CVN 73), JOHN C STENNIS (CVN 74), UNITED STATES
(CVN 75)

Recognition Features:
● Large island well aft of midships.
● Square profile air search radar aerial mounted atop forward end of island, above bridge.
● Large complex pole mainmast atop central bridge supporting array of radar, EW and WT
aerials.
● Enclosed mast immediately aft of island supporting curved lattice bedstead radar aerial.
● Two CIWS mountings fitted right aft, one port, one starboard, below flight deck overhang.
● Second two CIWS mountings, port and starboard, immediately forward of point where flight
deck narrows.

Displacement full load, tons: 91,487.0 (CVN 68-70),
96,386.0 (CVN 71), 102,000.0 (CVN 72-73)
Length, feet (metres): 1040.0 (317.0)
Beam, feet (metres): 134.0 (40.8)
Draught, feet (metres): 37.0 (11.3) CVN 68-70, 38.7
(11.8)
CVN 71, 39.0 (11.9) CVN 72-73
Flight deck length, feet (metres): 1092.0 (332.9)
Flight deck angled, feet (metres): 779.8 (237.7)
Flight deck width, feet (metres): 252.0 (76.8)
Speed, knots: 30.0+

Missiles:
SAM – 3 Raytheon GMLS Mk 29 octuple launchers.
Guns: 4 GE/GD 20 mm Vulcan Phalanx Mk 15 (3 in CVN 68 and 69).
Decoys: 4 Loral Hycor SRBOC 6-barrelled Mk 36.
SSTDS (torpedo defence system).
SLQ 36 Nixie (Phase I).
Radars:
Air search – ITT SPS 48E, 3D.
Raytheon SPS 49(V)5.
Hughes Mk 23 TAS.
Surface search – Norden SPS 67V.
Navigation – Raytheon SPS 64(V)9.
Fire control – 6 Mk 95.

Fixed wing aircraft: (Transitional air wing including)
20 F14 Tomcat.
20 F/A-18 Hornet.
4 EA-6B Prowler. 16 A-6E Intruders.
4 E-2C Hawkeye.
6 S-3A/B Viking.
Power Projection Airwing substitutes 4 more Hornets for 4 Intruders and reduces Prowlers and
Hawkeyes by one each.
Helicopters: 8 SH-3G/H Sea King or SH-60F Seahawk.

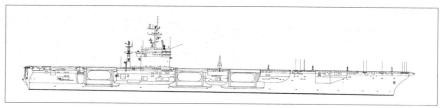

Nimitz Class

ABRAHAM LINCOLN

Vittorio Veneto Class

Country: ITALY
Ship type: CRUISERS
Class: VITTORIO VENETO
Active: 1

Name (Pennant Number): VITTORIO VENETO (C 550)

Recognition Features:
- Two large enclosed masts just forward and aft of midships.
- Twin funnels in vee formation at after end of each mast.
- Forward mast supports distinctive, square, long range air search radar aerial.
- Lattice crane derrick and ship's boat sited between masts.
- Very unusual break in deck level, just aft of bridge, up from maindeck to flight deck.
- 40 mm/70 mountings situated port and starboard at forward end of long flight deck.
- SAM launcher at after end of forecastle.
- Four SSM launchers amidships, two port two starboard, adjacent to forward funnel.

Displacement full load, tons: 9500.0
Length, feet (metres): 589.0 (179.6)
Beam, feet (metres): 63.6 (19.4)
Draught, feet (metres): 19.7 (6.0)
Flight deck length, feet (metres): 131.0 (40.6)
Flight deck width, feet (metres): 61.0 (18.6)
Speed, knots: 32.0
Range, miles: 5000 at 17 kts

Missiles:
  SSM – 4 OTO Melara Teseo Mk 2.
  SAM – GDC Pomona Standard SM-1ER; Aster twin Mk 10 Mod 9 launcher.
  A/S – Honeywell ASROC launcher.
Guns: 8 OTO Melara 3 in (76 mm)/62 MMK.
6 Breda 40 mm/70 (3 twin).

Torpedoes: 6 – 324 mm US Mk 32 (2 triple) tubes; Honeywell Mk 46; anti-submarine.
Decoys: 2 Breda SCLAR.
SLQ 25 Nixie torpedo decoy.
Radars:
  Long range air search – Hughes SPS 52C, 3D.
  Air search – Selenia SPS 768 (RAN 3L).
  Surface search/target indication – SMA SPS 702.
  Navigation – SMA SPS 748.
  Fire control – 4 Selenia SPG 70 (RTN 10X) (Argo).
              2 Selenia SPG 74 (RTN 20X) (Dardo).
              2 Sperry/RCA SPG 55C (Standard).
Sonars: Sangamo SQS 23G; bow-mounted.

Helicopters: 6 AB 212ASW.

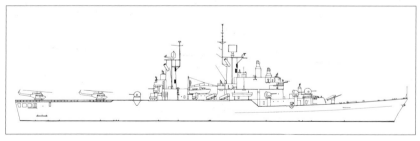

Vittorio Veneto Class

VITTORIO VENETO

De Ruyter Class

Country: PERU
Ship type: CRUISERS
Class: DE RUYTER
Active: 2

Name (Pennant Number): ALMIRANTE GRAU (ex-HrMs *De Ruyter*)
(CH 81), AGUIRRE (ex-HrMs *De Zeven Provincien*) (CH 84)

Recognition Features:

(*Aguirre*)

● Two 6 in and one 57 mm/60 mountings forward of bridge.
● Forward funnel at after end of forward superstructure with mast above.
● After funnel close to midships, tapered towards top with smoke deflector at top after end.
● Air search radar aerial atop after funnel.
● Lattice mast aft of after funnel.
● Helicopter hangar and flight deck aft of lattice mast (*Grau*).
● Two 6 in mountings only forward of bridge.
● Forward superstructure similar to *Aguirre*.
● Cylindrical after funnel sloped slightly aft with lattice mast built around it.
● Upper deck superstructure sited astern of after funnel with fire control director atop.
● Two 6 in mountings on afterdeck.
● No flight deck.

Displacement full load, tons: 12,165.0 (*Grau*), 12,250.0 (*Aguirre*)
Length, feet (metres): 609.0 (185.6) (*Aguirre*), 624.5 (190.3) (*Grau*)
Beam, feet (metres): 56.7 (17.3)
Draught, feet (metres): 22.0 (6.7)
Flight deck length, feet (metres): 115.0 (35.0) (*Aguirre*)
Flight deck width, feet (metres): 56.0 (17.0) (*Aguirre*)
Speed, knots: 32.0
Range, miles: 7000 at 12 kts

Missiles:
   SSM – 8 Aerospatiale MM 38 Exocet (*Grau* only).
Guns: 8 Bofors 6 in *(152 mm)*/53 (4 twin) (4 in *Aguirre*).
6 Bofors 57 mm/60 (3 twin) (these guns removed from *Grau*).
6 Bofors 40 mm/70 (4 in *Aguirre*) (removed from *Grau* during modernisation).
Depth charges: 2 racks.
Decoys: 2 Dagaie and 1 Sagaie launchers (*Grau*).
Radars:
   Air search – Signaal LW 08 (*Grau*).
                   Signaal LW 02 (*Aguirre*).
   Surface search/target indication – Signaal DA 08 (*Grau*).
                   Signaal DA 02 (*Aguirre*).
   Navigation – Signaal ZW 03 (*Aguirre*).
                   Racal Decca 1226 (*Grau*).
   Fire control – Signaal WM25 (*Grau*).
                   2 M45 (*Aguirre*).
                   1 M25 (*Aguirre*). Signaal STIR (*Grau*).
Sonars: CWE 10N (*Aguirre*), CWE 610 (*Grau*); hull-mounted.

Helicopters: 3 Agusta ASH-3D Sea Kings (*Aguirre*).

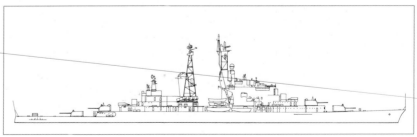

ALMIRANTE GRAU

J L M van der Burg

Country: RUSSIA AND ASSOCIATED STATES
Ship type: CRUISERS
Class: KARA (TYPE 1134B/1136B)
Active: 5

Name (Pennant Number): OCHAKOV, KERCH, AZOV, PETROPAVLOVSK, VLADIVOSTOK (ex-*Tallinn*)

Recognition Features:
● SAM (twin) launcher (1 in *Azov*) sited on raised forecastle structure forward of bridge.
● Head Light B or C fire control director mounted on bridge roof.
● Forward tripod mast aft of bridge supporting air/surface search radar aerial.
● Large pyramid mainmast sited amidships supporting, square profile air search radar aerial.
● Two 3 in mountings, port and starboard, sited between forward and aftermasts.
● Large, slightly tapered, square section funnel situated immediately aft of mainmast.
● Head Light B or C fire control director sited aft of funnel.
● SAM launcher on raised deck forward of small flight deck.

Displacement full load, tons: 9900.0
Length, feet (metres): 568.0 (173.2)
Beam, feet (metres): 61.0 (18.6)
Draught, feet (metres): 22.0 (6.7)
Speed, knots: 34.0
Range, miles: 9000 at 15 kts

Missiles:
　　SAM – 2 SA-N-3 Goblet twin launchers (1 in *Azov*).
　　　　6 SA-N-6 Grumble vertical launchers (*Azov* only).
　　　　2 SA-N-4 Gecko twin launchers.
　　A/S – 2 SS-N-14 Silex quad launchers.
Guns: 4 – 3 in *(76 mm)*/60 (2 twin).
4 – 30 mm/65; 6 barrels per mounting.

Torpedoes: 10 or 4 – 21 in *(533 mm)* (2 quin) (2 twin in *Azov*) Type 53.
A/S mortars: 2 RBU 6000 12-tubed.
2 RBU 1000 6-tubed (aft) (not in *Petropavlovsk*).
Decoys: 2 twin launchers.
1 BAT-1 torpedo decoy.
Radars:
　　Air search – Top Sail or Flat Screen, 3D.
　　Air/surface search – Head Net C, 3D.
　　Navigation – 2 Don Kay.
　　　　　　　　2 Palm Frond.
　　　　　　　　Don 2 (not in *Azov*).
　　Fire control – 2 Head Light B or C (one in *Azov*).
　　　　　　　　2 Pop Group.
　　　　　　　　Top Dome (aft in *Azov* in place of one Head Light C).
　　　　　　　　2 Owl Screech.
　　　　　　　　2 Bass Tilt.
Sonars: Bull Nose; hull-mounted. Mare Tail; VDS.

Helicopters: 1 Ka-25 Hormone A.

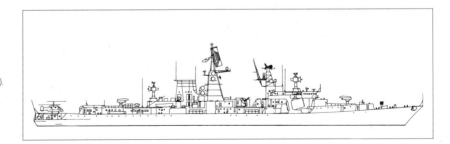

Kara Class

AZOV

Country: RUSSIA AND ASSOCIATED STATES
Ship type: CRUISERS
Class: KIROV (TYPE 1144)
Active: 3
Building: 1

Name (Pennant Number): ADMIRAL USHAKOV (ex-*Kirov*), ADMIRAL LAZAREV (ex-*Frunze*), ADMIRAL NAKHIMOV (ex-*Kalinin*), PYOTR VELIKIY (ex-*Yuri Andropov*)

Recognition Features:
(*Ushakov*)
- Very large mast and funnel combined sited amidships supporting air search radar aerials.
- Secondary masts and upper deck structures aft of mainmast supporting (from forward to aft) air/surface search and Top Dome and Kite Screech fire control radar aerials.
- Two 3.9 in mountings fitted fore and aft immediately forward of flight deck (X and Y position).
- Forward of bridge Eye Bowl Fire Control Radar.

(*Lazarev* and subsequent ships) – similar to *Ushakov* except-
- Forward radar aerial on secondary mast and upper deck structures aft of mainmast is Top Plate.
- Only one 130mm/70 mounting fitted forward of flight deck.
- Cross Sword and Pop Group fire control radars fitted forward of bridge.
- CADS-N-1 mounting fitted after end of forecastle deck.

Displacement full load, tons: 24,300.0
Length, feet (metres): 826.8 (252.0)
Beam, feet (metres): 93.5 (28.5)
Draught, feet (metres): 29.5 (9.1)
Speed, knots: 30.0
Range, miles: 14,000 at 30 kts

Missiles:
SSM – 20 SS-N-19 Shipwreck.
SAM – 12 SA-N-6 Grumble vertical launchers.
    2 SA-N-4 Gecko twin launchers.
    2 SA-N-9 Gauntlet octuple vertical launchers (not in *Ushakov*).
SAM/Guns – 6 CADS-N-1 (*Nakhimov*); each has a twin 30 mm Gatling.
A/S – 1 twin SS-N-14 Silex launcher (*Ushakov*); SS-N-15 (not in *Ushakov*); fired from fixed torpedo tubes behind shutters in superstructure.
Guns: 2 – 3.9 in *(100 mm)*/59 (*Ushakov*).
2 – 130 mm/70 (twin) (not in *Ushakov*).
8 – 30 mm/65 (*Ushakov* and *Lazarev*); 6 barrels per mounting.
Torpedoes: 10 – 21 in *(533 mm)* (2 quin); Type 53.
A/S mortars: 1 RBU 6000 12-tubed fwd (*Ushakov* and *Lazarev*).
1 RBU 12000 (*Lazarev*); 10 tubes per launcher.
2 RBU 1000 6-tubed.
Decoys: 2 twin 150 mm chaff launchers.
Towed torpedo decoy.
Radars:
Air search – Top Pair (Top Sail + Big Net).
Air/surface search – Top Steer (Top Plate in *Lazarev*).
Navigation – 3 Palm Frond.

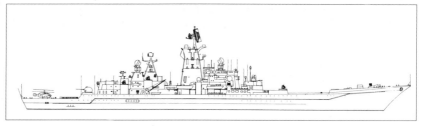

Kirov Class

ADMIRAL NAKHIMOV

Fire control – 2 Eye Bowl (*Ushakov* only).
Cross Sword (not in *Ushakov*).
2 Top Dome.
2 Pop Group.
Kite Screech.
4 Bass Tilt (not in *Lazarev*).

Aircraft control – Flyscreen A (*Ushakov*) or B.
Sonars: Horse Jaw; hull-mounted.
Horse Tail; VDS.

Helicopters: 3 Ka-25 Hormone or Ka-27 Helix.

Slava Class

Country: RUSSIA AND ASSOCIATED STATES
Ship type: CRUISERS
Class: SLAVA (TYPE 1164)
Active: 3
Building: 1

Name (Pennant Number): SLAVA, MARSHAL USTINOV, CHERVONA UKRAINA, VILNA UKRAINA (Ex-*Admiral Lobov*)

Recognition Features:
- High bow, sloping forecastle.
- 130 mm/70 mounting at after end of forecastle.
- Distinctive SSM launchers mounted in pairs adjacent to the bridge structure, four pairs port and four pairs starboard.
- Large pyramid mainmast at after end of bridge structure with lattice gantry protruding horizontally astern at the top. Mainmast supports the air/surface search Top Steer or Top Plate radar aerial.
- Smaller aftermast supporting the air search radar aerial.
- Short, squat twin funnels, side by side, immediately astern of aftermast.
- Notable gap abaft the twin funnels (SA-N-6 area) is traversed by a large crane which stows between the funnels.
- Prominent Top Dome fire control director aft situated just forward of small flight deck.

Displacement full load, tons: 11,200.0
Length, feet (metres): 610.2 (186.0)
Beam, feet (metres): 68.2 (20.8)
Draught, feet (metres): 24.9 (7.6)
Speed, knots: 32.0
Range, miles: 6000 at 15 kts

Missiles:
SSM – 16 SS-N-12 Sandbox (8 twin) launchers.

SAM – 8 SA-N-6 Grumble vertical launchers.
2 SA-N-4 Gecko twin launchers.
Guns: 2 – 130 mm/70 (twin).
6 – 30 mm/65; 6 barrels per mounting.
Torpedoes: 10 – 21 in *(533 mm)* (2 quin). Type 53.
A/S mortars: 2 RBU 6000 12-tubed.
Decoys: 2 twin 12-tubed chaff launchers.
Radars:
Air search – Top Pair (Top Sail + Big Net), 3D.
Air/surface search – Top Steer or Top Plate, 3D.
Navigation – 3 Palm Frond.
Fire control – Front Door.
Top Dome.
2 Pop Group.
3 Bass Tilt.
Kite Screech.
Sonars: Bull Horn; hull-mounted.
Mare Tail; VDS.

Helicopters: 1 Ka-25 Hormone B.

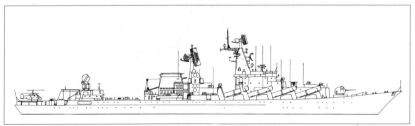

CHERVONA UKRAINA

Country: UNITED STATES OF AMERICA
Ship type: CRUISERS
Class: TICONDEROGA (AEGIS) (CG)
Active: 27

Name (Pennant Number): TICONDEROGA (CG 47), YORKTOWN (CG 48), VINCENNES (CG 49), VALLEY FORGE (CG 50), THOMAS S GATES (CG 51), BUNKER HILL (CG 52), MOBILE BAY (CG 53), ANTIETAM (CG 54), LEYTE GULF (CG 55), SAN JACINTO (CG 56), LAKE CHAMPLAIN (CG 57), PHILIPPINE SEA (CG 58), PRINCETON (CG 59), NORMANDY (CG 60), MONTEREY (CG 61), CHANCELLORSVILLE (CG 62), COWPENS (CG 63), GETTYSBURG (CG 64), CHOSIN (CG 65), HUE CITY (CG 66), SHILOH (CG 67), ANZIO (CG 68), VICKSBURG (CG 69), LAKE ERIE (CG 70), CAPE ST GEORGE (CG 71), VELLA GULF (CG 72), PORT ROYAL (CG 73)

Recognition Features:
● High raked bow with unusual raised solid sides surrounding forecastle.
● 5 in mounting on forecastle at break in maindeck profile.
● Two SAM or A/S Mk 26 Mod 5 launchers (CG 47-51), or two Mk 41 Mod 0 vertical launchers (CG 52 onwards), one between forward turret and bridge structure and one at the after break to quarterdeck. This is the clearest way to differentiate between the two versions of the class.
● Large, boxlike forward superstructure just forward of midships. Bridge at forward end, small lattice mast on bridge roof supporting dome for SPQ 9A fire control radar.
● Twin funnels, both with three exhausts. Forward funnel has two larger diameter exhausts forward of a smaller one, after funnel has smaller diameter exhaust of three at the forward end.
● Tall lattice mainmast supporting radar aerials situated between funnels, exactly amidships.
● Both versions have 5 in mounting on quarterdeck.
● Note – *Vincennes* and later ships have a lighter tripod mainmast vice the square quadruped of the first two.

Displacement full load, tons: 9590.0 (CG 47-48); 9407.0 (CG 49-51); 9466.0 (remainder)
Length, feet (metres): 567.0 (172.8)
Beam, feet (metres): 55.0 (16.8)
Draught, feet (metres): 31.0 (9.5) (sonar)
Speed, knots: 30.0+
Range, miles: 6000 at 20 kts

Missiles:
 SLCM/SSM – GDC Tomahawk (CG 52 onwards).
  8 McDonnell Douglas Harpoon (2 quad).
 SAM – 68 (CG 47-51); 122 (CG 52 onwards) GDC Standard SM-2MR.
 A/S – 20 Honeywell ASROC.
SAM and A/S missiles are fired from 2 twin Mk 26 Mod 5 launchers (CG 47-51) and 2 Mk 41 Mod 0 vertical launchers (CG 52 onwards). Tomahawk is carried in CG 52 onwards with 8 missiles in each VLS launcher. Vertical launch ASROC will be back fitted when available.
Guns: 2 FMC 5 in *(127 mm)*/54 Mk 45 (Mod 0 (CG 47-50); Mod 1 (CG 51 onwards)). 2 GE/GD 20 mm/76 Vulcan Phalanx 6-barrelled Mk 15.
4 – 12.7 mm MGs.
Torpedoes: 6 – 324 mm Mk 32 (2 triple) tubes. Honeywell Mk 46 Mod 5. To be replaced by Mk 50 in due course.
Decoys: 4 or 6 Loral Hycor SRBOC 6-barrelled Mk 36.

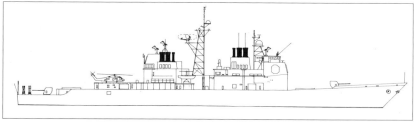

Ticonderoga Class

MOBILE BAY AND LAKE CHAMPLAIN

Ingalls

SLQ-25 Nixie; towed torpedo decoy.
Radars:
    Air search/fire control – RCA SPY 1A phased arrays, 3D.
                          Raytheon SPY 1B phased arrays, 3D (CG 59 on).
    Air search – Raytheon SPS 49(V)7.
    Surface search – ISC Cardion SPS 55.
    Navigation – Raytheon SPS 64(V)9.
    Fire control – Lockheed SPQ 9A.
                  4 Raytheon/RCA SPG 62.

Sonars: General Electric/Hughes SQS 53A/B (CG 47-55); bow-mounted.
Gould SQR 19 (CG 54-55); passive towed array.
Gould/Raytheon SQQ 89(V)3 (CG 56 onwards); combines hull-mounted SQS 53B (CG 56-67) or SQS 53C (CG 68-73) and passive towed array SQR 19.

Helicopters: 2 SH-60B Seahawk LAMPS III.
2 SH-2F LAMPS I (CG 47-48).

Country: UNITED STATES OF AMERICA
Ship type: CRUISERS
Class: VIRGINIA (CGN)
Active: 2

Name (Pennant Number): MISSISSIPPI (CGN 40), ARKANSAS (CGN 41)

Recognition Features:
● Very long forecastle with SAM-A/S GMLS Mk 26 launcher just aft of midway between bows and bridge.
● SSM Harpoon launcher sited immediately forward of bridge.
● 5 in mounting just forward of Harpoon launcher.
● Two pyramid masts, taller forward one supporting ITT SPS 48C air search radar aerial atop and SPQ 9A fire control aerial forward; the aftermast supporting one of two SPG 51 D fire control radar aerials.
● On afterdeck, from aft, SLCM/SSM Tomahawk launcher, SAM-A/S GMLS Mk 26 launcher and 5 in mounting.

Displacement full load, tons: 11,300.0
Length, feet (metres): 585.0 (178.3)
Beam, feet (metres): 63.0 (19.2)
Draught, feet (metres): 31.5 (9.6)
Speed, knots: 30.0+

Missiles:
SLCM/SSM – 8 GDC Tomahawk (2 quad).
8 McDonnell Douglas Harpoon (2 quad).
SAM – GDC Standard SM-2MR.
A/S – Honeywell ASROC; payload Mk 46 or Mk 50 torpedoes in due course.
SAM and A/S missiles are fired from 2 twin GMLS Mk 26 launchers.

Guns: 2 FMC 5 in *(127 mm)*/54 Mk 45 Mod 0.
2 GE/GD 20 mm Vulcan Phalanx 6-barrelled Mk 15.
4 – 12.7 mm MGs.
Torpedoes: 6 – 324 mm Mk 32 (2 triple) tubes. Honeywell Mk 46 Mod 5.
Decoys: 4 Loral Hycor SRBOC 6-barrelled Mk 36.
2 Mk 6 Fanfare or SLQ-26 Nixie.
Radars:
Air search – ITT SPS 48C or 48D/E, 3D.
Lockheed SPS 40B or Raytheon SPS 49(V)5.
Surface search – ISC Cardion SPS 55.
Navigation – Raytheon SPS 64(V)9.
Fire control – 2 SPG 51D.
SPG 60D.
SPQ 9A.
Sonars: EDO/GE SQS 53A; bow-mounted.

Virginia Class

ARKANSAS

Scott Connolly, RAN

Country: ARGENTINA
Ship type: DESTROYERS
Class: ALMIRANTE BROWN (MEKO 360 TYPE)
Active: 4

Name (Pennant Number): ALMIRANTE BROWN (D 10), LA ARGENTINA (D 11), HEROINA (D 12), SARANDI (D 13)

Recognition Features:
● Short forecastle, 5 in mounting (A position).
● 40 mm/70 mounting immediately forward of bridge (B position).
● Pyramid mast at after end of bridge structure housing WM 25 fire control radar dome.
● SSM launchers, port and starboard, immediately forward of funnels.
● Two side-by-side funnels angled outboard in vee formation with pole mast at forward edge.
● Air/surface search and fire control radars sited on raised superstructure aft of funnels.
● Short flight deck right aft with open quarterdeck below.
● Note 1 – Also operated by Nigeria (active 1). Most obvious difference is lattice support structure aft of funnels on Nigerian ship, solid on Argentine ships.
● Note 2 – Nigeria classifies this class as frigates.

Displacement full load, tons: 3360.0
Length, feet (metres): 413.1 (125.9)
Beam, feet (metres): 46.0 (14.0)
Draught, feet (metres): 19.0 (5.8) (screws)
Speed, knots: 30.5
Range, miles: 4500 at 18 kts

Missiles:
  SSM – 8 Aerospatiale MM 40 Exocet (2 quad) launchers.
  SAM – Selenia/Elsag Albatros launcher.
Guns: 1 OTO Melara 5 in *(127 mm)*/54 automatic.
8 Breda/Bofors 40 mm/70 (4 twin).

Torpedoes: 6 – 324 mm ILAS 3 (2 triple) tubes; Whitehead A 244.
Decoys: CSEE Dagaie mounting.
Graseby G1738 towed torpedo decoy system.
2 Breda 105 mm SCLAR launchers.
Radars:
  Air/surface search – Signaal DA 08A.
  Surface search – Signaal ZW 06.
  Navigation – Decca 1226.
  Fire control – Signaal STIR.
Sonars: Atlas Elektronik 80; hull-mounted.
DSQS 21BZ.

Helicopters: 2 SA 319B Alouette III.

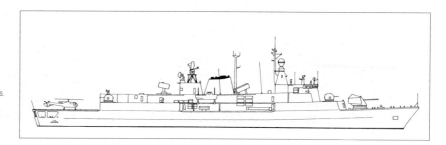

Almirante Brown Class

ALMIRANTE BROWN

Country: AUSTRALIA
Ship type: DESTROYERS
Class: PERTH (MODIFIED CHARLES F ADAMS)
Active: 3

Name (Pennant Number): PERTH (38), HOBART (39), BRISBANE (41)

Recognition Features:
- High bow, sweeping forecastle to 5 in mounting (A position).
- High bridge structure with SATCOM dome atop.
- Twin funnels sloped aft. Tripod mainmast astride forward funnel.
- Distinctive SPS 52C air search radar aerial mounted on aftermast and funnel combined.
- Two Raytheon SPG 51C fire control radar aerials immediately aft of after funnel.
- SAM launcher immediately forward of quarterdeck.
- Unusual tapered black tops to funnels.
- Note 1– Generally similar to the US *Charles F Adams* class, but differ by the addition of a broad deckhouse between the funnels.
- Note 2– Almost identical to the Greek *Kimon* class.

Displacement full load, tons: 4618.0
Length, feet (metres): 440.8 (134.3)
Beam, feet (metres): 47.1 (14.3)
Draught, feet (metres): 20.1 (6.1)
Speed, knots: 30.0+.
Range, miles: 6000 at 15 kts

Missiles:
   SAM –GDC Pomona Standard SM-1MR; Mk 13 Mod 6 launcher.
   Dual capability launcher for SSM.
Guns: 2 FMC 5 in *(127 mm)*/54 Mk 42 Mod 10.
2 GE/GD 20 mm Mk 15 Vulcan Phalanx.
Up to 6 – 12.7 mm MGs.

Torpedoes: 6 – 324 mm Mk 32 Mod 5 (2 triple) tubes; Honeywell Mk 46 Mod 5.
Decoys: 2 Loral Hycor SRBOC 6-barrelled Mk 36.
Nulka quad decoy launcher in *Brisbane* for trials.
SLQ 25; towed torpedo decoy.
Radars:
   Air search – Hughes SPS 52C.
            Lockheed SPS 40C.
   Surface search – Norden SPS 67V.
   Fire control – 2 Raytheon SPG 51C.
            Western Electric SPG 53F.
Sonars: Sangamo SQS 23KL; hull-mounted.

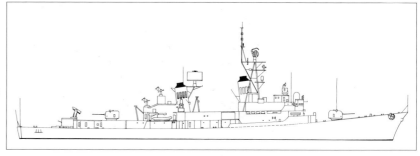

PERTH

S Poynton, RAN

Country: CANADA
Ship type: DESTROYERS
Class: IROQUOIS
Active: 4

Name (Pennant Number): IROQUOIS (280), HURON (281), ATHABASKAN (282), ALGONQUIN (283)

Recognition Features:
- SAM VLS at after end of forecastle.
- 3 in mounting (B position).
- Distinctive, curved, air search radar aerial atop after end of bridge structure.
- Tall lattice mainmast immediately forward of funnel.
- Unusual, large, square funnel amidships.
- CIWS mounting immediately aft of funnel atop after superstructure.
- Helicopter flight deck raised above quarterdeck level with torpedo tubes visible below.

Displacement full load, tons: 5100.0
Length, feet (metres): 426.0 (129.8)
Beam, feet (metres): 50.0 (15.2)
Draught, feet (metres): 15.5 (4.7)
Speed, knots: 29.0+
Range, miles: 4500 at 20 kts

Missiles:
SAM – 1 Martin Marietta Mk 41 VLS.
Guns: 1 OTO Melara 3 in *(76 mm)*/62 Super Rapid.
1 GE/GD 20 mm/76 6-barrelled Vulcan Phalanx Mk 15.
Torpedoes: 6 – 324 mm Mk 32 (2 triple) tubes. Honeywell Mk 46.
Decoys: 2 Plessey Shield launchers.
SLQ 25 Nixie; torpedo decoy.

Radars:
Air search – Signaal LW 08.
Surface search/navigation – Signaal DA 08.
Fire control – 2 Signaal STIR 1.8.
Sonars: Westinghouse SQS 505; combined VDS and hull-mounted. Westinghouse SQS 501; hull-mounted.

Helicopters: 2 CH-124A Sea King ASW.

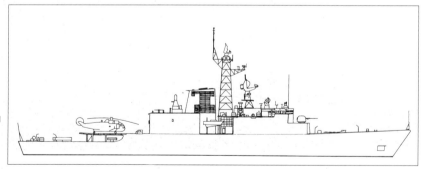

Iroquois Class

ALGONQUIN

Canadian Maritime Command

Country: CHILE
Ship type: DESTROYERS
Class: ALMIRANTE
Active: 2

Name (Pennant Number): ALMIRANTE RIVEROS (18), ALMIRANTE WILLIAMS (19)

Recognition Features:
- High freeboard to break at midships.
- Two 4 in mountings (A and B positions).
- Pole mainmast at after end of main superstructure supporting radar aerials.
- Two narrow funnels sloping aft with distinctive angled funnel caps.
- Two SSM launchers sited between after funnel and pole aftermast which supports large curved air search radar aerial.
- Two 4 in gun mountings aft (X and Y positions).

Displacement full load, tons: 3300.0
Length, feet (metres): 402.0 (122.5)
Beam, feet (metres): 43.0 (13.1)
Draught, feet (metres): 13.3 (4.0)
Speed, knots: 34.5
Range, miles: 6000 at 16 kts

Missiles:
   SSM – 4 Aerospatiale MM 38 Exocet.
   SAM – 2 Short Bros Seacat quad launchers.
Guns: 3 or 4 Vickers 4 in *(102 mm)*/60 Mk(N)R.
4 Bofors 40 mm/70.
Torpedoes: 6 – 324 mm Mk 32 (2 triple) tubes. Honeywell Mk 44 Mod 1.
A/S mortars: 2 Admiralty Squid DC mortars (3-barrelled).

Radars:
   Air search – Plessey AWS 1.
   Air/surface search – Marconi SNW 10.
   Navigation – Racal Decca 1629.
   Fire control – 2 SGR 102 Signaal M4/3.
Sonars: Graseby Type 184 B; hull-mounted.
Type 170; hull mounted.

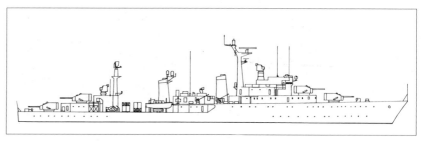

Almirante Class

ALMIRANTE WILLIAMS

Chilean Navy

Country: CHILE
Ship type: DESTROYERS
Class: PRAT (COUNTY)
Active: 4

Name (Pennant Number): PRAT (ex-*Norfolk*) (11), COCHRANE (ex-*Antrim*) (12), LATORRE (ex-*Glamorgan*) (14), BLANCO ENCALADA (ex-*Fife*) (15)

Recognition Features:
- High freeboard.
- 4.5 in mounting (A position) immediately forward of SSM launchers (B mounting position).
- Slim pyramid mast aft of bridge.
- Squat funnels with pyramid mainmast centrally situated between them. Double bedstead air search radar aerial atop.
- Seaslug SAM director on raised structure forward of flight deck with lattice Seaslug launcher on quarterdeck.
- Note - *Blanco Encalada* and *Cochrane* are different in appearance with greatly enlarged flight deck continued right aft making them effectively flush-decked and Seaslug system has been removed.

Displacement full load, tons: 6200.0
Length, feet (metres): 520.5 (158.7)
Beam, feet (metres): 54.0 (16.5)
Draught, feet (metres): 20.5 (6.3)
Speed, knots: 30.0
Range, miles: 3500 at 28 kts

Missiles:
SSM – 4 Aerospatiale MM 38 Exocet.
SAM – Short Bros Seaslug Mk 2 (11 and 14 only).
2 Shorts Seacat quad launchers (not in 14). 2 Israeli Barak I (To be fitted in all).

Guns: 2 Vickers 4.5 in *(115 mm)* Mk 6.
2 or 4 Oerlikon 20 mm Mk 9.
2 Bofors 40 mm/60 (14 only).
12.7 mm (single or twin) MGs.
Torpedoes: 6 – 324 mm Mk 32 (2 triple) tubes; Honeywell Mk 44 Mod 1.
Decoys: 2 Corvus launchers.
2 Wallop Barricade double layer launchers.
Radars:
Air search – Marconi Type 965 M or 966 (14 and 15).
Admiralty Type 277 M.
Surface search – Marconi Type 992 Q or R.
Navigation – Decca Type 978/1006.
Fire control – Plessey Type 903.
Marconi Type 901 (in 11 and 14).
2 Elta EL/M-22L IGM.
2 Plessey Type 904 (not in 14).
Sonars: Kelvin Hughes Type 162 M; hull-mounted.
Graseby Type 184 M or Type 184 S (in 15); hull-mounted.
Helicopters: 1 Bell 206B (11 and 14). 2 NAS 332F Super Puma (12 and 15).

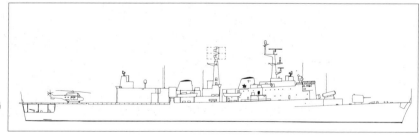

PRAT

Chilean Navy

Country: CHINA
Ship type: DESTROYERS
Class: LUDA (TYPE 051) (DDG)
Active: 17
Building: 1

Name (Pennant Number): JINAN (105), XIAN (106), YINCHUAN (107), XINING (108), KAIFENG (109), DALIAN (110), NANJING (131), HEFEI (132), CHONGQING (133), ZUNYI (134), CHANGSHA (161), NANNING (162), NANCHANG (163), GUILIN (164), ZHANJIANG (165), ZHUHAI (166), – (177)

Recognition Features:

Type III

● High bow with sweeping forecastle, aft to bridge. One maindeck level through to stern.
● Large distinctive 5.1 in mounting (A position) with 37 mm/63 mounting (B position).
● Lattice mainmast with sloping forward edge just forward of forward funnel. Smaller lattice tapered aftermast about midships.
● Twin, black-capped funnels angled astern.
● Two YJ-1 SSM missile launchers. One set immediately aft of forward funnel, the second immediately aft of after funnel.
● Isolated after superstructure supports fire control director at forward end and 37 mm/63 mounting.
● 5.1 in mounting (Y position).
● Note – Type I (modified) varies mainly from the Type III in that the YJ-1 SSM launchers are substituted by the larger HY-2 SSM launchers.

Displacement full load, tons: 3670.0
Length, feet (metres): 433.1 (132.0)
Beam, feet (metres): 42.0 (12.8)
Draught, feet (metres): 15.1 (4.6)
Speed, knots: 32.0
Range, miles: 2970 at 18 kts

Missiles:
    SSM – 6 HY-2 (C-201) launchers; (Types I and II).
        8 YJ-1 (Eagle Strike) (C-801) launchers (Type III).
    SAM – Thomson-CSF Crotale octuple launcher (*Kaifeng*).
    A/S – After set of launchers in *Zhuhai* may also be used for CY-1; payload anti-submarine torpedoes.
Guns: 4 (Type I) or 2 (Type II) USSR 5.1 in *(130 mm)*/58; (2 twin) (Type I).
8 China 57 mm/70 (4 twin). Fitted in some of the class, the others have 37 mm.
8 China 37 mm/63 (4 twin) (some Type I and Type III).
8 USSR 25 mm/60 (4 twin).
Torpedoes: 6 – 324 mm Whitehead B515 (2 triple tubes) (fitted in some Type I and Type III). Whitehead A 244S.
A/S mortars: 2 FQF 2500 12-tubed launchers.
Depth charges: 2 or 4 projectors; 2 or 4 racks.
Decoys: Chaff launchers (fitted to some).
Radars:
    Air search – Knife Rest or Cross Slot, Bean Sticks or Pea Sticks.
        Rice Screen, 3D (on mainmast in some). Surface search – Eye Shield or Thomson-CSF Sea Tiger.
        Square Tie (not in all).

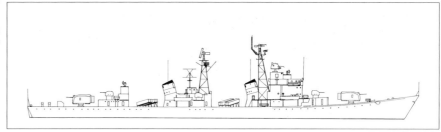

NANJING

Navigation – Fin Curve.
Fire control – Wasp Head or Type 343 Sun Visor B (Series 2).
    2 Rice Lamp (series 2).
    2 Type 347G.

Sonars: Pegas 2M and Tamir 2; hull-mounted.
VDS (Type III).

Helicopters: 2 Harbin Z-9A (Dauphin) (Type II).

Country: CHINA
Ship type: DESTROYERS
Class: LUHU (TYPE 052) (DDG)
Building: 1
Ordered: 1
Proposed: 2

Name (Pennant Number): HARIBING (112), – (113)

Recognition Features:
● Acute angled high bow. Single maindeck level from stem to stern.
● Sloping forecastle with 3.9 in mounting (A position).
● SAM launcher (B mounting position).
● 37 mm /63 mounting immediately forward of bridge.
● Tapered, lattice mainmast at after end of main superstructure.
● Single funnel amidships with black, wedge-shaped, Rad-Haz screen at after end.
● Two SSM missile launchers. One set between enclosed aftermast and funnel, second aft of aftermast.
● Square after superstructure supports large curved Hai Ying air search radar aerial at forward end and 37 mm/63 mounting at after end.
● Helicopter flight deck aft with open quarterdeck below.

Displacement standard, tons: 4200
Length, feet (metres): 475.7 (145.0)
Beam, feet (metres): 49.9 (15.2)
Draught, feet (metres): 16.7 (5.1)
Speed, knots: 30.0

Missiles:
    SSM – 8 YJ-1 (Eagle Strike) (C-801).
    SAM – 1 Thomson-CSF Crotale octuple launcher.
Guns: 2 – 3.9 in *(100 mm)*/56 (twin).

8 – 37 mm/63 (4 twin).
Torpedoes: 6 – 324 mm Whitehead B515 (2 triple) tubes; Whitehead A 244S.
A/S mortars: 2 FQF 2500 launchers.
Decoys: 2 SRBOC Mk 33 launchers.
2 China 26-barrelled launchers.
Radars:
    Air search – Rice Screen, 3D.
            Hai Ying.
    Air/surface search – Thomson-CSF Sea Tiger.
    Fire control – Typo 347G.
            2 Rice Lamp.
Sonars: Hull-mounted.
VDS.

Helicopters: 2 Harbin Z9A (Dauphin).

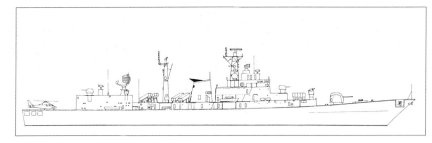

Luhu Class

HARIBING

Country: FRANCE
Ship type: DESTROYERS
Class: CASSARD (TYPE F 70 (A/A))
Active: 2

Name (Pennant Number): CASSARD (D 614), JEAN BART (D 615)

Recognition Features:
- Continuous maindeck from stem to stern.
- Long forecastle with 3.9 in mounting (A position).
- High forward superstructure with tall lattice mainmast towards after end.
- Large curved air/surface search radar aerial immediately forward of mainmast.
- High superstructure amidships with very distinctive air search radar dome atop.
- Two SPG 51C fire control directors on after end of central superstructure.
- Mk 13 Mod 5 SAM launcher aft of central superstructure.
- Matra Sadral PDMS SAM launchers outboard at after end of hangar.
- Hangar and small flight deck right aft.

Displacement full load, tons: 4700.0
Length, feet (metres): 455.9 (139.0)
Beam, feet (metres): 45.9 (14.0)
Draught, feet (metres): 21.3 (6.5) (sonar)
Speed, knots: 29.5.
Range, miles: 8200 at 17 kts

Missiles:
    SSM – 8 Aerospatiale MM 40 Exocet.
    SAM – GDC Pomona Standard SM-1MR; Mk 13 Mod 5
      launcher.
      2 Matra Sadral PDMS sextuple launchers; Mistral.
Guns: 1 DCN 3.9 in *(100 mm)*/55 Mod 68 CADAM.
2 Oerlikon 20 mm.
4 – 12.7 mm MGs.

Torpedoes: 2 launchers model KD 59E. ECAN L5 Mod 4.
Decoys: 2 CSEE Dagaie and 2 Sagaie launchers.
Nixie; towed torpedo decoy.
Radars:
    Air search – Thomson-CSF DRBJ 11B, 3D.
    Air/surface search – DRBV 26C.
    Navigation – 2 Racal DRBN 34A.
    Fire control – Thomson-CSF DRBC 33A.
               2 Raytheon SPG 51C.
Sonars: Thomson Sintra DUBA 25A (D 614) or DUBV 24C (D 615); hull-mounted.

Helicopters: 1 Lynx Mk 4.

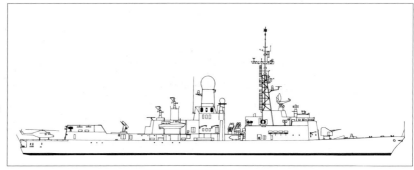

JEAN BART

Giorgio Ghiglione

Country: FRANCE
Ship type: DESTROYERS
Class: GEORGES LEYGUES (TYPE F 70 (ASW))
Active: 7

Name (Pennant Number): GEORGES LEYGUES (D 640), DUPLEIX
(D 641), MONTCALM (D 642), JEAN DE VIENNE (D 643), PRIMAUGUET
(D 644), LA MOTTE-PICQUET (D 645), LATOUCHE-TRÉVILLE (D 646)

Recognition Features:
● Long forecastle with 3.9 in mounting (A position).
● Tall lattice mainmast at after end of bridge with vertical after edge and sloping forward edge.
● Funnel amidships with vertical forward edge and sloping after edge, funnel cap angled down at after end.
● Two SSM launchers atop forward end of after superstructure immediately aft of funnel.
● Crotale SAM launcher atop after superstructure.
● Flight deck aft of hangar
● VDS towing equipment on quarterdeck.
● Note – Bridge raised one deck in the last three of the class.

Displacement full load, tons: 4300.0 (D 640-643), 4490.0
(D 644-646)
Length, feet (metres): 455.9 (139.0)
Beam, feet (metres): 45.9 (14.0)
Draught, feet (metres): 18.7 (5.7)
Speed, knots: 30.0; 21.0 on diesels
Range, miles: 8500 at 18 kts on diesels

Missiles:
SSM – 4 Aerospatiale MM 38 Exocet (MM 40 in D 642-646).
SAM – Thomson-CSF Crotale Naval EDIR launcher.

Guns: 1 – 3.9 in *(100 mm)*/55 Mod 68 CADAM automatic.
2 Oerlikon 20 mm.
4 M2HB 12.7 mm MGs.
Torpedoes: 2 launchers. ECAN L5; Honeywell Mk 46.
Decoys: 2 CSEE Dagaie launcher (replacing Syllex).
Radars:
Air search – DRBV 26 (not in D 644-646).
Air/surface search – Thomson-CSF DRBV 51C (DRBV 15A in D 644-646).
Navigation – 2 Decca 1226.
Fire control – Thomson-CSF Vega with DRBC 32E (D 640-643), DRBC 33A (D 644-646).
Crotale.
Sonars: Thomson Sintra DUBV 23D (DUBV 24C in D 644-646); bow-mounted.
DUBV 43B (43C in D 643-646) VDS; paired with DUBV 23D/24.
DSBV 61B (in D 644 onward).

Helicopters: 2 Lynx Mk 4.

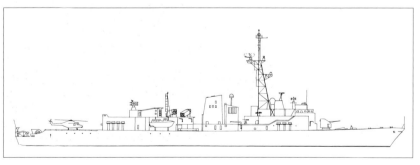

PRIMAUGUET

Maritime Photographic

Country: FRANCE
Ship type: DESTROYERS
Class: SUFFREN
Active: 2

Name (Pennant Number): SUFFREN (D 602), DUQUESNE (D 603)

Recognition Features:
● Two 3.9 in mountings (A and B positions).
● Large and distinctive air search radome at after end of bridge structure.
● Solid, rounded mast and funnel combined amidships with main engine exhausts at top.
● A/S missile launcher immediately aft of mainmast.
● SSM launcher on slightly raised after superstructure immediately forward of short lattice aftermast.
● SAM launcher at forward end of quarter deck.
● VDS towing equipment at after end of quarter deck.

Displacement full load, tons: 6910.0
Length, feet (metres): 517.1 (157.6)
Beam, feet (metres): 50.9 (15.5)
Draught, feet (metres): 20.0 (6.1)
Speed, knots: 34.0
Range, miles: 5100 at 18 kts

Missiles:
   SSM – 4 Aerospatiale MM 38 Exocet.
   SAM – ECAN Ruelle Masurca twin launcher.
   A/S – Latecoere Malafon; payload L4 torpedo.
Guns: 2 DCN 3.9 in *(100 mm)*/55 Mod 68 CADAM.
4 or 6 Oerlikon 20 mm.
Torpedoes: 4 launchers (2 each side). 10 ECAN L5.
Decoys: 2 CSEE Sagaie launchers.
2 Dagaie launchers.

Radars:
   Air search (radome) – DRBI 23.
   Air/surface search – DRBV 15A.
   Navigation – Racal Decca 1226.
   Fire control – 2 Thomson-CSF DRBR 51.
             Thomson-CSF DRBC 33A.
Sonars: Thomson Sintra DUBV 23; hull-mounted.
DUBV 43; VDS.

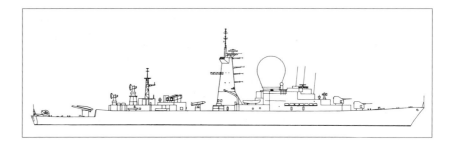

Suffren Class

SUFFREN

Tourville Class

Country: FRANCE
Ship type: DESTROYERS
Class: TOURVILLE (TYPE F 67)
Active: 3

Name (Pennant Number): TOURVILLE (D 610), DUGUAY-TROUIN (D 611), DE GRASSE (D 612)

Recognition Features:

● Two 3.9 in mountings (A and B positions).
● Short lattice mast atop after end of forward superstructure.
● SSM launchers immediately aft of forward superstructure.
● Large solid combined mainmast and funnel amidships.
● Distinctive air search radar aerial supported on projecting gantry forward end of mainmast.
● Two domed SATCOM aerials, port and starboard, immediately aft of mainmast.
● SAM launcher atop raised after superstructure.
● VDS towing gear on quarterdeck down from after end of flight deck.

Displacement full load, tons: 5950.0
Length, feet (metres): 501.6 (152.8)
Beam, feet (metres): 52.4 (16.0)
Draught, feet (metres): 18.7 (5.7)
Speed, knots: 32.0
Range, miles: 5000 at 18 kts

Missiles:

SSM – 6 Aerospatiale MM 38 Exocet.
SAM – Thomson-CSF Crotale Naval EDIR.
A/S – Latecoere Malafon; payload L4 torpedo.
Guns: 2 DCN 3.9 in *(100 mm)*/55 Mod 68 CADAM.
2 Oerlikon 20 mm.
Torpedoes: 2 launchers. 10 ECAN L5.
Decoys: 2 CSEE/VSEL Syllex launchers.

Radars:

Air search – DRBV 26.
Air/surface search – Thomson-CSF DRBV 51B.
Navigation – 2 Racal Decca Type 1226.
Fire control – Thomson-CSF DRBC 32D.
Crotale.
Sonars: Thomson Sintra DUBV 23; bow-mounted.
DSBV 62C; linear towed array.

Helicopters: 2 Lynx Mk 4.

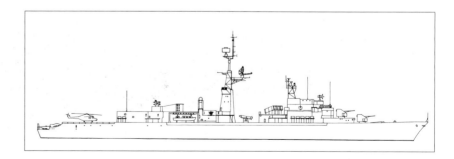

Tourville Class

TOURVILLE

Gunnar Olsen

Country: GERMANY
Ship type: DESTROYERS
Class: LÜTJENS (MODIFIED CHARLES F ADAMS) (TYPE 103B) (DDGs)
Active: 3

Name (Pennant Number): LÜTJENS (ex-US DDG 28) (D 185), MÖLDERS (ex-US DDG 29) (D 186), ROMMEL (ex-US DDG 30) (D 187)

Recognition Features:

● High bow, sweeping maindeck from stem to stern.
● 5 in mounting (A position).
● High, complex forward superstructure.
● Two funnels slightly angled aft. Forward one with tripod/lattice mainmast astride. After one is a mast and funnel combined with distinctive SPS 52 air search radar aerial atop. Both have two exhausts at top after end angled outboard.
● A/S missile launcher central between funnels.
● After superstructure supports after 5 in mounting and SSM missile launcher.
● Note – Some differences from unmodified *Charles F Adams* in W/T aerials and general outline, particularly the funnels.

Displacement full load, tons: 4500.0
Length, feet (metres): 437.0 (133.2)
Beam, feet (metres): 47.0 (14.3)
Draught, feet (metres): 20.0 (6.1)
Speed, knots: 32.0
Range, miles: 4500 at 20 kts

Missiles:

SSM – McDonnell Douglas Harpoon. Combined Mk 13 single-arm launcher with SAM system.

SAM – GDC Pomona Standard SM-1MR; Mk 13 Mod 0 launcher.
A/S – Honeywell ASROC Mk 112 octuple launcher; payload Mk 46 torpedoes.
Guns: 2 FMC 5 in *(127 mm)*/54 Mk 42 Mod 10 automatic.
Torpedoes: 6 – 324 mm US Mk 32 (2 triple) tubes. Honeywell Mk 46.
Depth charges: 1 projector.
Decoys: Loral Hycor SRBOC 6-barrelled Mk 36.
Radars:
Air search – Lockheed SPS 40.
Hughes SPS 52.
Surface search – Raytheon/Sylvania SPS 10.
Fire control – 2 Raytheon SPG 51.
Lockheed SPQ 9.
Lockheed SPG 60.
Sonars: Atlas Elektronik DSQS 21B; hull-mounted.

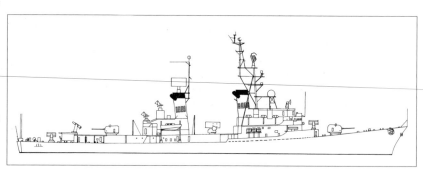

Lütjens Class

MÖLDERS

F Gámez

Country: ITALY
Ship type: DESTROYERS
Class: AUDACE (DDG)
Active: 2

Name (Pennant Number): ARDITO (D 550), AUDACE (D 551)

Recognition Features:

● Continuous maindeck from stem to stern.
● 5 in mounting (A position) with Aspide SAM launcher (B mounting position).
● Unusually high forward superstructure.
● Forward mast and funnel combined at after end of forward superstructure supports air search radar aerial. Twin exhausts in vee protruding aft.
● Aftermast and funnel combined has sloping forward edge supporting square-shaped long range air search radar aerial.
● SSM launchers sited between funnels.
● Pomona SAM launcher atop forward end of hangar.
● Flight deck right aft with open quarterdeck below.

Displacement full load, tons: 4400.0
Length, feet (metres): 448.0 (136.6)
Beam, feet (metres): 46.6 (14.2)
Draught, feet (metres): 15.1 (4.6)
Speed, knots: 34.0
Range, miles: 3000 at 20 kts

Missiles:

SSM – 8 OTO Melara/Matra Teseo Mk 2 (TG 2) (4 twin).
SAM – GDC Pomona Standard SM-1MR; Mk 13 Mod 4 launcher.
Selenia Albatros octuple launcher for Aspide.

Guns: 1 OTO Melara 5 in *(127 mm)*/54.
3 OTO Melara 3 in *(76 mm)*/62 Compact (*Ardito*) and 1 (*Ardito*) or 4 (*Audace*) Super Rapid.
Torpedoes: 6 – 324 mm US Mk 32 (2 triple) tubes. Honeywell Mk 46.
Decoys: 2 Breda 105 mm SCLAR 20-barrelled.
SLQ 25 Nixie; towed torpedo decoy.
Radars:
Long range air search – Hughes SPS 52C, 3D.
Air search – Selenia SPS 768 (RAN 3L).
Air/surface search – Selenia SPS 774 (RAN 10S).
Surface search – SMA SPQ 2D.
Navigation – SMA SPN 748.
Fire control – 3 Selenia SPG 76 (RTN 30X).
2 Raytheon SPG 51.
Sonars: CWE 610; hull-mounted.

Helicopters: 2 AB 212ASW.

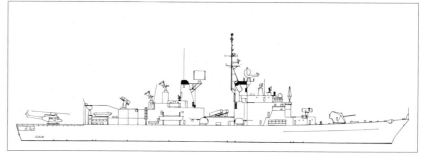

Audace Class

AUDACE

Giorgio Ghiglione

Country: ITALY
Ship type: DESTROYERS
Class: DE LA PENNE (ex-ANIMOSO) (DDG)
Active: 2

Name (Pennant Number): LUIGI DURAND DE LA PENNE (ex-*Animoso*) (D 560), FRANCESCO MIMBELLI (ex-*Ardimentoso*) (D 561)

Recognition Features:
- High bow, continuous maindeck from stem to stern.
- 5 in mounting (A position) with Aspide SAM launcher (B mounting position).
- Slim, pyramid foremast atop forward superstructure.
- Slightly shorter, enclosed aftermast supporting long range air search 3D radar aerial on platform protruding aft. Pole mast atop aftermast.
- Three square section funnels, one at after end of forward superstructure and twin vee funnels just abaft aftermast. Both sets slightly tapered towards top.
- SSM launchers amidships between forward funnel and aftermast.
- Pomona SAM launcher and 3 in mounting atop after superstructure.
- Flight deck right aft with open quarterdeck below.

Displacement full load, tons: 5400.0
Length, feet (metres): 487.4 (147.7)
Beam, feet (metres): 52.8 (16.1)
Draught, feet (metres): 16.5 (5.0)
Speed, knots: 31.5
Range, miles: 7000 at 18 kts

Missiles:
SSM – 4 or 8 OTO Melara/Matra Teseo Mk 2 (TG 2) (2 or 4 twin).

SAM – GDC Pomona Standard SM-1MR; Mk 13 Mod 4 launcher.
Selenia Albatros Mk 2 octuple launcher for Aspide.
Guns: 1 OTO Melara 5 in *(127 mm)*/54.
3 OTO Melara 3 in *(76 mm)*/62 Super Rapid.
Torpedoes: 6 – 324 mm B-515 (2 triple) tubes. Whitehead A 290.
Decoys: 2 CSEE Sagaie launchers.
1 Elmer anti-torpedo system.
Radars:
Long range air search – Hughes SPS 52C, 3D.
Air search – Selenia SPS 768 (RAN 3L).
Air/surface search – Selenia SPS 774 (RAN 10S).
Surface search – SMA SPS 702.
Fire control – 4 Selenia SPG 76 (RTN 30X).
2 Raytheon SPG 51D.
Navigation – SMA SPN 703 (3 RM 20).
Sonars: Raytheon, DE 1164; integrated hull, VDS.

Helicopters: 2 AB 212ASW.

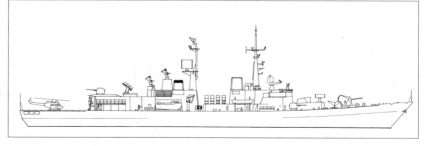

De La Penne Class

FRANCESCO MIMBELLI

Erminio Bagnasco

Country: JAPAN
Ship type: DESTROYERS
Class: ASAGIRI
Active: 8

Name (Pennant Number): ASAGIRI (DD 151), YAMAGIRI (DD 152), YUUGIRI (DD 153), AMAGIRI (DD 154), HAMAGIRI (DD 155), SETOGIRI (DD 156), SAWAGIRI (DD 157), UMIGIRI (DD 158)

Recognition Features:

● Continuous maindeck line from stem to stern.
● 3 in mounting (A position).
● A/S missile launcher immediately forward of bridge.
● Two black-capped funnels, after one partially obscured by superstructure.
● Lattice mainmast at aft of bridge supporting several radar aerials. Lattice aftermast just abaft after funnel.
● Fire control radar dome sited aft of aftermast.
● Helicopter deck aft, raised above maindeck with SAM launcher right aft at maindeck level.
● Note – The mainmast in *Asagiri* is offset to port. In the others of the class the mast has retained its central position but the after funnel has been offset to starboard.

Displacement full load, tons: 4200.0
Length, feet (metres): 449.4 (137.0)
Beam, feet (metres): 48.0 (14.6)
Draught, feet (metres): 14.6 (4.5)
Speed, knots: 30.0+

Missiles:

SSM – 8 McDonnell Douglas Harpoon (2 quad) launchers.
SAM – Raytheon Sea Sparrow Mk 29 octuple launcher.
A/S – Honeywell ASROC Mk 112 octuple launcher; payload Mk 46 torpedoes.

Guns: 1 OTO Melara 3 in *(76 mm)*/62 compact.
2 GE/GD 20 mm Phalanx Mk 15 CIWS.
Torpedoes: 6 – 324 mm Type 68 (2 triple) HOS 301 tubes. Honeywell Mk 46 Mod 5 Neartip.
Decoys: 2 Loral Hycor SRBOC 6-barrelled Mk 36.
1 SLQ 51 Nixie or Type 4; towed anti-torpedo decoy.
Radars:
Air search – Melco OPS 14C (DD 151-154).
Melco OPS 24 (DD 155-158), 3D.
Surface search – JRC OPS 28C.
Fire control – Type 2-22.
Type 2-12E (DD 151-154).
Type 2-12G (DD 155-158).
Sonars: Mitsubishi OQS 4A (II); hull-mounted.

Helicopters: 1 Mitsubishi HSS-2B Sea King or SH-60J Sea Hawk (DD 153-156, 158).

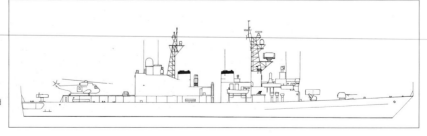

Asagiri Class

UMIGIRI

Hachiro Nakai

Haruna Class

Country: JAPAN
Ship type: DESTROYERS
Class: HARUNA
Active: 2

Name (Pennant Number): HARUNA (DD 141), HIEI (DD 142)

Recognition Features:
- Continuous maindeck line from bows to stern.
- Forecastle identical to *Shirane* class.
- Similar large central superstructure to *Shirane* class.
- Main difference is single mast and funnel combined offset slightly to port.
- Lattice mast and curved air search radar aerial atop funnel.
- Aft of funnel almost identical to *Shirane* class.
- Note – A heavy crane is fitted atop the hangar, starboard side.

Displacement standard, tons: 4950 (5050, DD 142)
Length, feet (metres): 502.0 (153.0)
Beam, feet (metres): 57.4 (17.5)
Draught, feet (metres): 17.1 (5.2)
Speed, knots: 31.0

Missiles:
SAM – Raytheon Sea Sparrow Mk 29 octuple launcher.
A/S – Honeywell ASROC Mk 112 octuple launcher; payload
Mk 46 torpedoes.
Guns: 2 FMC 5 in *(127 mm)*/54 Mk 42 automatic.
2 GE/GD 20 mm Phalanx Mk 15 CIWS.
Torpedoes: 6 – 324 mm Type 68 (2 triple) tubes. Honeywell
Mk 46 Mod 5 Neartip.
Decoys: 4 Loral Hycor SRBOC 6-barrelled Mk 36.

Radars:
Air search – Melco OPS 11C.
Surface search – JRC OPS 28.
Fire control – 1 Type 1A.
1 Type 2-12.
Sonars: Sangamo/Mitsubishi OQS 3; hull-mounted.

Helicopters: 3 Mitsubishi HSS-2B Sea King.

Haruna Class

HIEI

Hachiro Nakai

Hatakaze Class

Country: JAPAN
Ship type: DESTROYERS
Class: HATAKAZE
Active: 2

Name (Pennant Number): HATAKAZE (DD 171), SHIMAKAZE (DD 172)

Recognition Features:
● Break in upper deck profile just aft from bow, continuous maindeck from stem to stern.
● Three weapons fitted on long forecastle, from forward to aft, SAM launcher, 5 in mounting, A/S missile launcher.
● Central superstructure with lattice mainmast atop after end supporting square profile SPS 52C radar aerial.
● Black-capped, slightly tapered funnel just aft of midships.
● Short lattice aftermast supporting curved, OPS 11C air search radar.
● 5 in mounting forward end flight deck (Y position).
● Long flight deck with open quarterdeck below.

Displacement full load, tons: 5500.0
Length, feet (metres): 492.0 (150.0)
Beam, feet (metres): 53.8 (16.4)
Draught, feet (metres): 15.7 (4.8)
Speed, knots: 30.0

Missiles:
SSM – 8 McDonnell Douglas Harpoon.
SAM – GDC Pomona Standard SM-1MR; Mk 13 Mod 4 launcher.
A/S – Honeywell ASROC Mk 112 octuple launcher; payload Mk 46 torpedoes.
Guns: 2 FMC 5 in *(127 mm)*/54 Mk 42 automatic.
2 GE/GD 20 mm Phalanx Mk 15 CIWS.

Torpedoes: 6 – 324 mm Type 68 (2 triple) tubes. Honeywell Mk 46 Mod 5 Neartip.
Decoys: 2 Loral Hycor SRBOC 6-barrelled Mk 36.
Radars:
Air search – Hughes SPS 52C, 3D.
Melco OPS 11C.
Surface search – JRC OPS 28 B.
Fire control – 2 Raytheon SPG 51C.
Melco 2-21.
Type 2-12.
Sonars: Nec OQS 4; hull-mounted.

Helicopters: Platform for 1 Mitsubishi HSS-2B Sea King or SH-60J Sea Hawk.

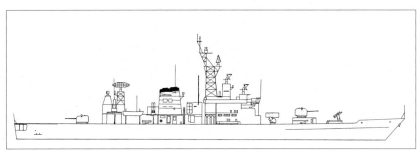

SHIMAKAZE

Hachiro Nakai

Country: JAPAN
Ship type: DESTROYERS
Class: HATSUYUKI
Active: 12

Name (Pennant Number): HATSUYUKI (DD 122), SHIRAYUKI (DD 123), MINEYUKI (DD 124), SAWAYUKI (DD 125), HAMAYUKI (DD 126), ISOYUKI (DD 127), HARUYUKI (DD 128), YAMAYUKI (DD 129), MATSUYUKI (DD 130), SETOYUKI (DD 131), ASAYUKI (DD 132), SHIMAYUKI (DD 133)

Recognition Features:
● Continuous maindeck with break down to quarterdeck.
● 3 in mounting (A position).
● A/S missile launcher immediately forward of bridge.
● Large black-capped funnel, slightly tapered, amidships.
● Lattice mainmast at after end of bridge structure supporting several radar aerials.
● Fire control radar dome mounted atop hangar, offset to starboard.
● Flight deck aft raised above maindeck level.
● SAM launcher just forward of quarterdeck.

Displacement full load, tons: 3700.0 (3800.0, DD 129 onwards)
Length, feet (metres): 426.4 (130.0)
Beam, feet (metres): 44.6 (13.6)
Draught, feet (metres): 13.8 (4.2), (14.4 (4.4) DD 129 onwards)
Speed, knots: 30.0

Missiles:
SSM – McDonnell Douglas Harpoon (2 quad) launchers.

SAM – Raytheon Sea Sparrow Type 3 (A-1) launcher.
A/S – Honeywell ASROC Mk 112 octuple launcher; payload Mk 46 torpedoes.
Guns: 1 OTO Melara 3 in *(76 mm)*/62 compact.
2 GE/GD 20 mm Phalanx Mk 15 CIWS.
Torpedoes: 6 – 324 mm Type 68 (2 triple) tubes. Honeywell Mk 46 Mod 5 Neartip.
Decoys: 2 Loral Hycor SRBOC 6-barrelled Mk 36.
Radars:
Air search – Melco OPS 14B.
Surface search – JRC OPS 18.
Fire control – Type 2-12 A.
2 Type 2-2½1A.
Sonars: Nec OQS 4A (II) (SQS 23 type); hull-mounted.

Helicopters: 1 Mitsubishi HSS-2B Sea King.

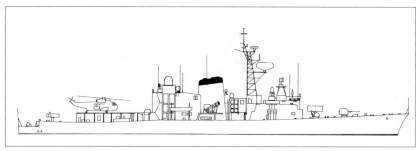

Hatsuyuki Class

SHIMAYUKI

J Mortimer

Kongo Class

Country: JAPAN
Ship type: DESTROYERS
Class: KONGO
Active: 2
Building: 2

Name (Pennant Number): KONGO (DD 173), KIRISHIMA (DD 174), – (DD 175), – (DD 176)

Recognition Features:
● Continuous maindeck line from stem to stern.
● Sole visable armament on long foredeck 5 in mounting (A position).
● CIWS mounting immediately forward of bridge and at after end of after superstructure.
● High forward superstructure topped by lattice mast sloping aft.
● Two unusually large angular funnels, close together amidships. Funnels tapered and with several black exhausts protruding at top.
● SSM launchers between funnels.
● SAM VLS cells at after end foredeck and forward end flight deck; not obvious from side aspect of ship.
● Long flight deck aft.
● Note – This is an enlarged and improved version of the USA *Arleigh Burke* class.

Displacement full load, tons: 9485.0
Length, feet (metres): 528.2 (161.0)
Beam, feet (metres): 68.9 (21.0)
Draught, feet (metres): 20.3 (6.2)
Speed, knots: 30.0
Range, miles: 4500 at 20 kts

Missiles:
SSM – 8 McDonnell Douglas Harpoon (2 quad) launchers.
SAM – GDC Pomona Standard SM-2MR. FMC Mk 41 (29 cells) forward.

Martin Marietta Mk 41 VLS (61 cells) aft.
A/S – Vertical launch ASROC; payload Mk 46 torpedoes.
Guns: 1 OTO Melara 5 in *(127 mm)*/54 Compatto.
2 GE/GD 20 mm/76 Mk 15 Vulcan Phalanx.
Torpedoes: 6 – 324 mm (2 triple) tubes. Honeywell Mk 46 Mod 5 Neartip.
Decoys: 4 Loral Hycor SRBOC 6-barrelled Mk 36.
Towed torpedo decoy.
Radars:
Air search – RCA SPY 1D, 3D.
Surface search – JRC OPS 28C or D.
Navigation – JRC OPS 20.
Fire control – 3 SPG 62; 1 Mk 2/21.
Sonars: Nec OQS 102 (SQS 53B/C) hull-mounted.
Oki OQR 2 (SQR 19A (V)) TACTASS; towed array.

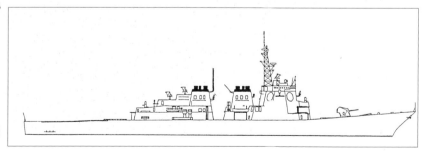

KONGO

Hachiro Nakai

Country: JAPAN
Ship type: DESTROYERS
Class: MINEGUMO
Active: 3

Name (Pennant Number): MINEGUMO (DD 116), NATSUGUMO (DD 117), MURAKUMO (DD 118)

Recognition Features:
● High bow, sweeping continuous maindeck to stern.
● 3 in mounting (A position).
● A/S mortar launcher (B mounting position).
● Single tapered funnel amidships.
● Type 2-12B fire control radar dome atop forward end of after superstructure.
● 3 in mounting aft of fire control dome.
● A/S missile launcher on afterdeck.
● Note – Almost identical to and easily confused with Yamagumo class from bow to mainmast.

Displacement standard, tons: 2100 (2150, DD 118)
Length, feet (metres): 373.9 (114.0), 377.2 (115.0) (DD 118)
Beam, feet (metres): 38.7 (11.8)
Draught, feet (metres): 13.1 (4.0)
Speed, knots: 27.0
Range, miles: 7000 at 20 kts

Missiles:
   A/S – Honeywell ASROC Mk 112 octuple launcher; payload Mk 46 torpedoes.
Guns: 4 USN 3 in *(76 mm)*/50 Mk 33 (2 twin) (only 2 in DD 118). 1 FMC/OTO Melara 3 in *(76 mm)*/62 Mk 75 compact (DD 118 only).

Torpedoes: 6 – 324 mm Type 68 (2 triple) tubes. Honeywell Mk 46 Mod 5 Neartip.
A/S mortars: 1 Bofors 375 mm Type 71 4-barrelled launcher.
Radars:
   Air search – Melco OPS 11.
   Surface search – JRC OPS 17.
   Fire control – Type 2-12B.
                Western Electric SPG 34 (DD 118 only).
                Type 1A FCS.
Sonars: Nec OQS 3; hull-mounted.
EDO SQS 36(J) (DD 118); VDS.

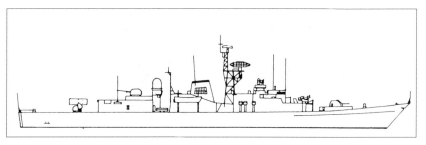

Minegumo Class

MURAKUMO

Murasame (DDG)

Country: JAPAN
Ship type: DESTROYERS
Class: MURASAME (DDG)
Building: 2
Proposed: 2

Name (Pennant Numbers): DD101, SS102, DD103, DD104

Recognition Features:
- Curved sweeping bow, square, near vertical stern
- 3-in mounting sited at mid-forecastle
- VL ASROC abaft forward gun mounting
- CIWS mounting on raised platform immediately forward of bridge
- Forward superstructure has bridge at forward end and large lattice mainmast at after end
- Two large, twin, square profile funnels, one at after end of forward superstructure and one at forward end of after superstructure
- Large flight deck at after end of superstructure

Displacement full load, tons: 5100
Length, feet (metres): 494.4 (151.0)
Beam, feet (metres): 57.1 (17.4)
Draught, feet (metres): 17.1 (5.2)
Speed, knots: 30

Missiles:
  SSM - 8 SSM-1B Harpoon
  SAM - Raytheon Mk48 VLS Sparrow
Guns: 1 OTO Melara 3 in (76 mm)/62 compact
2 GE/GD 20 mm Vulcan Phalanx Mk 15
Torpedoes: 6 - 324 mm Type 68 tubes. Type 89 (Mk 46 Mod 5)
Decoys: 4 Chaff launchers
Radars:
  Air search - Melco OPS 24, 3D
  Surface search - JRC OPS 28D
  Navigation - OPS 20
  Fire control - Two Type 2-31
Sonars: Mitsubishi OQS-5, hull mounted
OQE-1 towed array

Helicopters: 1 SH-60J Seahawk

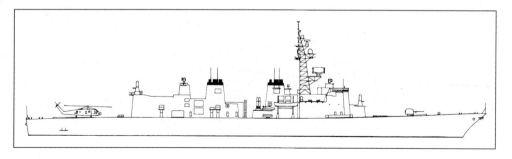

Murasame (DDG)

MURASAME

Hachiro Nakai

Country: JAPAN
Ship type: DESTROYERS
Class: SHIRANE
Active: 2

Name (Pennant Number): SHIRANE (DD 143), KURAMA (DD 144)

Recognition Features:
- High bow, sweeping continuous maindeck line from stem to stern.
- Two 5 in mountings (A and B positions) with A/S missile launcher between after mounting and bridge.
- High centrally sited superstructure.
- Two funnels and masts combined with distinctive black, wedge-shaped exhaust diffusers/RAD-HAZ screens atop. The after funnel is set to starboard and the forward one to port.
- Lattice mast mounted atop forward funnel and WM 25 fire control radar dome on atop after one.
- Long flight deck with open quarterdeck below.
- SAM launcher atop hangar.

Displacement standard, tons: 5200
Length, feet (metres): 521.5 (159.0)
Beam, feet (metres): 57.5 (17.5)
Draught, feet (metres): 17.5 (5.3)
Speed, knots: 32.0

Missiles:
   SAM – Raytheon Sea Sparrow Mk 29 octuple launcher.
   A/S – Honeywell ASROC Mk 112 octuple launcher; payload Mk 46 torpedoes.
Guns: 2 FMC 5 in *(127 mm)*/54 Mk 42 automatic.
2 GE/GD 20 mm Phalanx Mk 15 CIWS.
Torpedoes: 6 – 324 mm Type 68 (2 triple) tubes. Honeywell Mk 46 Mod 5 Neartip.

Radars:
   Air search – Nec OPS 12, 3D.
   Surface search – JRC OPS 28.
   Navigation – Koden OPN-11.
   Fire control – Signaal WM 25.
            Two Type 72-1A FCS.
Sonars: EDO/Nec SQS 35(J); VDS.
Nec OQS 101; hull-mounted.
EDO/Nec SQR 18A; towed array.

Helicopters: 3 SH-60J Sea Hawk.

SHIRANE

Hachiro Nakai

Tachikaze Class

Country: JAPAN
Ship type: DESTROYERS
Class: TACHIKAZE
Active: 3

Name (Pennant Number): TACHIKAZE (DD 168), ASAKAZE (DD 169), SAWAKAZE (DD 170)

Recognition Features:
- High bow, continuous sweeping maindeck line from stem to stern.
- 5 in mounting (A position).
- A/S missile launcher immediately forward of bridge.
- Forward mast and funnel combined at after end of main superstructure topped by lattice mast.
- Aftermast and funnel combined has SPS 52C square profile radar aerial mounted atop.
- Two sets of torpedo tubes mounted between funnels.
- After 5 in mounting (X position).
- SSM launcher on long afterdeck.

Displacement standard, tons: 3850 (3950, DD 170)
Length, feet (metres): 469.0 (143.0)
Beam, feet (metres): 47.0 (14.3)
Draught, feet (metres): 15.4 (4.7)
Speed, knots: 32.0

Missiles:
SSM – 8 McDonnell Douglas Harpoon.
SAM – GDC Pomona Standard SM-1MR; Mk 13 Mod 3 or 4 launcher.
A/S – Honeywell ASROC Mk 112 octuple launcher; payload Mk 46 torpedoes.
Guns: 2 FMC 5 in *(127 mm)*/54 Mk 42 automatic.
2 GE/GD 20 mm Phalanx CIWS Mk 15.

Torpedoes: 6 – 324 mm Type 68 (2 triple) tubes. Honeywell Mk 46 Mod 5 Neartip.
Decoys: 4 Loral Hycor SRBOC 6-barrelled Mk 36.
Radars:
Air search – Melco OPS 11.
Hughes SPS 52C, 3D.
Surface search – JRC OPS 16.
JRC OPS 28 (DD 170).
Fire control – 2 Raytheon SPG 51.
Type 2 FCS.
Sonars: Nec OQS-3A; hull-mounted.

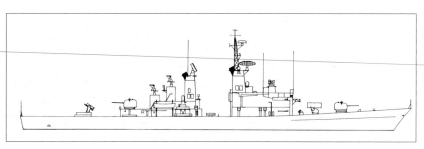

Tachikaze Class

ASAKAZE

Hachiro Nakai

Country: RUSSIA AND ASSOCIATED STATES
Ship type: DESTROYERS
Class: SOVREMENNY (DDG)
Active: 17
Building: 3

Name (Pennant Number): SOVREMENNY, OTCHYANNY, OTLICHNNY, OSMOTRITELNY, BEZUPRECHNY, BOYEVOY, STOYKY, OKRYLENNY, BURNY, GREMYASHCHY, BYSTRY, RASTOROPNY, BEZBOYAZNENNY, BEZUDERZHNY, BESPOKOINY, NASTOYCHIVY, BESSTRASHNY, VAZHNY, VDUMCHIVY, + 1

Recognition Features:
● High bow. Sweeping maindeck aft to break at bridge where SSM launchers are fitted, port and starboard.
● 130 mm/70 mounting (A position).
● SAM launcher (B mounting position).
● High forward superstructure with large enclosed mainmast at its after end. Large distinctive air search radar aerial atop.
● Single, large, square funnel just aft of midships.
● Lattice aftermast immediately aft of funnel.
● Small raised flight deck forward of SAM launcher.
● 130 mm/70 mounting (Y position).

Displacement full load, tons: 7300.0
Length, feet (metres): 511.8 (156.0)
Beam, feet (metres): 56.8 (17.3)
Draught, feet (metres): 21.3 (6.5)
Speed, knots: 32.0
Range, miles: 14 000 at 14 kts

Missiles:
SSM – 8 SS-N-22 Sunburn (2 quad) launchers.
SAM – 2 SA-N-7 Gadfly.

Guns: 4 – 130 mm/70 (2 twin).
4 – 30 mm/65 ADG 630.
Torpedoes: 4 – 21 in *(533 mm)* (2 twin) tubes. Type 53.
A/S mortars: 2 RBU 1000 6-barrelled.
Mines: Have mine rails for up to 40.
Decoys: 8 ten-barrelled launchers.
Radars:
Air search – Top Steer (in first three).
Plate Steer (in 4th and 5th).
Top Plate (remainder), 3D.
Surface search – 3 Palm Frond.
Fire control – Band Stand.
6 Front Dome.
Kite Screech.
2 Bass Tilt.
Sonars: Bull Horn and Steer Hide; hull-mounted.

Helicopters: 1 Ka-25 Hormone B or Ka-27 Helix.

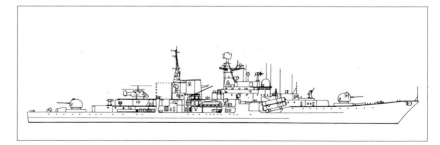

Sovremenny Class

GREMYASHCHY

Udaloy Class

Country: RUSSIA AND ASSOCIATED STATES
Ship type: DESTROYERS
Class: UDALOY (DDG)
Active: 11

Name (Pennant Number): UDALOY, VITSE-ADMIRAL KULAKOV, MARSHAL VASILEVSKY, ADMIRAL SPIRIDONOV, ADMIRAL TRIBUTS, MARSHAL SHAPOSHNIKOV, SIMFEROPOL (ex-*Marshal Budienny*), ADMIRAL LEVCHENKO, ADMIRAL VINOGRADOV, ADMIRAL KHARLAMOV, ADMIRAL PANTELEYEV

Recognition Features:
- High bow with sweeping maindeck aft to break at after funnel.
- 3.9 in mountings (A and B positions).
- SAM VLS launcher set into the ships' structure on the forecastle.
- A/S missile launchers on maindeck level, outboard of bridge, port and starboard.
- Two square section, twin funnels with tapered RAD-HAZ screens at after end.
- Two lattice masts forward of funnels. After mainmast is larger with Top Plate air search radar aerial atop.
- Smaller pyramid mast on bridge roof supports fire control radar.
- Large crane derrick aft of after funnels.
- Two hangars set side by side with inclined elevating ramps to the flight deck.

Displacement full load, tons: 8700.0
Length, feet (metres): 536.4 (163.5)
Beam, feet (metres): 63.3 (19.3)
Draught, feet (metres): 24.6 (7.5)
Speed, knots: 30.0
Range, miles: 4000 at 18 kts

Missiles:
SAM – 8 SA-N-9 Gauntlet vertical launchers.

A/S – 2 SS-N-14 Silex quad launchers; payload nuclear or Type E53 torpedo.
Guns: 2 – 3.9 in *(100 mm)*/59.
4 – 30 mm/65.
Torpedoes: 8 – 21 in *(533 mm)* (2 quad) tubes. Type 53.
A/S mortars: 2 RBU 6000 12-tubed.
Mines: Rails for 30 mines.
Decoys: 8 ten-barrelled chaff launchers.
US Masker type noise reduction.
Radars:
Air search – 1 or 2 (*Udaloy* and *Kulakov*) Strut Pair.
Top Plate (not *Udaloy* and *Kulakov*), 3D.
Surface search – 3 Palm Frond.
Fire Control – 2 Eye Bowl.
2 Cross Sword.
Kite Screech.
2 Bass Tilt.
Sonars: Horse Jaw; hull-mounted.
Horse Tail; VDS.
Helicopters: 2 Ka-27 Helix A.

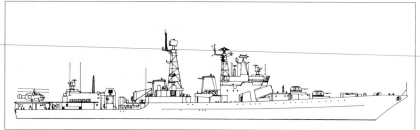

Udaloy Class

ADMIRAL VINOGRADOV

Guy Toremans

Country: TAIWAN
Ship type: DESTROYERS
Class: GEARING (FRAM I) (WU CHIN III CONVERSION)
Active: 7

Name (Pennant Number): CHIEN YANG (ex-USS *James E Kyes* DD 787) (912), LIAO YANG (ex-USS *Hanson* DD 832) (921), CHEN YANG (ex-USS *Hollister* DD 788) (923), TE YANG (ex-USS *Sarsfield* DD 837) (925), YUN YANG, (ex-USS *Johnston* DD 821) (927), SHEN YANG (ex-USS *Power* DD 839) (928), CHAO YANG (ex-USS *Hamner* DD 718) (929)

Recognition Features:
- Blunt bow, low freeboard.
- Continuous maindeck from stem to stern.
- Gun mounting (A position).
- Twin funnels sloping aft with distinctive black tapered tops.
- Large lattice mainmast astride forward funnel, smaller lattice mast aft of after funnel.
- Note 1 – The general recognition features above apply to all of the class. There are too many variants to be covered in this publication. Further details can be obtained from *Jane's Fighting Ships* yearbook.
- Note 2 – Class can be confused with Allen M Sumners.
- Note 3 – Also operated by Brazil (active 2), Greece (active 1), South Korea (active 7), Mexico (active 2), Pakistan (active 3 plus 1 MSA), Turkey (active 6).

Displacement full load, tons: approx 3500.0
Length, feet (metres): 390.5 (119.0)
Beam, feet (metres): 41.2 (12.6)
Draught, feet (metres): 19.0 (5.8)
Speed, knots: 32.5
Range, miles: 5800 at 15 kts

Missiles:
  SAM – 10 General Dynamics Standard SM1-MR (2 triple; 2 twin)
  A/S – Honeywell ASROC Mk 112 octupal launcher; payload Mk 46 torpedoes.
Guns: 1 OTO Melara 3 in (*76 mm*)/62.
1 GE/GD 20 mm Vulcan Phalanx Block 1, 6 barrelled Mk 15.
2 Bofors 40 mm/70.
4 or 6 12.7 mm MGs.
Torpedoes: 6 – 324 mm US Mk 32 (2 triple) tubes. Honeywell Mk 46.
Decoys: 4 Kung Fen 6 16-tubed launchers.
Mk T-6 Fanfare torpedo decoy.
Radars:
  Air search – Signaal DA-08.
  Surface search – Raytheon SPS 10/SPS 58.
  Fire control – Signaal STIR.
            Westinghouse W-160.
Sonars: Raytheon SQS 23 H; hull mounted.
Helicopters: 1 McDonnell Douglas 500MD.

TE-YANG

Leo Van Ginderen

Type 42 Class (Batch 1 and 2)

Country: UNITED KINGDOM
Ship type: DESTROYERS
Class: TYPE 42 (BATCH 1 AND 2)
Active: 8

Batch 1
Name (Pennant Number): BIRMINGHAM (D 86), NEWCASTLE (D 87), GLASGOW (D 88), CARDIFF (D 108)

Batch 2
Name (Pennant Number): EXETER (D 89), SOUTHAMPTON (D 90), NOTTINGHAM (D 91), LIVERPOOL (D 92)

Recognition Features:
● Continuous maindeck line from stem to stern, high freeboard.
● 4.5 in mounting half way between bow and bridge.
● SAM launcher immediately forward of bridge.
● High forward superstructure with large fire control radar dome atop.
● Large single, black-capped funnel with sloping after end, just aft of midships.
● Large lattice air search radar aerial at after end of forward superstructure.
● Tall, black-topped pole foremast forward of funnel.
● Tall, enclosed, black-topped mainmast aft of funnel, supporting surface search radar aerial.
● Hangar superstructure at forward end of flight deck with large fire control radar dome at forward end.
● Open quarterdeck below after end of flight deck.
● Note – Also operated by Argentina (active 2). Most obvious differences are air search bedstead radar aerial atop forward superstructure, large black exhausts on side of funnel, SSM launchers outboard of funnels.

Displacement full load, tons: 4100.0
Length, feet (metres): 412.0 (125.0)
Beam, feet (metres): 47.0 (14.3)
Draught, feet (metres): 19.0 (5.8)

Speed, knots: 29.0
Range, miles: 4000 at 18 kts

Missiles:
    SAM – British Aerospace Sea Dart twin launcher.
Guns: 1 Vickers 4.5 in (114 mm)/55 Mk 8.
2 or 4 Oerlikon/BMARC 20 mm GAM-BO1.
2 Oerlikon 20 mm Mk 7A (in those with only 2 BMARC).
2 GE/GD 20 mm Vulcan Phalanx Mk 15.
Torpedoes: 6 – 324 mm Plessey STWS Mk 3 (2 triple) tubes.
Decoys: 4 Marconi Sea Gnat 130 mm 6 barrelled launchers.
Graseby Type 182; towed torpedo decoy.
Radars:
    Air search – Marconi/Signaal Type 1022.
    Surface search – Plessey Type 996.
    Navigation – Kelvin Hughes Type 1006.
    Fire control – 2 Marconi Type 909.
Sonars: Ferranti Type 2050 or Plessey Type 2016; hull-mounted. Kelvin Hughes Type 162M.

Helicopters: 1 Westland Lynx HAS 3.

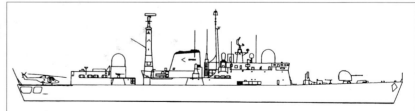

NOTTINGHAM

C & S Taylor

Country: UNITED KINGDOM
Ship type: DESTROYERS
Class: TYPE 42 (BATCH 3)
Active: 4

Batch 3
Name (Pennant Number): MANCHESTER (D 95), GLOUCESTER (D 96), EDINBURGH (D 97), YORK (D 98)

Recognition Features:
● Easily identified by their extremely long forecastle, some 50 ft more than Batches 1 and 2.
● Otherwise very similar to Batch 1 and 2 of the class.
● The stretched Batch 3s are fitted with a strengthening beam on each side which increases width by 2 feet.

Displacement full load, tons: 4675.0
Length, feet (metres): 462.8 (141.4)
Beam, feet (metres): 49.0 (14.9)
Draught, feet (metres): 19.0 (5.8) (screws)
Speed, knots: 30.0+
Range, miles: 4000 at 18 kts

Missiles:
SAM – British Aerospace Sea Dart twin launcher.
Guns: 1 Vickers 4.5 in *(114 mm)*/55 Mk 8.
2 Oerlikon/BMARC 20 mm GAM-BO1.
2 Oerlikon 20 mm Mk 7A.
1 or 2 GE/GD 20 mm Vulcan Phalanx Mk 15.
Torpedoes: 6 – 324 mm STWS Mk 2 (2 triple) tubes. Marconi Stingray.
Decoys: 4 Marconi Sea Gnat 130 mm 6 barrelled launchers. Graseby Type 182; towed torpedo decoy.

Radars:
Air search – Marconi/Signaal Type 1022.
Air/surface search – Marconi Type 992R or Plessey Type 996.
Navigation – Kelvin Hughes Type 1006.
Fire control – 2 Marconi Type 909 or 909 Mod 1.
Sonars: Ferranti Type 2050 or Plessey Type 2016; hull-mounted. Kelvin Hughes Type 162M; hull-mounted.

Helicopters: 1 Westland Lynx HAS 3.

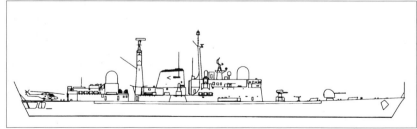

Type 42 Class (Batch 3)

MANCHESTER

H M Steele

Country: UNITED STATES OF AMERICA
Ship type: DESTROYERS
Class: ARLEIGH BURKE (FLIGHTS I and II) – (AEGIS) (DDG)
Active: 5
Building: 12
Proposed: 9

Name (Pennant Number): ARLEIGH BURKE (DDG 51), BARRY (ex-*John Barry*) (DDG 52), JOHN PAUL JONES (DDG 53), CURTIS WILBUR (DDG 54), STOUT (DDG 55), JOHN S McCAIN (DDG 56), MITSCHER (DDG 57), LABOON (DDG 58), RUSSELL (DDG 59), PAUL HAMILTON (DDG 60), RAMAGE (DDG 61), FITZGERALD (DDG 62), STETHEM (DDG 63), CARNEY (DDG 64), BENFOLD (DDG 65), GONZALEZ (DDG 66), COLE (DDG 67)
Only ships Active and Building named.

Recognition Features:
● High bow with sweeping maindeck aft to break down to flight deck.
● Only obvious armament on forecastle is 5 in mounting mid-way between bow and bridge.
● A/S missile VLS tubes situated between forward gun mounting and bridge and just forward of flight deck.
● High main superstructure with aft-sloping pole mainmast atop.
● Large twin funnels of unusual square section with black exhausts protruding at top. Funnels sited either side of midships.
● CIWS mountings on raised platform immediately forward of bridge and forward of Harpoon SSM launcher.
● Flight deck right aft.
● Note 1 – Helicopter hangar version is to be incorporated. Flight 2A version.
● Note 2 – Japan operate an improved Arleigh Burke class named Kongo class, see Japanese entry.

Displacement full load, tons: 8422.0
Length, feet (metres): 504.5 (153.8)
Beam, feet (metres): 66.9 (20.4)
Draught, feet (metres): 20.7 (6.3)
Speed, knots: 32.0
Range, miles: 4400 at 20 kts

Missiles:
SLCM/SSM – 56 GDC Tomahawk; combination of (a) land attack; TAINS (b) anti-ship (TASM). 8 McDonnell Douglas Harpoon (2 quad).
SAM – GDC Standard SM-2MR Block 4.
A/S – Honeywell ASROC; payload Mk 46 torpedoes.
2 Martin Marietta Mk 41 Vertical Launch Systems (VLS) for Tomahawk, Standard and ASROC.
Guns: 1 FMC 5 in *(127 mm)*/54 Mk 45 Mod 1 or 2.
2 GE/GD 20 mm Vulcan Phalanx 6-barrelled Mk 15.
Torpedoes: 6 – 324 mm Mk 32 Mod 14 (2 triple) tubes. Honeywell Mk 46 Mod 5.
Decoys: 2 Loral Hycor SRBOC 6-barrelled Mk 36.
SLQ 25 Nixie; torpedo decoy.
NATO Sea Gnat. SLQ-95 AEB. SLQ-39 chaff buoy.

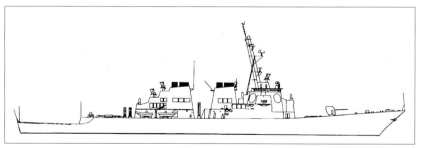

Arleigh Burke Class

BARRY

Ingalls

Radars:
Air search/fire control – RCA SPY 1D, 3D.
Surface search – Norden SPS 67(V)3.
Navigation – Raytheon SPS 64(V)9. Fire control – 3 Raytheon/RCA SPG 62.

Sonars: Gould/Raytheon/GE SQQ 89(V)6; combines SQS 53C; hull-mounted.
SQR 19 passive towed array.

Kidd Class

Country: UNITED STATES OF AMERICA
Ship type: DESTROYERS
Class: KIDD (DDG)
Active: 4

Name (Pennant Number): KIDD (ex-*Iranian Kouroosh*) (DDG 993) (ex-US DD 993), CALLAGHAN (ex-*Iranian Daryush*) (DDG 994) (ex-US DD 994), SCOTT (ex-*Iranian Nader*) (DDG 995) (ex-US DD 995, ex-US DD*996), CHANDLER (ex-*Iranian Anoushirvan*) (DDG 996) (ex-US DD 996, ex-US DD 998)

Recognition Features:
- High bow, high freeboard, sweeping maindeck aft to break at flight deck.
- 5 in mounting forward of A/S missile launcher on forecastle.
- Unusually high and long main superstructure giving a slab-sided profile.
- Two funnels, just proud of superstructure, each with several black exhausts protruding at the top.
- Complex lattice foremast supporting various aerials atop bridge roof.
- Large, central mainmast between funnels supporting the square, SPS 48E air search radar aerial.
- Raised flight deck immediately aft of superstructure.
- A/S missile launcher aft of flight deck with 5 in mounting (Y position).

Displacement full load, tons: 9574.0
Length, feet (metres): 563.3 (171.7)
Beam, feet (metres): 55.0 (16.8)
Draught, feet (metres): 20.0 (6.2)
Speed, knots: 33.0
Range, miles: 8000 at 17 kts

Missiles:
SSM – 8 McDonnell Douglas Harpoon (2 quad) launchers.
SAM – 52 GDC Standard SM-2MR.

A/S – 16 Honeywell ASROC; payload Mk 46 torpedoes.
Twin Mk 26 (Mod 3 and Mod 4) launchers for Standard and ASROC.
Guns: 2 FMC 5 in *(127 mm)*/54 Mk 45 Mod 0.
2 GE/GD 20 mm Vulcan Phalanx 6-barrelled Mk 15.
4 – 12.7 mm MGs.
Torpedoes: 6 – 324 mm Mk 32 (2 triple) tubes. Honeywell Mk 46.
Decoys: 4 Loral Hycor SRBOC 6-barrelled Mk 36.
SLQ 25 Nixie; torpedo decoy.
Radars:
Air search – ITT SPS 48E, 3D.
Raytheon SPS 49(V)5.
Surface search – ISC Cardion SPS 55.
Navigation – Raytheon SPS 64.
Fire control – Two SPG 51D, 1 SPG 60, 1 SPQ 9A.
Sonars: General Electric/Hughes SQS 53A; bow-mounted.
Gould SQR 19 (TACTAS); passive towed array (may be fitted).

Helicopters: 2 SH-2F LAMPS I or 1 SH-60 LAMPS III.

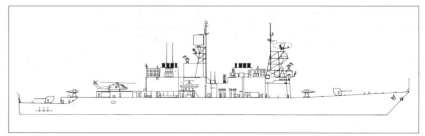

CALLAGHAN

Albert Campanera i Rovira

Country: UNITED STATES OF AMERICA
Ship type: DESTROYERS
Class: SPRUANCE (DD)
Active: 31

Name (Pennant Number): SPRUANCE (DD 963), PAUL F FOSTER (DD 964), KINKAID (DD 965), HEWITT (DD 966), ELLIOTT (DD 967), ARTHUR W RADFORD (DD 968), PETERSON (DD 969), CARON (DD 970), DAVID R RAY (DD 971), OLDENDORF (DD 972), JOHN YOUNG (DD 973), COMTE DE GRASSE (DD 974), O'BRIEN (DD 975), MERRILL (DD 976), BRISCOE (DD 977), STUMP (DD 978), CONOLLY (DD 979), MOOSBRUGGER (DD 980), JOHN HANCOCK (DD 981), NICHOLSON (DD 982), JOHN RODGERS (DD 983), LEFTWICH (DD 984), CUSHING (DD 985), HARRY W HILL (DD 986), O'BANNON (DD 987), THORN (DD 988), DEYO (DD 989), INGERSOLL (DD 990), FIFE (DD 991), FLETCHER (DD 992), HAYLER (DD 997)

Recognition Features:
- High bow, high freeboard, sweeping maindeck aft to break at flight deck.
- 5 in mounting on forecastle forward of A/S missile launcher and SSM or VLS tubes on some.
- Unusually high and long main superstructure giving a slab-sided impression.
- Large, square section twin funnels just proud of superstructure, each with several exhausts protruding at the top. After funnel offset to starboard.
- Complex lattice foremast supporting various aerials immediately atop bridge roof.
- Large central, lattice mainmast between funnels supporting air search radar aerial.
- Raised flight deck immediately aft of superstructure.
- SAM launcher just aft of flight deck with 5 in mounting in (Y position).
- GDC RAM SAM launcher (DD 971), starboard side aft.
- 5 in mounting on quarterdeck.
- Note – Modular construction makes these ships very similar to *Kidd* class.

Displacement full load, tons: 8040.0
Length, feet (metres): 563.2 (171.7)
Beam, feet (metres): 55.1 (16.8)

Draught, feet (metres): 19.0 (5.8)
Speed, knots: 33.0
Range, miles: 6000 at 20 kts

Missiles:
SLCM/SSM – GDC Tomahawk; combination of (a) land attack TAINS and (b) anti-ship (TASM).
8 McDonnell Douglas Harpoon (2 quad).
SAM – Raytheon GMLS Mk 29 octuple launcher.
GDC RAM quadruple launcher (DD 971).
A/S – Honeywell ASROC Mk 16 octuple launcher; payload Mk 46/Mk 50 torpedoes.
Guns: 2 FMC 5 in *(127 mm)*/54 Mk 45 Mod 0.
2 GE/GD 20 mm/76 6-barrelled Mk 15 Vulcan Phalanx. 4 – 12.7 mm MGs.
Torpedoes: 6 – 324 mm Mk 32 (2 triple) tubes. Honeywell Mk 46.
Decoys: 4 Loral Hycor SRBOC 6-barrelled Mk 36.
SLQ 25 Nixie; torpedo decoy.
Radars:
Air search – Lockheed SPS 40B/C/D (not in DD 997).
Raytheon SPS 49V (DD 997).
Hughes Mk 23 TAS.
Surface search – ISC Cardion SPS 55.
Navigation – Marconi LN 66 or SPS 53.

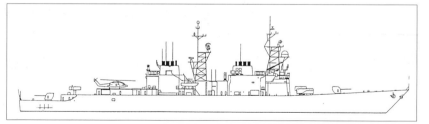

O'BRIEN

Giorgio Arra

Fire control – Lockheed SPG 60.
Lockheed SPQ 9A.
Raytheon Mk 95.

Sonars: SQQ 89(V)6 including GE/Hughes SQS 53B/C; bow-mounted; Gould SQR 19 (TACTAS); passive towed array.
Helicopters: 1 SH-60B LAMPS III or 1 SH-2F LAMPS I.

Destroyers – United States of America   **139**

Country: ALGERIA
Ship type: FRIGATES
Class: MOURAD RAIS (KONI) (TYPE II)
Active: 3

Name (Pennant Number): MOURAD RAIS (901), RAIS KELLICH (902), RAIS KORFOU (903)

Recognition Features:

● High bow, sweeping maindeck line through to stern.
● 3 in mounting (A position).
● A/S mortar in B mounting position.
● Stepped superstructure with enclosed mast at after end supporting air/surface or air search radar aerials.
● Single, squat funnel just aft of midships.
● Short enclosed mast just forward of funnel supporting Drum Tilt fire control radar aerial.
● SAM launcher in X mounting position.
● 3 in mounting (Y position).
● Pop Group fire control director just forward of SAM launcher.
● Note – Also operated by Bulgaria (active 1), Cuba (active 3) and Libya (active 2). The above features apply to Bulgarian and Cuban ships which could easily be confused. Obvious differences in Libyan ships are, forward end of superstructure removed to fit SS-N-2C SSM launcher and lattice mast fitted forward of Pop Group fire control director.

Displacement full load, tons: 1900.0
Length, feet (metres): 316.3 (96.4)
Beam, feet (metres): 41.3 (12.6)
Draught, feet (metres): 11.5 (3.5)
Speed, knots: 27.0 gas; 22.0 diesel
Range, miles: 1800 at 14 kts

Missiles:

  SAM – SA-N-4 Gecko twin launcher.

Guns: 4 – 3 in *(76 mm)*/60 (2 twin).
4 – 30 mm/65 (2 twin).
A/S mortars: 2 – 12-barrelled RBU 6000.
Depth charges: 2 racks.
Mines: Rails.
Decoys: 2 – 16-barrelled launchers.
Radars:
  Air/surface search – Strut Curve.
  Navigation – Don 2.
  Fire Control – Hawk screech.
       Drum tilt.
       Pop Group.
Sonars: Hull-mounted.

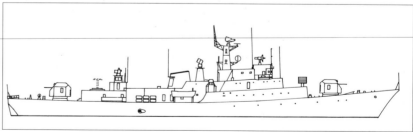

Mourad Rais Class

RAIS KELLICH

Leo Van Ginderen

Country: ARGENTINA
Ship type: FRIGATES
Class: ESPORA (MEKO 140) TYPE
Active: 4
Building: 2

Name (Pennant Number): ESPORA (41), ROSALES (42), SPIRO (43), PARKER (44), ROBINSON (45), GOMEZ ROCA (46)

Recognition Features:
- Blunt bow. Maindeck level raised for the length of the superstructure.
- 3 in mounting (A position).
- 40 mm/70 mountings (B and Y positions).
- Low integral funnel at after end of upper superstructure. Black exhaust protrudes from centre of main funnel.
- Tripod style mainmast atop after end of bridge structure supporting fire control radar dome.
- Raised flight deck.
- SSM launchers between after mounting and after end of flight deck.
- *Parker* and later ships fitted with a telescopic hangar.

Displacement full load, tons: 1790.0
Length, feet (metres): 299.1 (91.2)
Beam, feet (metres): 36.4 (11.1)
Draught, feet (metres): 11.2 (3.4)
Speed, knots: 27.0
Range, miles: 4000 at 18 kts

Missiles:
    SSM – 4 Aerospatiale MM 38 Exocet or 8 MM 40.
Guns: 1 OTO Melara 3 in *(76 mm)*/62 compact.
4 Breda 40 mm/70 (2 twin).
2 – 12.7 mm MGs.

Torpedoes: 6 – 324 mm ILAS 3 (2 triple) tubes. Whitehead A 244/S.
Decoys: CSEE Dagaie double mounting.
Radars:
    Air/surface search – Signaal DA 05.
    Navigation – Decca TM 1226.
    Fire Control – Signaal WM 28.
Sonars: Atlas Elektronik ASQ 4; hull-mounted.

Helicopters: 1 SA 319B Alouette III.

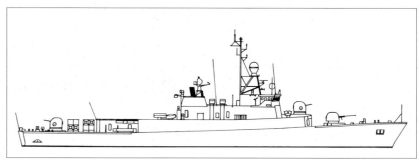

Espora Class

SPIRO

Country: AUSTRALIA
Ship type: FRIGATES
Class: ADELAIDE (OLIVER HAZARD PERRY) (FFGs)
Active: 6

Name (Pennant Number): ADELAIDE (01), CANBERRA (02), SYDNEY (03), DARWIN (04), MELBOURNE (05), NEWCASTLE (06)

Recognition Features:
- High bow with raised, solid sides to forward end of forecastle.
- SAM/SSM launcher in (A mounting position).
- High, box-like superstructure running from forecastle to flight deck.
- Distinctive fire control radar dome atop the bridge with the lattice foremast immediately aft supporting large curved air search radar aerial.
- Large lattice mainmast just forward of midships.
- 3 in mounting forward of funnel.
- Single funnel just showing towards after end of superstructure.
- After end of superstructure flush with ships side.
- CIWS mounting atop after end of hangar roof.
- Note – See Oliver Hazard Perry entry, USA.

Displacement full load, tons: 4100
Length, feet (metres): 453.0 (138.1)
Beam, feet (metres): 45.0 (13.7)
Draught, feet (metres): 14.8 (4.5)
Speed, knots: 29.0
Range, miles: 4500 at 20 kts

Missiles:
    SSM – 8 McDonnell Douglas Harpoon.
    SAM – GDC Pomona Standard SM-1MR.
Mk 13 Mod 4 launcher for both SAM and SSM systems.
Guns: 1 OTO Melara 3 in (76 mm)/62 Mk 75 compact.

1 GE/GD 20 mm Mk 15 Vulcan Phalanx.
Up to 6 – 12.7 mm MGs.
Torpedoes: 6 – 324 mm Mk 32 (2 triple) tubes. Honeywell Mk 46. Some Mk 44 torpedoes are still in service.
Decoys: 2 Loral Hycor SRBOC 6-barrelled Mk 36.
SLQ 25; towed torpedo decoy.
Radars:
    Air search – Raytheon SPS 49.
    Surface search/navigation – ISC Cardion SPS 55.
    Fire control – Lockheed SPG 60.
            Sperry Mk 92 (Signaal WM 28).
Sonars: Raytheon SQS 56; hull-mounted.
Commercial derivative of DE 1160 series.

Helicopters: 2 Sikorsky S-70B-2 Seahawks or 1 Seahawk and 1 Squirrel.

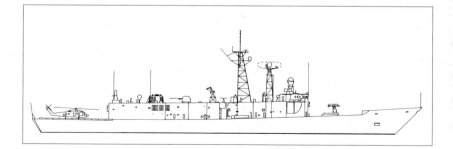

MELBOURNE

J Mortimer

Leopard Class

Country: BANGLADESH
Ship type: FRIGATES
Class: LEOPARD (TYPE 41)
Active: 2

Name (Pennant Number): ABU BAKR (ex-HMS *Lynx*) (F 15), ALI HAIDER (ex-HMS *Jaguar*)
(F 17)

Recognition Features:
● Raised forecastle with break down to 4.5 in mounting.
● Fire control director atop after end of bridge roof.
● Two masts, lattice foremast immediately aft of fire control director, enclosed mainmast supporting single bedstead air search radar aerial.
● Engine exhausts from short funnel inside lattice mainmast and at top after end of aftermast.
● 4.5 in mounting (Y position).
● Break in maindeck down to short quarterdeck.

Displacement full load, tons: 2520.0
Length, feet (metres): 339.8 (103.6)
Beam, feet (metres): 40.0 (12.2)
Draught, feet (metres): 15.5 (4.7) (screws)
Speed, knots: 24.0
Range, miles: 7500 at 16 kts

Guns: 4 Vickers 4.5 in *(115 mm)*/45 (2 twin) Mk 6.
1 Bofors 40 mm/60.
Radars:
 Air search – Marconi Type 965 with single AKE 1 array.
 Air/surface search – Plessey Type 993.
 Navigation – Decca Type 978; Kelvin Hughes Type 1007.
 Fire control – Type 275.

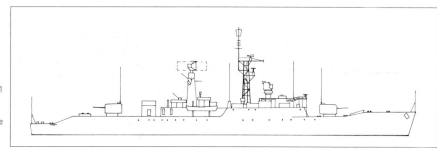

Leopard Class

ALI HAIDER

Country: BANGLADESH
Ship type: FRIGATES
Class: SALISBURY (TYPE 61)
Active: 1

Name (Pennant Number): UMAR FAROOQ (ex-HMS *Llandaff*) (F 16)

Recognition Features:
● Raised forecastle with break down to 4.5 in mounting (A position).
● Low superstructure with fire control director at after end of bridge.
● Two large, black-topped mast and funnel combined structures, aftermast supporting double bedstead air search radar aerial.
● Engine exhausts at top after end of masts.
● Short lattice mast supporting height finder radar aerial between forward mast and fire control director.
● 40 mm/60 mounting (Y position).
● Break down to short quarterdeck.

Displacement full load, tons: 2408.0
Length, feet (metres): 339.8 (103.6)
Beam, feet (metres): 40.0 (12.2)
Draught, feet (metres): 15.5 (4.7)
Speed, knots: 24.0
Range, miles: 7500 at 16 kts

Guns: 2 Vickers 4.5 in *(115 mm)*/45 (twin) Mk 6.
2 Bofors 40 mm/60.
A/S mortars: 1 triple-barrelled Squid Mk 4.
Radars:
    Air search – Marconi Type 965 with double AKE 2 array.
    Air/surface search – Plessey Type 993.
    Height finder – Type 278M.
    Surface search – Kelvin Hughes Type 1007.

    Navigation – Decca Type 978.
    Fire control – Type 275.
Sonars: Type 174; hull-mounted.
Graseby Type 170B; hull-mounted.

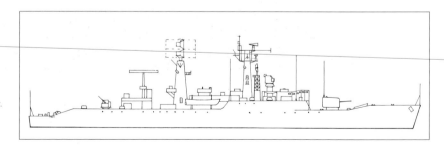

Salisbury Class

UMAR FAROOQ

J Mortimer

Country: BELGIUM
Ship type: FRIGATES
Class: WIELINGEN (E-71)
Active: 3

Name (Pennant Number): WIELINGEN (F 910), WESTDIEP (F 911), WANDELAAR (F 912)

Recognition Features:
- High freeboard with continuous maindeck from bow aft to break for very short quarterdeck.
- 3.9 in mounting (A position).
- A/S mortar launcher (B mounting position).
- Enclosed mainmast atop superstructure supporting surface search/fire control radar dome.
- Large distinctive funnel amidships with large central exhaust and smaller exhausts protruding at top.
- Short enclosed aftermast supporting air/surface search radar aerial.
- Two SSM launchers (X mounting position).
- SAM launcher forward of quarterdeck.

Displacement full load, tons: 2430.0
Length, feet (metres): 349.0 (106.4)
Beam, feet (metres): 40.3 (12.3)
Draught, feet (metres): 18.4 (5.6)
Speed, knots: 26.0
Range, miles: 6000 at 15 kts

Missiles:
   SSM – 4 Aerospatiale MM 38 Exocet (2 twin) launchers.
   SAM – Raytheon Sea Sparrow Mk 29 octuple launcher.
Guns: 1 Creusot Loire 3.9 in *(100 mm)*/55 Mod 68.
Torpedoes: 2 – 21 in *(533 mm)* launchers. ECAN L5 Mod 4.
A/S Mortars: 1 Creusot Loire 375 mm 6-barrelled.
Decoys: 2 Tracor MBA SRBOC 6-barrelled Mk 36.
Nixie SLQ 25; towed anti-torpedo decoy.

Radars:
   Air/surface search – Signaal DA 05.
   Surface search/fire control – Signaal WM 25.
   Navigation – Raytheon TM 1645/9X.
Sonars: Westinghouse SQS 505A; hull-mounted.

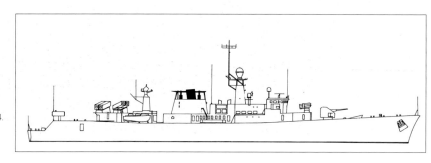

WESTDIEP

Guy Toremans

Country: BRAZIL
Ship type: FRIGATES
Class: INHAÚMA
Active: 4
Proposed: 1

Name (Pennant Number): INHAÚMA (V 30), JACEGUAY (V 31), JULIO DE NORONHA (V 32), FRONTIN (V 33)

Recognition Features:
● Apart from forecastle and quarterdeck, unusually high freeboard superstructure flush with ship's side.
● 4.5 in mounting (A position).
● Steep fronted, high forward superstructure.
● Large enclosed mainmast at after end of forward superstructure topped by slender lattice mast.
● Lattice aftermast atop forward end of after superstructure.
● Squat, tapered, black-capped funnel aft of midships atop after superstructure.
● 40 mm/70 mountings at after end of superstructure, port and starboard.
● Flight deck on maindeck level forward of break down to quarterdeck.

Displacement full load, tons: 1970.0
Length, feet (metres): 314.2 (95.8)
Beam, feet (metres): 37.4 (11.4)
Draught, feet (metres): 12.1 (5.3)
Speed, knots: 27.0
Range, miles: 4000 at 15 kts

Missiles:
　SSM – 4 Aerospatiale MM 40 Exocet.

Guns: 1 Vickers 4.5 in *(115 mm)* Mk 8.
2 Bofors 40 mm/70.
Torpedoes: 6 – 324 mm Mk 32 (2 triple) tubes. Honeywell Mk 46 Mod 5.
Decoys: 2 Plessey Shield launchers.
Radars:
　Surface search – Plessey ASW 4.
　Navigation – Kelvin Hughes Type 1007.
　Fire control – Selenia Orion RTN 10X.
Sonars: Atlas Elektronik DSQS 21C; hull-mounted.

Helicopters: 1 Westland Lynx.

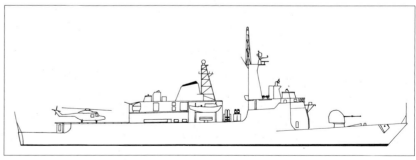

Inhaúma Class

FRONTIN

Verolme

Niteroi Class

Country: BRAZIL
Ship type: FRIGATES
Class: NITEROI
Active: 6

Name (Pennant Number): NITEROI (F 40), DEFENSORA (F 41), CONSTITUIÇÃO (F 42 *), LIBERAL (F 43*), INDEPENDÊNCIA (F 44), UNIÃO (F 45) (* GP design)

Recognition Features:
GP design -
● Short forecastle with 4.5 in mounting (A position) and A/S mortar launcher (B mounting position).
● High forward superstructure flush with ships side.
● Foremast at after end of forward superstructure.
● Pyramid mainmast immediately forward of funnel supporting air/surface search radar aerial.
● Squat, wide, black-capped funnel sited just aft of midships. Funnel has sloping top from forward to aft.
● Flight deck on maindeck level with break down to long quarterdeck with 4.5 in mounting (Y position).
● Ships boats, in davits, port and starboard, adjacent to funnel.
● Note – Standard design have longer flight deck (hence shorter quarterdeck) and A/S missile launcher (Y mounting position).

Displacement full load, tons: 3707.0
Length, feet (metres): 424.0 (129.2)
Beam, feet (metres): 44.2 (13.5)
Draught, feet (metres): 18.2 (5.5)
Speed, knots: 30.0
Range, miles: 5300 at 17 kts

Missiles:
SSM – 4 Aerospatiale MM 40 Exocet (2 twin) launchers.

SAM – 2 Short Bros Seacat triple launchers.
A/S – 1 Ikara launcher (Branik standard) (A/S version); payload Mk 46 torpedoes.
Guns: 2 Vickers 4.5 in *(115 mm)*/55 Mk 8 (GP version).
A/S version only has 1 mounting.
2 Bofors 40 mm/70.
Torpedoes: 6 – 324 mm Plessey STWS-1 (2 triple) tubes. Honeywell Mk 46 Mod 5.
A/S mortars: 1 Bofors 375 mm rocket launcher (twin-tube).
Depth charges: 1 rail; 5 charges (GP version).
Decoys: 2 Plessey Shield launchers.
Radars:
Air/surface search – Plessey AWS 2.
Surface search – Signaal ZW 06.
Fire control – 2 Selenia Orion RTN 10X.
Sonars: EDO 610E; hull-mounted.
EDO 700E VDS (F 40 and 41).

Helicopters: 1 Westland Lynx SAH-11.

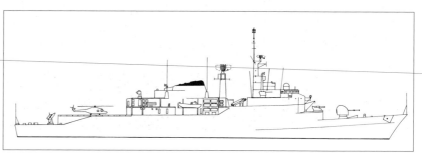

Niteroi Class

DEFENSORA

Erik Laursen

Pará Class

Country: BRAZIL
Ship type: FRIGATES
Class: PARÁ (ex-US GARCIA)
Active: 4

Name (Pennant Number): PARÁ (ex-*Albert David*) (D 27 (ex-FF 1050)), PARAÍBA (ex-*Davidson*) (D 28 (ex-FF 1045)), PARANÁ (ex-*Sample*) (D 29 (ex-FF 1048)), PERNAMBUCO (ex-*Bradley*) (D 30 (ex-FF 1041))

Recognition Features:
● Very long forecastle with continuous maindeck line from stem to stern.
● 5 in mounting on forecastle approximately mid-point between bow and bridge.
● A/S missile launcher between forward mounting and bridge.
● Single black-capped funnel amidships.
● Mast and funnel combined with pole mast atop after end. Large air search radar aerial at forward end of funnel.
● 5 in mounting atop after superstructure forward of hangar.
● Flight deck right aft.

Displacement full load, tons: 3403.0
Length, feet (metres): 414.5 (126.3)
Beam, feet (metres): 44.2 (13.5)
Draught, feet (metres): 14.5 (4.4)
Speed, knots: 27.5
Range, miles: 4000 at 20 kts

Missiles:
  A/S – Honeywell ASROC Mk 112 octuple launcher.
Guns: 2 USN 5 in *(127 mm)*/38 Mk 30.
Torpedoes: 6 – 324 mm Mk 32 (2 triple) tubes. 14 Honeywell Mk 46 Mod 5.

Decoys: 2 Loral Hycor Mk 33 RBOC 6 tubed launchers.
T-Mk 6 Fanfare; torpedo decoy system.
Prairie/Masker; hull/blade rate noise suppression.
Radars:
  Air search – Lockheed SPS 40.
  Surface search – Raytheon SPS 10.
  Navigation – Marconi LN 66.
  Fire control – General Electric Mk 35.
Sonars: EDO/General Electric SQS 26 AXR (D 29 and 30) or SQS 26B; bow-mounted.

Helicopters: Westland Lynx SAH-11.

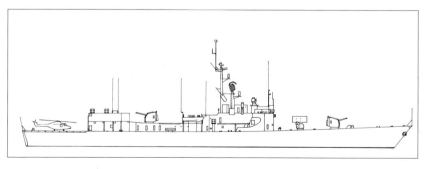

Pará Class

PERNAMBUCO

Hartmut Ehlers

Country: CANADA
Ship type: FRIGATES
Class: ANNAPOLIS
Active: 2

Name (Pennant Number): ANNAPOLIS (265), NIPIGON (266)

Recognition Features:
- Rounded, contoured forecastle from bow to breakwater.
- 3 in mounting aft of breakwater (A position).
- Low forward superstructure with very tall lattice mainmast at after end.
- Small, twin, side-by-side funnels aft of mainmast at forward end of hangar.
- Flight deck raised above maindeck level.
- Torpedo tubes, port and starboard, midway along flight deck length at maindeck level.
- Unusual shaped stern, sloping away (aft) from quarterdeck.

Displacement full load, tons: 2930.0
Length, feet (metres): 371.0 (113.1)
Beam, feet (metres): 42.0 (12.8)
Draught, feet (metres): 14.4 (4.4)
Speed, knots: 28
Range, miles: 4570 at 14 kts

Guns: 2 FMC 3 in *(76 mm)*/50 Mk 33 (twin).
Torpedoes: 6 – .324 mm Mk 32 (2 triple) tubes. Honeywell Mk 46 Mod 5.
Decoys: 4 Loral Hycor SRBOC 6-barrelled Mk 36.
Radars:
    Air/surface search – Marconi SPS 503 (CMR 1820).
    Surface search – Raytheon/Sylvania SPS 10.
    Fire control – Bell SPG 48.

Sonars: Westinghouse SQS 505 (*Annapolis*), SQS 510 (*Nipigon*); hull-mounted. SQS 501; hull-mounted.
Helicopters: 1 CH-124A Sea King ASW.

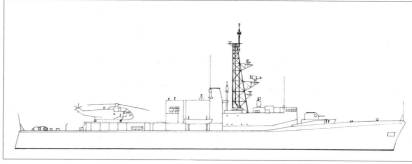

NIPIGON

Giorgio Arra

Improved Restigouche Class

Country: CANADA
Ship type: FRIGATES
Class: IMPROVED RESTIGOUCHE
Active: 3

Name (Pennant Number): GATINEAU (236), KOOTENAY (258), TERRA NOVA (259)

Recognition Features:
- Rounded, contoured forecastle aft to breakwater.
- 3 in mounting aft of breakwater (A position).
- Forward superstructure has very tall, slender lattice mainmast at after end.
- Small, single funnel aft of forward superstructure.
- Long afterdeck with SSM launcher forward end and CIWS mounting after end. (Gulf modified ships).
- Long afterdeck with torpedo tubes midway between after superstructure and stern and A/S missile launcher at forward end. (unmodified ships).

Displacement full load, tons: 2900.0
Length, feet (metres): 371.0 (113.1)
Beam, feet (metres): 42.0 (12.8)
Draught, feet (metres): 14.1 (4.3)
Speed, knots: 28.0
Range, miles: 4750 at 14 kts

Missiles:
SSM – 8 McDonnell Douglas Harpoon 2 quad launchers
A/S – Honeywell ASROC Mk 112 octuple launcher; payload Mk 46 torpedoes.
Guns: 2 Vickers 3 in *(76 mm)*/70 (twin) Mk 6.
1 GE/GD 20 mm/76 6-barrelled Vulcan Phalanx Mk 15 (modified).
2 Bofors 40 mm/60.

Torpedoes: 6 – 324 mm Mk 32 (2 triple) tubes. Honeywell Mk 46 Mod 5.
Decoys: 4 Loral Hycor SRBOC 6-barrelled Mk 36.
Plessey Shield launchers.
Radars:
Air search – Marconi SPS 503 (CMR 1820) or Ericsson Sea Giraffe HC 150.
Surface search – Raytheon SPS 10.
Navigation – Sperry 127E.
Fire control – Bell SPG 48.
Sonars: Westinghouse SQS 505 (SQS 510 in *Terra Nova*); combined VDS and hull-mounted.
C-Tech mine avoidance.
SQS 501; hull-mounted.

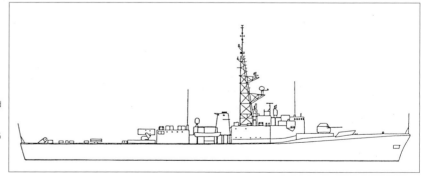

Improved Restigouche Class

GATINEAU

Halifax Class

Country: CANADA
Ship type: FRIGATES
Class: HALIFAX (FFH)
Active: 8
Building: 4

Name (Pennant Number): HALIFAX (330), VANCOUVER (331), VILLE DE QUEBEC (332), TORONTO (333), REGINA (334), CALGARY (335), MONTREAL (336), FREDERICTON (337), WINNIPEG (338), CHARLOTTETOWN (339), ST JOHN'S (340), OTTAWA (341)

Recognition Features:
● 57 mm/70 mounting mid-forecastle.
● Short lattice mast supporting large air search radar aerial mid- forward superstructure.
● Tall lattice mainmast after end of forward superstructure.
● Unusually large, square section funnel amidships, offset to port, with grilled intakes top, forward.
● High after superstructure with CIWS mounting at after end.
● Flight deck aft of hangar with small break down to short quarterdeck.
● Note – Large displacement for a frigate.

Displacement full load, tons: 5235.0
Length, feet (metres): 441.9 (134.7)
Beam, feet (metres): 53.8 (16.4)
Draught, feet (metres): 16.1 (4.9)
Speed, knots: 28.0
Range, miles: 7100 at 15 kts

Missiles:
SSM – 8 McDonnell Douglas Harpoon Block 1C (2 quad) launchers.
SAM – 2 Raytheon Sea Sparrow Mk 48 octuple vertical launchers.

Guns: 1 Bofors 57 mm/70 Mk 2.
1 GE/GD 20 mm Vulcan Phalanx Mk 15 Mod 1.
8-12.7 mm MGs.
Torpedoes: 4-324 mm Mk 32 Mod 9 (2 twin) tubes. Honeywell Mk 46 Mod 5.
Decoys: 4 Plessey Shield launchers.
Nixie SLQ 25; towed acoustic decoy.
Radars:
   Air search – Raytheon SPS 49(V)5.
   Air/surface search – Ericsson Sea Giraffe HC 150.
   Fire control – 2 Signaal VM 25 STIR.
   Navigation – Sperry Mk 340.
Sonars: Westinghouse SQS 505(V)6; hull-mounted.

Helicopters: 1 CH-124A ASW or 1 CH-124B Heltas Sea King.

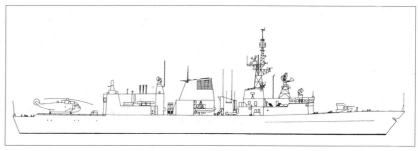

Halifax Class

TORONTO

St John Shipbuilding

Country: CHINA
Ship type: FRIGATES
Class: JIANGHU I (TYPE 053) (FFG)
Active: 25
Building: 2

Name (Pennant Number): CHANG DE (509), SHAOXING (510), NANTONG (511), WUXI (512), HUAYIN (513), ZENJIANG (514), XIAMEN (515), JIUJIANG (516), NANPING (517), JIAN (518), CHANGZHI (519), NINGPO (533), JINHUA (534), DANDONG (543), LINFEN (545), MAOMING (551), YIBIN (552), SHAOGUAN (553), ANSHUN (554), ZHAOTONG (555), JISHOU (557), ZIGONG (558), KANGDING (559), DONGGUAN (560), SHANTOU (561)

Recognition Features:

● Long slim hull with a high bow, low in water.
● 3.9 in mounting (A position).
● Squat funnel aft of midships.
● SSM launchers forward and aft of funnel.
● Tall lattice mainmast aft of forward superstructure.
● Two 37 mm/63 mountings forward of bridge, two outboard of mainmast and two atop after superstructure (X position).
● 3.9 in mounting (Y position).
● Note 1 – There are several variants of the Jianghu I class, but the basic outline is similar.
● Note 2 – Jianghu II are similar to Jianghu I except that aft of the funnel is a through deck with hangar forward of flight deck.
● Note 3 – Also operated by Bangladesh (active 1), Egypt (active 2). Both Type I but Egyptian ships have China 57 mm/70 mountings.

Displacement full load, tons: 1702, 1820 (Type II)
Length, feet (metres): 338.5 (103.2)
Beam, feet (metres): 35.4 (10.8)
Draught, feet (metres): 10.2 (3.1)
Speed, knots: 26.0

Range, miles: 4000 at 15 kts; 2700 at 18 kts

Missiles:
    SSM – 4 HY-2 (C-201) (2 twin) launchers (2 in Type II).
Guns: 2 or 4 China 3.9 in *(100 mm)*/56 (2 twin).
1 Creusot Loire 3.9 in *(100 mm)*/55 (Type II).
12 China 37 mm/63 (6 twin) (8 (4 twin) (in some).
Torpedoes: 6 – 324 mm ILAS (2 triple) tubes (Type II).
Whitehead A 244S.
A/S mortars: 2 RBU 1200 5-tubed launchers (4 in some).
Depth charges: 2 BMB-2 projectors; 2 racks.
Decoys: 2 SRBOC 6-barrelled Mk 33 or 2 China 26-barrelled launchers.
Radars:
    Air/surface search – MX 902 Eye Shield.
    Surface search/fire control – Square Tie.
    Navigation – Don 2 or Fin Curve.
    Fire control – Wok Won or Rice Lamp.
        Sun Visor (some Type I).
Sonars: Echo Type 5; hull-mounted.

Helicopters: Harbin Z-9A (Dauphin) (in Type II).

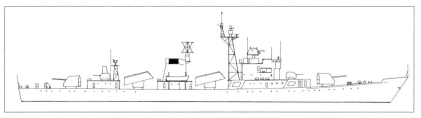

DANDONG

Country: CHINA
Ship type: FRIGATES
Class: JIANGHU III and IV (TYPE 053 HT) (FFG)
Active: 3
Building: 1

Name (Pennant Number): HUANGSHI (535), WU HU (536), ZHOUSHAN (537) (535, 536 – Type III) (537 – Type IV)

Recognition Features:
● High bow, with 3.9 in mounting (A position).
● The maindeck is higher in the midships section.
● Forward superstructure with enclosed mainmast at after end, enclosed lower section lattice top.
● Large, low funnel aft of midships with ship's boats in davits outboard.
● Two 37 mm/63 mountings forward of bridge and two at after end of maindeck level, port and starboard.
● SSM launchers trained outboard, port and starboard, forward and aft of funnel.
● 3.9 mounting (Y position).

Displacement full load, tons: 1924.0
Length, feet (metres): 338.5 (103.2)
Beam, feet (metres): 35.4 (10.8)
Draught, feet (metres): 10.2 (3.1)
Speed, knots: 26.0
Range, miles: 4000 at 15 kts

Missiles:
   SSM – 8 YJ-1 (Eagle Strike) (C-801).
Guns: 4 China 3.9 in *(100 mm)*/56 (2 twin).
8 China 37 mm/63 (4 twin).
A/S mortars: 2 RBU 1200 5-tubed launchers.
Depth charges: 2 BMB-2 projectors; 2 racks.

Decoys: 2 China 26-barrelled launchers.
Radars:
   Air/surface search – MX 902 Eye Shield.
   Surface search/fire control – Square Tie.
   Navigation – Fin Curve.
   Fire Control – Rice Lamp, Sun Visor.
Sonars: Echo Type 5; hull-mounted.

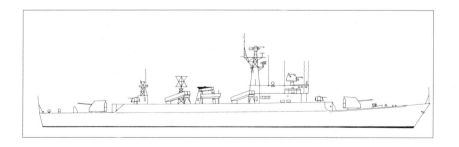

WU HU

Country: CHINA
Ship type: FRIGATES
Class: JIANGWEI (FFG)
Active: 4
Building: 1
Proposed: 1

Name (Pennant Number): ANQING (539), HUAINAN (540), HUABEI (541), TONGLING (542)

Recognition Features:
- Long forecastle, one third length of ship.
- Weapons on forecastle from forward to aft, A/S mortar launcher, 3.9 in mounting and SAM launcher.
- Stepped superstructure with 37 mm/63 mountings, port and starboard, outboard at forward end of bridge.
- Large Sun Visor fire control radar dome atop bridge.
- Mainmast, enclosed bottom lattice topped, at after end of forward superstructure.
- Single, squat funnel just aft of midships.
- Ship's boats in davits, port and starboard, adjacent to funnel.
- SSM launchers forward (trained to starboard) and aft (trained to port) of funnel.
- Large hangar with flight deck right aft and open quarterdeck below.

Displacement standard, tons: 2180.0
Length, feet (metres): 367.5 (112.0)
Beam, feet (metres): 40.7 (12.4)
Draught, feet (metres): 14.1 (4.3)
Speed, knots: 25.0
Range, miles: 4000 at 18 kts

Missiles:
   SSM – 6 YJ-1 (Eagle Strike) (C-801) (2 triple) launchers.
   SAM – 1 HQ-61 sextuple launcher.
Guns: 2 China 3.9 in *(100 mm)*/56 (twin).
8 China 37 mm/63 (4 twin).
A/S mortars: 2 RBU 1200; 5-tubed launchers.
Decoys: 2 SRBOC Mk 33 6-barrelled launchers.
2 China 26-barrelled launchers.
Radars:
   Air/surface search – Rice Screen.
   Fire control – Sun Visor.
                           2 Rice Lamp.
                           Navigation – Fin Curve.
Sonars: Echo Type 5; hull-mounted.

Helicopters: 1 Harbin Z9A (Dauphin).

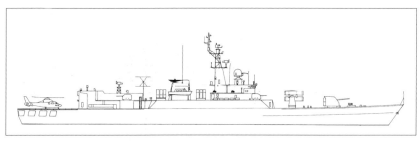

Jiangwei Class

ANQING

Country: COLOMBIA
Ship type: FRIGATES
Class: ALMIRANTE PADILLA (TYPE FS 1500)
Active: 4

Name (Pennant Number): ALMIRANTE PADILLA (CM 51), CALDAS (CM 52), ANTIOQUIA (CM 53), INDEPENDIENTE (CM 54)

Recognition Features:
- Low forecastle with break up to high midships maindeck and down to short quarterdeck.
- 3 in mounting (A position).
- Tall flat fronted bridge structure with large enclosed mainmast at after end. Pole mast atop after end of mainmast.
- Large, tapered funnel with wedge shaped smoke deflector atop.
- SSM launchers between funnel and forward superstructure.
- Flight deck aft of after superstructure at maindeck level.
- 40 mm/70 mounting (Y position).
- Note – Also operated by Malaysia (active 2), and classified as Corvettes. Main differences are; large pyramid mast with single pole mast immediately aft; surface search radar aerial on raised platform atop after superstructure.

Displacement full load, tons: 2100.0
Length, feet (metres): 325.1 (99.1)
Beam, feet (metres): 37.1 (11.3)
Draught, feet (metres): 12.1 (3.7)
Speed, knots: 27.0
Range, miles: 7000 at 14 kts

Missiles:
SSM – 8 Aerospatiale MM 40 Exocet.
Guns: 1 OTO Melara 3 in *(76 mm)*/62 compact.
2 Breda 40 mm/70 (twin).

4 Oerlikon 30 mm/75 Mk 74 (2 twin).
Torpedoes: 6 – 324 mm Mk 32 (2 triple) tubes.
Decoys: 1 CSEE Dagaie double mounting.
Radars:
Combined search – Thomson-CSF Sea Tiger.
Fire control – Castor II B.
Sonars: Atlas Elektronik ASO 4-2; hull-mounted.

Helicopters: 1 MBB BO 105 CB, ASW.

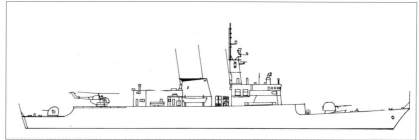

Almirante Padilla Class

ANTIOQUIA

Hartmut Ehlers

Modified Hvidbjørnen Class

Country: DENMARK
Ship type: FRIGATES
Class: MODIFIED HVIDBJØRNEN
Active: 1

Name (Pennant Number): BESKYTTEREN (F 340)

Recognition Features:
- Short forecastle with 3 in mounting (A position).
- Continuous maindeck from stem to stern.
- Square section enclosed mainmast at after end of forward superstructure with large air/surface search radar dome atop.
- Slim, tapered, black-capped funnel amidships.
- Ship's boats in davits, outboard of funnel, port and starboard.
- Flight deck extends from hangar to stern with open quarterdeck below.

Displacement full load, tons: 1970.0
Length, feet (metres): 245.0 (74.7)
Beam, feet (metres): 40.0 (12.2)
Draught, feet (metres): 17.4 (5.3)
Speed, knots: 18.0
Range, miles: 6000 at 13 kts on 1 engine

Guns: 1 USN 3 in *(76 mm)*/50.
Decoys: THORN EMI Sea Gnat 6-barrelled launchers.
Radars:
    Air/surface search – Plessey AWS 6; G band.
    Navigation – Burmeister & Wain Elektronik Scanter Mil 009.
Sonars: Plessey PMS 26; hull-mounted.

Helicopters: 1 Westland Lynx Mk 91.

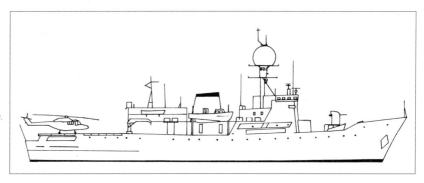

Modified Hvidbjørnen Class

BESKYTTEREN

Royal Danish Navy

Country: DENMARK
Ship type: FRIGATES
Class: NIELS JUEL
Active: 3

Name (Pennant Number): NIELS JUEL (F 354), OLFERT FISCHER (F 355), PETER TORDENSKIOLD (F 356)

Recognition Features:
● Unusual profile and easily identified frigate.
● Low forecastle with 3 in mounting (A position).
● High midships maindeck section, slab-sided.
● Unusually robust enclosed mainmast amidships, supporting surface search radar aerial.
● Large, black-capped funnel with sloping top sited well aft of midships.
● SSM launchers, port and starboard, aft of funnel.
● Two 9 LV 200 fire control directors mounted on sturdy pedestals aft of bridge and forward of quarterdeck.
● SAM launcher on quarterdeck.

Displacement full load, tons: 1320.0
Length, feet (metres): 275.5 (84.0)
Beam, feet (metres): 33.8 (10.3)
Draught, feet (metres): 10.2 (3.1)
Speed, knots: 28.0
Range, miles: 2500 at 18 kts

Missiles:
SSM – 8 McDonnell Douglas Harpoon (2 quad) launchers.
SAM – Raytheon NATO Sea Sparrow Mk 29 octuple launcher.

Guns: 1 OTO Melara 3 in (76 mm)/62 compact.
4 Oerlikon 20 mm (one each side of the funnel and two abaft the mast).
Depth charges: 1 rack.
Decoys: 2 THORN EMI Sea Gnat 6-barrelled launchers.
Radars:
Air search – Plessey AWS 5, 3D.
Surface search – Philips 9GR 600.
Fire control – 2 Mk 95.
Philips 9LV 200.
Navigation – Burmeister & Wain Elektronik Scanter Mil 009.
Sonars: Plessey PMS 26; hull-mounted.

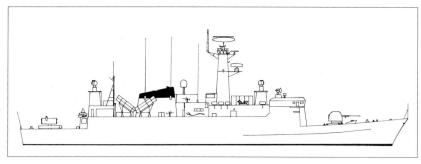

OLFERT FISCHER

Royal Danish Navy

Country: DENMARK
Ship type: FRIGATES
Class: THETIS
Active: 4

Name (Pennant Number): THETIS (F 357), TRITON (F 358), VAEDDEREN (F 359), HVIDBJØRNEN (F 360)

Recognition Features:
- Short forecastle with 3 in mounting (A position).
- High, slab-sided midships section.
- Large enclosed mainmast at after end of forward superstructure with distinctive air/surface search radar dome atop.
- Large, squat, black-capped funnel amidships.
- Ship's boats in davits outboard of funnel, port and starboard.
- Long flight deck with domed SATCOM aerial on pedestal atop hangar roof.
- Note – *Thetis* has a modified stern for seismological equipment.

Displacement full load, tons: 3500.0
Length, feet (metres): 369.1 (112.5)
Beam, feet (metres): 47.2 (14.4)
Draught, feet (metres): 19.7 (6.0)
Speed, knots: 20.0
Range, miles: 8500 at 15.5 kts

Guns: 1 OTO Melara 3 in *(76 mm)*/62 Super Rapid. 1 or 2 Oerlikon 20 mm.
Depth charges: 2 Rails (door in stern).
Radars:
Air/surface search – Plessey AWS 6.
Surface search – Terma Scanter Mil.
Navigation – Furuno FR1505DA.
Fire control – Bofors Electronic 9LV 200.

Sonars: Thomson Sintra TSM 2640 Salmon; hull-mounted and VDS.

Helicopters: 1 Westland Lynx Mk 91.

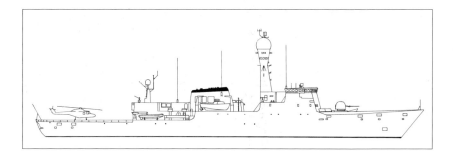

Thetis Class

THETIS

Royal Danish Navy

Country: FRANCE
Ship type: FRIGATES
Class: D'ESTIENNE D'ORVES (TYPE A 69)
Active: 17

Name (Pennant Number): D'ESTIENNE D'ORVES (F 781), AMYOT D'INVILLE (F 782), DROGOU (F 783), DÉTROYAT (F 784), JEAN MOULIN (F 785), QUARTIER MAÎTRE ANQUETIL (F 786), COMMANDANT DE PIMODAN (F 787), SECOND MAÎTRE LE BIHAN (F 788), LIEUTENANT DE VAISSEAU LE HÉNAFF (F 789), LIEUTENANT DE VAISSEAU LAVALLÉE (F 790), COMMANDANT L'HERMINIER (F 791), PREMIER MAÎTRE L'HER (F 792), COMMANDANT BLAISON (F 793), ENSEIGNE DE VAISSEAU JACOUBET (F 794), COMMANDANT DUCUING (F 795), COMMANDANT BIROT (F 796), COMMANDANT BOUAN (F 797)

Recognition Features:
● Low profile forecastle with 3.9 in mounting (A position).
● Substantial forward superstructure.
● Single funnel just aft of midships with vertical forward end and sloping after end.
● Mast and funnel combined with lattice mainmast atop.
● Break in deck level aft of funnel.
● SSM launchers, port and starboard, just aft of funnel.
● Ship's boat stowed in davits aft of SSM launchers.
● A/S mortar launcher atop after superstructure.
● Note – Also operated by Argentina (active 3). Most obvious difference 40 mm/70 mounting in place of A/S mortar launcher on after superstructure.

Displacement full load, tons: 1250.0 (1330.0 on later ships)
Length, feet (metres): 262.5 (80.0)
Beam, feet (metres): 33.8 (10.3)
Draught, feet (metres): 18.0 (5.5)
Speed, knots: 23.0

Range, miles: 4500 at 15 kts

Missiles:
    SSM – 4 Aerospatiale MM 40 (or 2 MM 38) Exocet.
Guns: 1 DCN 3.9 in *(100 mm)*/55 Mod 68 CADAM.
2 Oerlikon 20 mm.
Torpedoes: 4 tubes. ECAN L5.
A/S mortars: 1 Creusot Loire 375 mm Mk 54 6-tubed launcher.
Decoys: 2 CSEE Dagaie 10-barrelled launchers.
Nixie torpedo decoy.
Radars:
    Air/surface search – Thomson-CSF DRBV 51A.
    Navigation – Racal Decca 1226.
    Fire control – Thomson-CSF DRBC 32E.
Sonars: Thomson Sintra DUBA 25; hull-mounted.

DROGOU

Giorgio Ghiglione

Country: FRANCE
Ship type: FRIGATES
Class: FLORÉAL
Active: 6

Helicopters: 1 Dauphin II/Panther or 1 Alouette III or 1 AS 332F Super Puma.

Name (Pennant Number): FLORÉAL (F 730), PRAIRIAL (F 731), NIVÔSE (F 732), VENTÔSE (F 733), VENDÉMIAIRE (F 734), GERMINAL (F 735).

Recognition Features:

- Low forecastle with 3.9 in mounting (B position).
- High central superstructure with complex enclosed mainmast at after end of bridge.
- Unusual, twin, rectangular side-by-side funnels with exhausts protruding at top.
- SSM launcher sited between funnel and mainmast.
- 20 mm mounting on hangar roof.
- Long flight deck with break down to small quarterdeck.
- Ship's boat in starboard side davits adjacent to SSM launcher.

Displacement full load, tons: 2950.0
Length, feet (metres): 306.8 (93.5)
Beam, feet (metres): 45.9 (14.0)
Draught, feet (metres): 14.1 (4.3)
Speed, knots: 20.0
Range, miles: 10,000 at 15 kts

Missiles:
  SSM – 2 Aerospatiale MM 38 Exocet.
Guns: 1 DCN 3.9 in *(100 mm)*/55 Mod 68 CADAM. 2 Giat 20 F2 20 mm.
Decoys: 2 CSEE Dagaie II; 10-barrelled launchers.
Radars:
  Air/surface search – Thomson-CSF Mars DRBV 21A.
  Navigation – 2 Racal Decca DRBN 34A (1226).

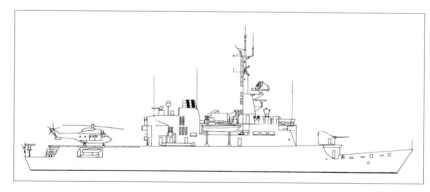

Floréal Class

FLORÉAL

Country: FRANCE
Ship type: FRIGATES
Class: LA FAYETTE
Building: 6

Name (Pennant Number): LA FAYETTE (F 710), SURCOUF (F 711), COURBET (F 712), JAUREGUIBERRY (F 713), GUEPRATTE (F 714), RONARC'H (F 715)

Recognition Features:

● 3.9 in mounting (A position).
● High, flush central superstructure with pyramid mainmast amidships.
● Unusual forward-sloping mast and funnel combined, supporting air/surface search radar aerial.
● SAM launcher at after end of main superstructure.
● Long flight deck right aft.
● Note 1 – All superstructure inclines at 10° to the vertical to reduce radar echo area.
● Note 2 – External equipment such as capstans and bollards are either hidden or installed as low as possible.
● Note 3 – Unusual smooth uncluttered profile for a warship.
● Note 4 – Also operated by Taiwan (6 building). Taiwan first of class 1994.

Displacement full load, tons: 3500.0
Length, feet (metres): 410.1 (125.0)
Beam, feet (metres): 50.5 (15.4)
Draught, feet (metres): 13.1 (4.4)
Speed, knots: 25.0
Range, miles: 9000 at 12 kts

Missiles:

SSM – 8 Aerospatiale MM 40 Exocet.
SAM – Thomson-CSF Crotale Naval CN 2 octuple launcher.

Guns: 1 DCN 3.9 in *(100 mm)*/55 Mod 68 CADAM.
2 Giat 20F2 20 mm.
2 – 12.7 mm MGs.
Decoys: 2 CSEE Dagaie 10-barrelled launchers.
SLAT anti-wake homing torpedoes system.
Radars:
Air/surface search – Thomson-CSF Sea Tiger (DRBV 15C).
Navigation – Racal Decca 1226.
Fire control – Thomson-CSF Castor II.
Crotale.
Arabel (for second three).

Helicopters: 1 Aerospatiale AS565 MA Panther.

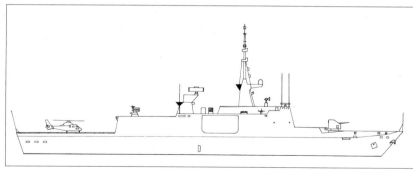

La Fayette Class

LA FAYETTE

Country: GERMANY
Ship type: FRIGATES
Class: BRANDENBURG (TYPE 123)
Building: 4

Name (Pennant Number): BRANDENBURG (F 215), SCHLESWIG-HOLSTEIN (F 216), BAYERN (F 217), MECKLENBURG-VORPOMMERN (F 218)

Recognition Features:

● High freeboard, continuous maindeck from bow to break down to flight deck.
● 76 mm/62 mounting (A position), SAM launcher (B position).
● High central superstructure with bridge well aft from bows.
● SAM (VLS) tubes immediately forward of bridge.
● Large, sturdy, enclosed mainmast forward of midships.
● Single, low, large funnel sited between forward and after superstructures.
● After superstructure with aftermast atop, supporting large air search radar aerial.
● SSM launcher atop hangar roof.
● Flight deck right aft with open quarterdeck below.
● Note – Also operated by Portugal (Active 3), Turkey (Active 4).

Displacement full load, tons: 4700.0
Length, feet (metres): 455.7 (138.9)
Beam, feet (metres): 54.8 (16.7)
Draught, feet (metres): 14.4 (4.4)
Speed, knots: 29.0
Range, miles: 4000 at 18 kts

Missiles:
  SSM – 4 Aerospatiale MM 38 Exocet.
  SAM – Martin Marietta VLS Mk 41.
       2 RAM 21 cell Mk 49 launchers.
Guns: 1 OTO Melara 76 mm/62.

Torpedoes: 4 – 324 mm Mk 32 (2 twin) tubes. Honeywell Mk 46.
Decoys: 2 Breda SCLAR.
Radars:
  Air search – Signaal LW 08.
  Air/Surface search – Signaal SMART, 3D.
  Fire control – 2 Signaal STIR 180 trackers.
  Navigation – 2 Raypath.
Sonars: Atlas Elektronik DSQS 23BZ; hull-mounted.

Helicopters: 2 Sea Lynx Mk 88.

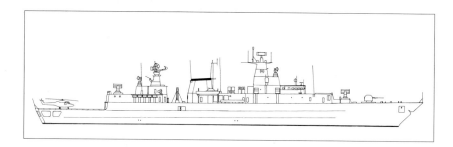

BRANDENBURG

M Nitz

Country: GERMANY
Ship type: FRIGATES
Class: BREMEN (TYPE 122)
Active: 8

Name (Pennant Number): BREMEN (F 207), NIEDERSACHSEN (F 208), RHEINLAND-PFALZ (F 209), EMDEN (F 210), KÖLN (F 211), KARLSRUHE (F 212), AUGSBURG (F 213), LÜBECK (F 214)

Recognition Features:
- 3 in mounting (A position) with Sea Sparrow SAM launcher (B mounting position).
- Forward superstructure dominated by WM 25 fire control director atop at after end.
- Unusual lattice mainmast immediately forward of funnel.
- SSM launchers sited between mainmast and forward superstructure.
- After superstructure has small lattice mast at forward end supporting air/surface search radar aerial.
- Two GDC RAM SAM launchers atop after end of hangar.
- Flight deck right aft with open quarterdeck below.
- Note – Goalkeeper fitted as a contingency for GDC RAM in three of the class.

Displacement full load, tons: 3600.0
Length, feet (metres): 426.4 (130.0)
Beam, feet (metres): 47.6 (14.5)
Draught, feet (metres): 21.3 (6.5)
Speed, knots: 30.0
Range, miles: 4000 at 18 kts

Missiles:
　　SSM – 8 McDonnell Douglas Harpoon (2 quad) launchers.
　　SAM – 16 Raytheon NATO Sea Sparrow Mk 29 octuple launcher.
Guns: 1 OTO Melara 3 in *(76 mm)*/62 Mk 75.

Torpedoes: 4 – 324 mm Mk 32 (2 twin) tubes. 8 Honeywell Mk 46 Mod 1.
Decoys: 4 Loral Hycor SRBOC 6-barrelled Mk 36.
SLQ 25 Nixie; towed torpedo decoy.
Prairie bubble noise reduction.
Radars:
　　Air/surface search – Signaal DA 08.
　　Navigation – SMA 3 RM 20.
　　Fire control – Signaal WM 25.
　　　　　　　　Signaal STIR.
Sonars: Atlas Elektronik DSQS 21 BZ (BO); hull-mounted.

Helicopters: 2 Westland Sea Lynx Mk 88.

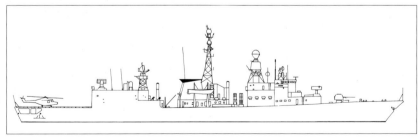

Bremen Class

BREMEN

Antonio Moreno

Country: GREECE
Ship type: FRIGATES
Class: HYDRA (MEKO 200HN)
Active: 1
Building: 3

Name (Pennant Number): HYDRA (F 452), SPETSAI (F 453), PSARA (F 454), SALAMIS (F 455)

Recognition Features:
● High bow with break down to after end of forecastle.
● 5 in mounting (A position).
● CIWS mounting (B mounting position).
● High, flat sided superstructure extending from bridge aft to flight deck.
● Lattice mainmast at after end of bridge structure.
● SSM launchers immediately aft of mainmast.
● Twin, outward sloping, side-by-side funnels aft of midships.
● Ship's boats hoisted unusually high on midship davits.
● CIWS mounting at after end of hangar roof.
● Flight deck right aft with open quarterdeck below.
● Note – Also operated by Portugal (active 3), Turkey (active 4).

Displacement full load, tons: 3200.0
Length, feet (metres): 383.9 (117.0)
Beam, feet (metres): 48.6 (14.8)
Draught, feet (metres): 13.5 (4.1)
Speed, knots: 31.0
Range, miles: 4100 at 16 kts

Missiles:
  SSM – 8 McDonnell Douglas Harpoon Block 1C; 2 quad launchers.

  SAM – Raytheon NATO Sea Sparrow Mk 48 vertical launcher.
Guns: 1 FMC Mk 45 Mod 2A 5 in (127 mm)/54.
  2 GD/GE Vulcan Phalanx 20 mm Mk 15 Mod 12.
Torpedoes: 6 – 324 mm Mk 32 Mod 5 (2 triple) tubes. Honeywell Mk 46.
Decoys: 4 Loral Hycor SRBOC 6-barrelled Mk 36.
  SLQ-25 Nixie; torpedo decoy.
Radars:
  Air search – Signaal MW 08, 3D.
  Air Surface search – Signaal/Magnavox; DA 08.
  Navigation – Racal Decca 2690 BT.
  Fire Control – 2 Signaal STIR.
Sonars: Raytheon SQS-56/DE 1160; hull-mounted and VDS.

Helicopters: 1 Sikorsky S-70B6 Seahawk (from 1995).

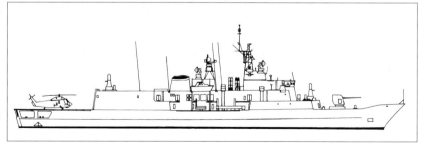

Hydra Class

HYDRA

Hartmut Ehlers

Country: INDIA
Ship type: FRIGATES
Class: GODAVARI
Active: 3
Building: 3

Name (Pennant Number): GODAVARI (F 20), GOMATI (F 21), GANGA (F 22), – (F 23), – (F 24), – (F 25)

Recognition Features:

● Unusually long forecastle.
● Three major weapons systems forward of the bridge; from the bow aft 57 mm/70 mounting, SSM launchers, SAM launchers.
● The bows are flared to accommodate the large SSM launchers sited either side of the Muff Cob fire control director.
● Midships superstructure with pyramid mainmast at after end.
● Small, tapered funnel just aft of midships.
● Slab-sided after superstructure (hangars) with small enclosed aftermast at forward end and air search radar aerial atop.
● Flight deck with break down to short quarterdeck.
● Note – The second three (improved) Godavari class will be larger and of a totally different profile.

Displacement full load, tons: 3850.0
Length, feet (metres): 414.9 (126.5)
Beam, feet (metres): 47.6 (14.5)
Draught, feet (metres): 14.8 (4.5)
Speed, knots: 27.0
Range, miles: 4500 at 12 kts

Missiles:

SSM – 4 SS-N-2D Styx. Indian designation P 20 or P 21.
SAM – SA-N-4 Gecko twin launcher.

Guns: 2 – 57 mm/70 (twin).
8 – 30 mm/65 (4 twin).
Torpedoes: 6 – 324 mm ILAS 3 (2 triple) tubes. Whitehead A244S.
Decoys: 2 launchers.
Graseby G738 towed torpedo decoy.
Radars:

Air search – Signaal LW 08.
Air/surface search – Head Net C, 3D.
Navigation/helo control – 2 Signaal ZW 06; or Don Kay.
Fire control – Two Drum Tilt.
Pop Group.
Muff Cob.

Sonars: Graseby 750 (*Godavari*); Bharat APSOH (*Ganga* and *Gomati*); hull-mounted. Fathoms Oceanic VDS (not in *Godavari*).
Type 162M.

Helicopters: 2 Sea King or 1 Sea King and 1 Chetak.

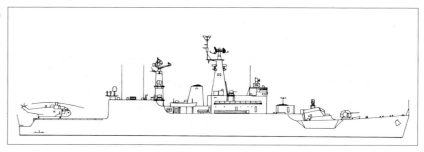

GANGA

Country: INDONESIA
Ship type: FRIGATES
Class: FATAHILLAH
Active: 3

Name (Pennant Number): FATAHILLAH (361), MALAHAYATI (362), NALA (363)

Recognition Features:
- 4.7 in mounting (A position) with A/S mortar launcher (B mounting position).
- Low, slab-sided superstructure centred forward of midships.
- Very substantial pyramid mainmast with pole mast atop its after end.
- Fire control radar dome atop mainmast.
- Large, square shaped, low profile funnel well aft of midships.
- SSM launchers between funnel and after superstructure.
- Large air/surface search radar aerial on pedestal atop small after superstructure.
- 40 mm/70 mounting aft of maindeck at break down to small quarterdeck.
- Note – *Nala* has no after mounting and the maindeck is extended to provide a hangar and flight deck.

Displacement full load, tons: 1450.0
Length, feet (metres): 276.0 (84.0)
Beam, feet (metres): 36.4 (11.1)
Draught, feet (metres): 10.7 (3.3)
Speed, knots: 30.0
Range, miles: 4250 at 16 kts

Missiles:
  SSM – 4 Aerospatiale MM 38 Exocet.
Guns: 1 Bofors 4.7 in *(120 mm)*/46.
1 or 2 Bofors 40 mm/70 (2 in *Nala*).
2 Rheinmetall 20 mm.
Torpedoes: 6 – 324 mm Mk 32 or ILAS 3 (2 triple) tubes (none in *Nala*). 12 Mk 46 (or A244S).

A/S mortars: 1 Bofors 375 mm twin-barrelled.
Decoys: 2 Knebworth Corvus 8-tubed launchers.
1 T-Mk 6 torpedo decoy.
Radars:
  Air/surface search – Signaal DA 05.
  Surface search – Racal Decca AC 1229.
  Fire control – Signaal WM 28.
Sonars: Signaal PHS 32; hull-mounted.

Helicopters: 1 Westland Wasp (*Nala* only).

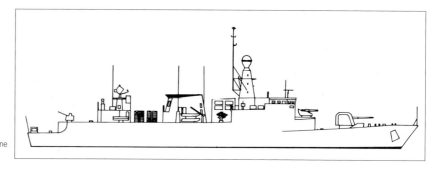

MALAHAYATI

92 Wing RAAF

Country: INDONESIA
Ship type: FRIGATES
Class: TRIBAL
Active: 3

Name (Pennant Number): MARTHA KRISTINA TIYAHAHU (ex-HMS *Zulu*) (331), WILHELMUS ZAKARIAS YOHANNES (ex-HMS *Gurkha*) (332), HASANUDDIN (ex-HMS *Tartar*) (333)

Recognition Features:
- 4.5 in mounting (A positions).
- Large lattice mainmast, forward of midships, supporting single bedstead air search radar.
- Twin funnels, after one slightly shorter.
- A/S mortar mounting between after funnel and hangar.
- Helicopter landing pad, on hangar roof, forward of after 4.5 in mounting (Y position).
- Note – Helicopter descends to hangar by flight deck lift and is covered by portable panels.

Displacement full load, tons: 2700.0
Length, feet (metres): 360.0 (109.7)
Beam, feet (metres): 42.5 (13.0)
Draught, feet (metres): 12.5 (3.8)
Speed, knots: 25.0
Range, miles: 5400 at 12 kts

Missiles:
SAM – 2 Short Bros Seacat quad launchers.
Guns: 2 Vickers 4.5 in *(114 mm)*.
2 Oerlikon 20 mm.
2 – 12.7 mm MGs.
A/S mortars: 1 Limbo 3-tubed Mk 10.
Decoys: 2 Knebworth Corvus 8-tubed launchers.

Radars:
Air search – Marconi Type 965.
Surface search – Type 993.
Navigation – Decca 978.
Fire control – Plessey Type 903.
Sonars: Graseby Type 177; hull-mounted.
Graseby Type 170 B; hull-mounted.
Kelvin Hughes Type 162.

Helicopters: 1 Westland Wasp.

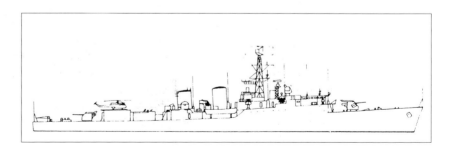

WILHELMUS ZAKARIAS YOHANNES

92 Wing RAAF

Country: INDONESIA
Ship type: FRIGATES
Class: VAN SPEIJK
Active: 6

Name (Pennant Number): AHMAD YANI (ex-*Tjerk Hiddes*) (351), SLAMET RIYADI (ex-*Van Speijk*) (352), YOS SUDARSO (ex-*Van Galen*) (353), OSWALD SIAHAAN (ex-*Van Nes*) (354), ABDUL HALIM PERDANA KUSUMA (ex-*Evertsen*) (355), KAREL SATSUITUBUN (ex-*Isaac Sweers*) (356)

Recognition Features:
● Similar to British *Leander* class.
● Long, raised forecastle with 3 in mounting (A position).
● Midships superstructure with pyramid mainmast atop, just aft of bridge.
● Single funnel just aft of midships.
● Short aftermast supporting large air search radar aerial.
● SAM launchers on hangar roof.
● Torpedo tubes, port and starboard, on maindeck at forward end of long flight deck.

Displacement full load, tons: 2835.0
Length, feet (metres): 372.0 (113.4)
Beam, feet (metres): 41.0 (12.5)
Draught, feet (metres): 13.8 (4.2)
Speed, knots: 28.5
Range, miles: 4500 at 12 kts

Missiles:
SSM – 8 McDonnell Douglas Harpoon.
SAM – 2 Short Bros Seacat quad launchers.
Guns: 1 OTO Melara 3 in *(76 mm)*/62 compact.
Torpedoes: 6 – 324 mm Mk 32 (2 triple) tubes. Honeywell Mk 46.
Decoys: 2 Knebworth Corvus 8-tubed.

Radars:
Air search – Signaal LW 03.
Air/surface search – Signaal DA 05.
Navigation – Racal Decca 1229.
Fire control – Signaal M 45.
2 Signaal M 44.
Sonars: Signaal CWE 610; hull-mounted; VDS.

Helicopters: 1 Westland Wasp.

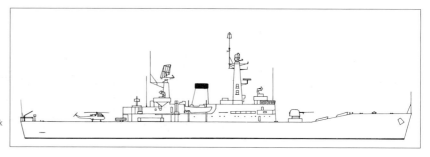

AHMAD YANI

L P Dunne, RAN

Country: IRAN
Ship type: FRIGATES
Class: ALVAND (VOSPER MARK 5)
Active: 3

Name (Pennant Number): ALVAND (ex-*Saam*) (71), ALBORZ (ex-*Zaal*) (72), SABALAN (ex-*Rostam*)

Recognition Features:

● Similar profile to the British Type 21 frigates.
● Long forecastle with 4.5 in mounting (A position).
● Pyramid mainmast just forward of midships.
● Low profile, sloping funnel well aft with distinctive gas turbine air intakes forward of funnel, port and starboard.
● Sited on afterdeck, from forward to aft, SSM launcher, A/S mortar and 35 mm/90 mounting.

Displacement full load, tons: 1350.0
Length, feet (metres): 310.0 (94.5)
Beam, feet (metres): 36.4 (11.1)
Draught, feet (metres): 14.1 (4.3)
Speed, knots: 39.0
Range, miles: 3650 at 18 kts

Missiles:

SSM – 1 Sistel Sea Killer II quin launcher.
Guns: 1 Vickers 4.5 in *(114 mm)*/55 Mk 8.
2 Oerlikon 35 mm/90 (twin).
3 Oerlikon GAM-BO1 20 mm.
2 – 12.7 mm MGs.
A/S mortars: 1 – 3-tubed Limbo Mk 10.
Decoys: 2 UK Mk 5 rocket flare launchers.

Radars:
Air/surface search – Plessey AWS 1.
Surface search – Racal Decca 1226.
Navigation – Decca 629.
Fire control – 2 Contraves Sea Hunter.
Sonars: Graseby 174; hull-mounted.
Graseby 170; hull-mounted.

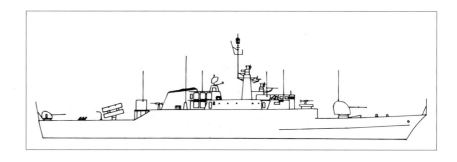

Alvand Class

ALBORZ

Lupo Class

Country: ITALY
Ship type: FRIGATES
Class: LUPO
Active: 4

Name (Pennant Number): LUPO (F 564), SAGITTARIO (F 565), PERSEO (F 566), ORSA (F 567)

Recognition Features:

● High bow, sweeping forecastle with 5 in mounting (A position).
● High forward superstructure with distinctive surface search/target indication radar dome atop bridge roof.
● Enclosed mast, with pole mast at after end, atop bridge superstructure.
● Shorter pyramid aftermast immediately forward of funnel.
● After superstructure (hangar) with SAM launcher on roof.
● Forward-trained SSM launchers on maindeck level, port and starboard, immediately aft of funnel.
● Two 40 mm/70 mountings on maindeck level, port and starboard, aft of SSM launchers.
● Flight deck right aft with open quarterdeck below.
● Note 1 – New Italian *Artigliere* class almost identical.
● Note 2 – Also operated by Peru (active 4) and Venezuela (active 6) Modified Lupo class. Most obvious difference being extended flight deck with break down to short quarterdeck.

Displacement full load, tons: 2525.0
Length, feet (metres): 371.3 (113.2)
Beam, feet (metres): 37.1 (11.3)
Draught, feet (metres): 12.1 (3.7)
Speed, knots: 35.0
Range, miles: 4350 at 16 kts on diesels

Missiles:
  SSM – 8 OTO Melara Teseo Mk 2 (TG 2).
  SAM – Raytheon NATO Sea Sparrow Mk 29 octuple launcher.
Guns: 1 OTO Melara 5 in *(127 mm)*/54.
4 Breda 40 mm/70 (2 twin) compact.
2 Oerlikon 20 mm can be fitted.
Torpedoes: 6 – 324 mm US Mk 32 tubes. Honeywell Mk 46.
Decoys: 2 Breda 105 mm SCLAR 20-tubed.
SLQ 25 Nixie; towed torpedo decoy.
Radars:
  Air search – Selenia SPS 774 (RAN 10S).
  Surface search/target indication – SMA SPS 702.
  Surface search – SMA SPQ2 F.
  Navigation – SMA SPN 748.
  Fire control – Selenia SPG 70 (RTN 10X).
            2 Selenia SPG 74 (RTN 20X)
            US Mk 95 Mod 1.
Sonars: Raytheon DE 1160B; hull-mounted.

Helicopters: 1 AB 212ASW.

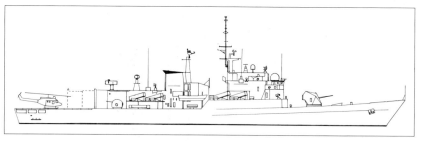

Lupo Class

SAGITTARIO

Guy Toremans

Country: ITALY
Ship type: FRIGATES
Class: MAESTRALE
Active: 8

Name (Pennant Number): MAESTRALE (F 570), GRECALE (F 571), LIBECCIO (F 572), SCIROCCO (F 573), ALISEO (F 574), EURO (F 575), ESPERO (F 576), ZEFFIRO (F 577)

Recognition Features:
● Bridge well aft from bows.
● 5 in mounting (A position).
● SAM launcher (B mounting postion).
● High forward superstructure with pointed pyramid mainmast atop.
● Single, rectangular funnel with wedge shaped, black smoke diffuser at top.
● SSM launchers, two port two starboard, angled outboard sited immediately aft of funnel.
● White, domed SATCOM aerial atop hangar roof.
● Flight deck right aft with open quarterdeck below.

Displacement full load, tons: 3200.0
Length, feet (metres): 405.0 (122.7)
Beam, feet (metres): 42.5 (12.9)
Draught, feet (metres): 15.1 (4.6)
Speed, knots: 32.0
Range, miles: 6000 at 16 kts

Missiles:
SSM – 4 OTO Melara Teseo Mk 2 (TG 2).
SAM – Selenia Albatros octuple launcher.
Guns: 1 OTO Melara 5 in (127 mm)/54 automatic.
4 Breda 40 mm/70 (2 twin) compact.
2 Oerlikon 20 mm.
Torpedoes: 6 – 324 mm US Mk 32 (2 triple) tubes. Honeywell Mk 46.

2 – 21 in (533 mm) B516 tubes in transom. Whitehead A184.
Decoys: 2 Breda 105 mm SCLAR 20-tubed rocket launchers.
SLQ 25; towed torpedo decoy.
Prairie Masker; noise suppression system.
Radars:
Air/surface search – Selenia SPS 774 (RAN 10S).
Surface search – SMA SPS 702.
Navigation – SMA SPN 703.
Fire control – Selenia SPG 75 (RTN 30X).
2 Selenia SPG 74 (RTN 20X).
Sonars: Raytheon DE 1164; hull-mounted; VDS.

Helicopters: 2 AB 212ASW.

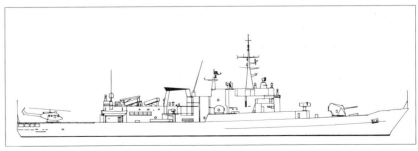

Maestrale Class

LIBECCIO

Aldo Fraccaroli

Country: JAPAN
Ship type: FRIGATES
Class: ABUKUMA
Active: 6

Name (Pennant Number): ABUKUMA (DE 229), JINTSU (DE 230), OHYODO (DE 231), SENDAI (DE 232), CHIKUMA (DE 233), TONE (DE 234)

Recognition Features:
- Long, sweeping, uncluttered forecastle with 3 in mounting midway between bow and bridge front.
- High forward superstructure with large lattice mainmast at after end, top half offset.
- Distinctive curved, lattice air search radar aerial on platform at forward end of mast.
- Two rectangular shaped black-capped funnels, forward one slightly taller.
- A/S missile launcher sited between funnels.
- Gas turbine air intakes aft of after funnel, port and starboard.
- Short lattice aftermast atop after superstructure.
- SSM launchers on raised structure immediately aft of aftermast.
- CIWS mounting on afterdeck.
- Note – Non-vertical and rounded surfaces are employed for stealth reasons.

Displacement full load, tons: 2550.0
Length, feet (metres): 357.6 (109.0)
Beam, feet (metres): 44.0 (13.4)
Draught, feet (metres): 12.5 (3.8)
Speed, knots: 27.0

Missiles:
SSM – 8 McDonnell Douglas Harpoon (2 quad) launchers.
A/S – Honeywell ASROC Mk 112 octuple launcher; payload Mk 46 torpedoes.

Guns: 1 OTO Melara 3 in (76 mm)/62 compact.
1 GE/GD 20 mm Phalanx CIWS Mk 15.
Torpedoes: 6 – 324 mm Type 68 (2 triple) tubes. Honeywell Mk 46 Mod 5 Neartip.
Decoys: 2 Loral Hycor SRBOC 6-barrelled Mk 36.
Radars:
Air search – Melco OPS 14C.
Surface search – JRC OPS 28.
Fire control – Type 2-21.
Sonars: Hitachi OQS-8; hull-mounted.

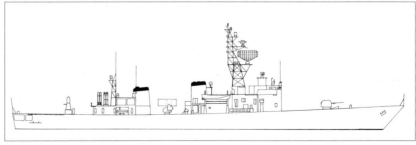

Abukuma Class

CHIKUMA

Hachiro Nakai

Country: JAPAN
Ship type: FRIGATES
Class: CHIKUGO
Active: 11

Name (Pennant Number): CHIKUGO (DE 215), AYASE (DE 216), MIKUMA (DE 217), TOKACHI (DE 218), IWASE (DE 219), CHITOSE (DE 220), NIYODO (DE 221), TESHIO (DE 222), YOSHINO (DE 223), KUMANO (DE 224), NOSHIRO (DE 225)

Recognition Features:
- High bow with continuous sweeping maindeck through to stern.
- 3 in mounting with high breakwater (A position).
- High forward superstructure with large lattice mainmast at after end.
- Mainmast supports air search and air/surface search radar aerials.
- Single, sloping, black-capped funnel amidships.
- Small lattice aftermast.
- A/S missile launcher sited between funnel and aftermast.
- 40 mm/60 mounting on sponson on afterdeck.

Displacement standard, tons: 1470 (DE 215, 217-219 and 221); 1480 (DE 216, 220); 1500 (DE 222 onwards)
Length, feet (metres): 305.0 (93.0)
Beam, feet (metres): 35.5 (10.8)
Draught, feet (metres): 11.5 (3.5)
Speed, knots: 25.0
Range, miles: 10,900 at 12 kts

Missiles:
A/S – Honeywell ASROC Mk 112 octuple launcher; payload Mk 46 torpedoes.
Guns: 2 USN 3 in *(76 mm)*/50 Mk 33 (twin).
2 Bofors 40 mm/60 (twin).

Torpedoes: 6 – 324 mm Type 68 (2 triple) tubes. Honeywell Mk 46 Mod 5 Neartip.
Radars:
Air search – Melco OPS 14.
Surface search – JRC OPS 16.
Fire control – Type 1B.
Sonars: Hitachi OQS 3A; hull-mounted.
EDO SPS 35(J) (in last five ships only); VDS.

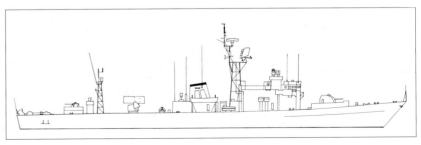

IWASE

Hachiro Nakai

Najin Class

Country: KOREA, NORTH
Ship type: FRIGATES
Class: NAJIN
Active: 2

Name (Pennant Number): (531), (631)

Recognition Features:
● High bow, sweeping forecastle.
● 3.9 in mounting (A position), 57 mm/80 mounting (B position).
● Large lattice mainmast astride forward funnel at after end of forward superstructure.
● Twin sloping funnels, well separated.
● Small lattice aftermast forward of after funnel, supporting fire control radar aerial.
● Large distinctive SSM launchers outboard of aftermast, port and starboard.
● 3.9 in mounting (Y position), 57 mm/80 mounting (X position).

Displacement full load, tons: 1500.0
Length, feet (metres): 334.6
Beam, feet (metres): 32.8
Draught, feet (metres): 8.9
Speed, knots: 24.0
Range, miles: 4000 at 13 kts

Missiles:
   SSM – 2 SS-N-2A Styx.
Guns: 2 – 3.9 in *(100 mm)*/56.
4 – 57 mm/80 (2 twin).
8 – 25 mm/70 (2 quad).
8 – 14.5 mm (4 twin) MGs.
A/S mortars: 2 RBU 1200 5-tubed launchers.
Depth charges: 2 projectors; 2 racks.

Radars:
   Air search – Slim Net.
   Surface search – Pot Head.
   Navigation – Pot Drum.
   Fire control – Drum Tilt.
Sonars: One hull-mounted type. One VDS type.

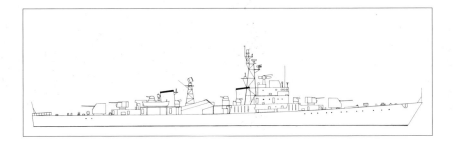

Najin Class

NAJIN

Ships of the World

Ulsan Class

Country: KOREA, SOUTH
Ship type: FRIGATES
Class: ULSAN
Active: 9

Name (Pennant Number): ULSAN (FF 951), SEOUL (FF 952), CHUNG NAM (FF 953), MASAN (FF 955), KYONG BUK (FF 956), CHON NAM (FF 957), CHE JU (FF 958), BUSAN (FF 959), CHUNG JU (FF 961)

Recognition Features:
● Continuous maindeck from stem to stern.
● 3 in mounting (B position).
● High superstructure at forward end with lower continuous superstructure to afterdeck.
● Single sloping funnel aft of midships.
● Large pyramid mainmast, supporting radar dome, at after end of bridge structure.
● Slim, enclosed aftermast supporting air/surface search radar aerial.
● SSM launchers aft of funnel.
● 3 in mounting (Y position).
● Note – There are three versions of this class. The first five ships are the same but *Kyong Buk* has four Emerson Electric 30 mm guns replaced by three Breda 40 mm, and the last four of the class have a built-up gun platform aft.

Displacement full load, tons: 2180.0, (2300 for FF 957 on)
Length, feet (metres): 334.6 (102.0)
Beam, feet (metres): 37.7 (11.5)
Draught, feet (metres): 11.5 (3.5)
Speed, knots: 34.0
Range, miles: 4000 at 15 kts

Missiles:
    SSM – 8 McDonnell Douglas Harpoon (4 twin) launchers.

Guns: 2 – 3 in *(76 mm)*/62 OTO Melara compact.
8 Emerson Electric 30 mm (4 twin) (FF 951-955).
6 Breda 40 mm/70 (3 twin) (FF 956-961).
Torpedoes: 6 – 324 mm Mk 32 (2 triple) tubes. Honeywell Mk 46 Mod 1.
Decoys: 4 Loral Hycor SRBOC 6-barrelled Mk 36.
Nixie; towed torpedo decoy.
Radars:
    Air/surface search – Signaal DA 05.
    Surface search – Signaal ZW 06 (FF 951-956).
                Marconi S 1810 (FF 957-961).
    Fire control – Signaal WM 28 (FF 951-956).
                Marconi ST 1802 (FF 957-961).
    Navigation – Raytheon SPS 10C (FF 957-961).
Sonars: Signaal PHS 32; hull-mounted.

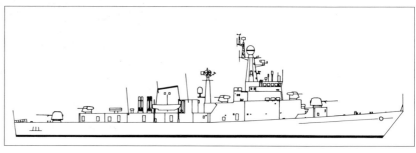

Ulsan Class

CHUNG NAM

Maritime Photographic

Country: MALAYSIA
Ship type: FRIGATES
Class: LEKIU
Active: 1
Building: 1

Name (Pennant Number): LEKIU (30), JEBAT (29)

Recognition Features:
- High bow with straight leading edge sloping down towards bridge
- 57 mm mounting (A position)
- VLS SAM launchers immediately forward of bridge (B position)
- Raised, angular bridge structure with all-round windows
- Large enclosed mainmast amidships with sloping forward edge and vertical after edge. Distinctive air search radar aerial atop aftermast
- Very large square section funnel with shallow sloping after edge abaft aftermast
- Steeply sloping hangar doors down to large, low profile flight deck

Displacement full load, tons: 2270
Length, feet (metres): 346 (105.5)
Beam, feet (metres): 42 (12.8)
Draught, feet (metres): 11.8 (3.6)
Speed, knots: 28
Range, miles: 5000 at 14 knots

Missiles:
 SSM - 8 Aerospatiale MM40 Exocet
 SAM - British Aerospace VLS Seawolf
Guns: 1 Bofors 57 mm/70 SAK Mk2
2 MSI Defense Systems 30 mm DS 30B
Torpedoes: 6 Whitehead B 515 324mm (2 triple) tubes
Decoys: 2 Super Barricade 12 barrelled launchers
Graseby Sea Siren torpedo decoy
Radars:
Air search - Signaal DA 08
Surface search - Ericcson Sea Giraffe 150HC
Navigation - Racal I band
Fire control - 2 Marconi 1802
Sonars: Thomson Sintra Spherion, hull mounted

Helicopters: 1 Westland Wasp HAS 1

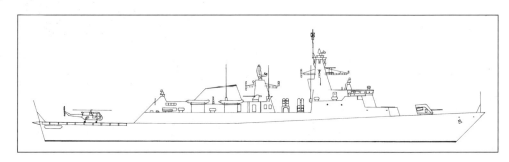

Lekiu Class

JEBAT (artists impression)

GEC Naval Systems

Country: MALAYSIA
Ship type: FRIGATES
Class: RAHMAT
Active: 1

Name (Pennant Number): RAHMAT (ex-*Hang Jebat*) (24)

Recognition Features:
- 4.5 in mounting (A position).
- Forward superstructure, with pyramid mainmast atop, supporting fire control radar dome.
- Single, black-capped funnel with sloping top just aft of midships.
- Large air search radar aerial atop superstructure (not mast) immediately aft of funnel.
- Unique maindeck overhang at break down to quarterdeck.

Displacement full load, tons: 1600.0
Length, feet (metres): 308.0 (93.9)
Beam, feet (metres): 34.1 (10.4)
Draught, feet (metres): 14.8 (4.5)
Speed, knots: 26.0
Range, miles: 6000 at 16 kts

Guns: 1 Vickers 4.5 in *(114 mm)*/45 Mk 5.
3 Bofors 40 mm/70.
A/S mortars: 1 Limbo Mk 10 3-tubed mortar.
Decoys: 2 UK Mk I rail launchers.
Radars:
    Air search – Signaal LW 02.
    Surface search – Decca 626.
    Navigation – Kelvin Hughes MS 32.
    Fire control – Signaal M 22.
Sonars: Graseby Type 170B and Type 174; hull-mounted.

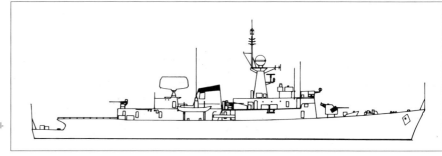

Rahmat Class

RAHMAT

Jacob Van Heemskerck Class

Country: NETHERLANDS
Ship type: FRIGATES
Class: JACOB VAN HEEMSKERCK
Active: 2

Name (Pennant Number): JACOB VAN HEEMSKERCK (F 812), WITTE DE WITH (F 813)

Recognition Features:

- Continuous maindeck from stem to stern.
- No weapons on forecastle.
- Sea Sparrow SAM launcher (B mounting position).
- Forward superstructure has large pyramid mast at after end supporting air/surface search radar aerial.
- Pole mast aft of mainmast.
- SSM launchers immediately aft of mainmast.
- Large funnel with sloping top just aft of midships.
- After superstructure with raised forward section supporting large air search radar aerial at forward end and STIR 240 fire control radar aft.
- SM-1MR SAM launcher aft of raised superstructure.
- CIWS mounting on quarterdeck.

Displacement full load, tons: 3750.0
Length, feet (metres): 428.0 (130.5)
Beam, feet (metres): 47.9 (14.6)
Draught, feet (metres): 14.1 (4.3)
Speed, knots: 30.0
Range, miles: 4700 at 16 kts

Missiles:

SSM – 8 McDonnell Douglas Harpoon (2 quad) launchers.

SAM – 40 GDC Pomona Standard SM-1MR; Mk 13 Mod 1 launcher.
Raytheon Sea Sparrow Mk 29 octuple launcher.
Guns: 1 Signaal SGE-30 Goalkeeper with General Electric 30 mm.
2 Oerlikon 20 mm.
Torpedoes: 4 – 324 mm US Mk 32 (2 twin) tubes. Honeywell Mk 46 Mod 5.
Decoys: 2 Loral Hycor SRBOC 6-barrelled Mk 36 (quad) launchers.
Radars:
Air search – Signaal LW 08.
Air/surface search – Signaal DA 05.
Surface search – Signaal ZW 06.
Fire control – Two Signaal STIR 240.
Signaal STIR 180.
Sonars: Westinghouse SQS 509; hull-mounted.

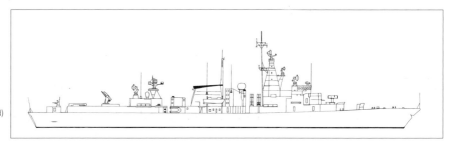

Jacob Van Heemskerck Class

WITTE DE WITH   *Albert Campanera i Rovira*

Country: NETHERLANDS
Ship type: FRIGATES
Class: KAREL DOORMAN
Active: 6
Building: 2

Name (Pennant Number): KAREL DOORMAN (F 827), WILLEM VAN DER ZAAN (F 829), TJERK HIDDES (F 830), VAN AMSTEL (F 831), ABRAHAM VAN DER HULST (F 832), VAN NES (F 833), VAN GALEN (F 834), VAN SPEIJK (F 828)

Recognition Features:
● Continuous maindeck from stem to stern.
● 3 in mounting (A position).
● High forward superstructure topped by tall enclosed mainmast at after end supporting air/ surface search radar aerial.
● Squat, square shaped funnel with sloping after end, just aft of midships.
● After superstructure has distinctive pedestal mounted air/surface search radar aerial at forward end.
● Large hangar with CIWS mounting atop at after end.
● Long flight deck with open quarterdeck below.

Displacement full load, tons: 3320.0
Length, feet (metres): 401.1 (122.3)
Beam, feet (metres): 47.2 (14.4)
Draught, feet (metres): 14.1 (4.3)
Speed, knots: 30.0
Range, miles: 5000 at 18 kts

Missiles:
SSM – 8 McDonnell Douglas Harpoon (2 quad) launchers.
SAM – Raytheon Sea Sparrow Mk 48 vertical launchers.
Guns: 1 – 3 in *(76 mm)*/62 OTO Melara compact Mk 100.
1 Signaal SGE-30 Goalkeeper with General Electric 30 mm.

2 Oerlikon 20 mm.
Torpedoes: 4 – 324 mm US Mk 32 (2 twin) tubes (mounted inside the after superstructure). Honeywell Mk 46 Mod 5. .
Decoys: 2 Loral Hycor SRBOC 6-barrelled Mk 36 (quad) launchers.
Radars:
Air/surface search – Signaal SMART, 3D.
Air/surface search – Signaal LW 08.
Surface search – Signaal ZW 06.
Navigation – Racal Decca 1226.
Fire control – 2 Signaal STIR.
Sonars: Signaal PHS 36; hull-mounted.
Thomson Sintra Anaconda DSBV 61; towed array.

Helicopters: 1 Westland SH-14 Lynx.

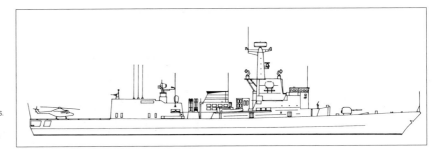

TJERK HIDDES

J L M van der Burg

Kortenaer Class

Country: NETHERLANDS
Ship type: FRIGATES
Class: KORTENAER
Active: 7

Name (Pennant Number): KORTENAER (F 807), PIET HEYN (F 811), ABRAHAM CRIJNSSEN (F 816), PHILIPS VAN ALMONDE (F 823), BLOYS VAN TRESLONG (F 824), JAN VAN BRAKEL (F 825), PIETER FLORISZ (ex-*Willem van der Zaan*) (F 826)

Recognition Features:
● Identical hull and basic profile to the *Jacob Van Heemskerck* class.
● Easily identifiable differences are: 3 in mounting (A position), WM 25 fire control radar dome atop mainmast, Pomona Standard SAM launcher not fitted, flight deck with open quarterdeck below.
● Note – Also operated by Greece (active 4, ordered 1).

Displacement full load, tons: 3630.0
Length, feet (metres): 428.0 (130.5)
Beam, feet (metres): 47.9 (14.6)
Draught, feet (metres): 14.1 (4.3)
Speed, knots: 30.0
Range, miles: 4700 at 16 kts

Missiles:
SSM – 8 McDonnell Douglas Harpoon (2 quad) launchers.
SAM – Raytheon Sea Sparrow Mk 29 octuple launcher.
Guns: 1 OTO Melara 3 in *(76 mm)*/62 compact.
Signaal SGE-30 Goalkeeper with General Electric 30 mm.
2 Oerlikon 20 mm.
Torpedoes: 4 – 324 mm US Mk 32 (2 twin) tubes. Honeywell Mk 46 Mod 5.
Decoys: 2 Loral Hycor SRBOC 6-barrelled Mk 36.

Radars:
Air search – Signaal LW 08.
Surface search – Signaal ZW 06.
Fire control – Signaal STIR.
Signaal WM 25.
Sonars: Westinghouse SQS 505 (F 807, 811 and 816).
SQS 509 (F 823-F 826); bow-mounted.

Helicopters: 2 Westland SH-14B Lynx.

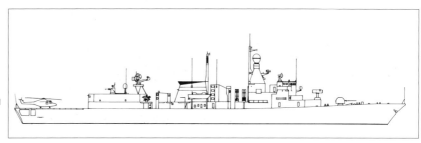

Kortenaer Class

BLOYS VAN TRESLONG

Wright & Logan

Country: NETHERLANDS
Ship type: FRIGATES
Class: TROMP
Active: 2

Name (Pennant Number): TROMP (F 801), DE RUYTER (F 806)

Recognition Features:

● 4.7 in mounting (A position), Sea Sparrow SAM launcher (B mounting position).
● WM 25 fire control radar aerial dome forward of bridge.
● High forward superstructure dominated by very large air/surface search radar dome.
● Low profile twin, side-by-side, vee formation funnels amidships.
● SSM launchers sited between funnels and forward superstructure.
● Large enclosed mainmast atop main superstructure aft of funnels and immediately forward of SPG 51C fire control director on pedestal.
● After superstructure with SM-1MR launcher at forward end and CIWS mounting starboard side aft on hangar roof.
● Short flight deck with open quarterdeck below.

Displacement full load, tons: 4308.0
Length, feet (metres): 454.0 (138.4)
Beam, feet (metres): 48.6 (14.8)
Draught, feet (metres): 15.1 (4.6)
Speed, knots: 30.0
Range, miles: 5000 at 18 kts

Missiles:
SSM – 8 McDonnell Douglas Harpoon (2 quad) launchers.
SAM – 40 GDC Pomona Standard SM-1MR; Mk 13 Mod 4 launcher.
Raytheon Sea Sparrow Mk 29 octuple launcher.

Guns: 2 Bofors 4.7 in *(120 mm)*/50 (twin).
Signaal SGE-30 Goalkeeper with GE 30 mm.
2 Oerlikon 20 mm.
Torpedoes: 6 – 324 mm US Mk 32 (2 triple) tubes. Honeywell Mk 46 Mod 5.
Decoys: 2 Loral Hycor SRBOC 6-barrelled Mk 36.
Radars:
Air/surface search – Signaal MTTR/SPS 01, 3D.
Navigation – 2 Decca 1226.
Fire control – 2 Raytheon SPG 51C.
Signaal WM 25.
Sonars: CWE 610; hull-mounted.

Helicopters: 1 Westland SH-14B Lynx.

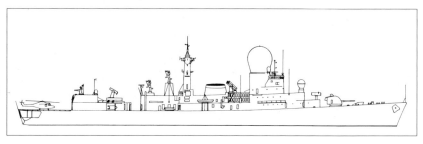

TROMP

Per Kornefeldt

Country: NEW ZEALAND
Ship type: FRIGATES
Class: LEANDER
Active: 4

Name (Pennant Number): WAIKATO (F 55), WELLINGTON (ex-HMS *Bacchante*) (F 69), SOUTHLAND (ex-HMS *Dido*) (F 104), CANTERBURY (F 421) (WELLINGTON and CANTERBURY Broad-beamed)

Recognition Features:
● High forecastle, break at after end of bridge with continuous maindeck to stern.
● 4.5 in mounting (A position).
● Substantial midships superstructure with tall enclosed mainmast aft of bridge.
● Single funnel just aft of bridge. Extensions fitted to funnel uptakes on *Waikato* and *Canterbury*.
● After superstructure has large enclosed aftermast atop.
● Long flight deck with hangar at forward end.
● Note 1 – Also operated by Chile (with substantially different superstructure profile) (active 4), Ecuador (active 2) with SSM and SAM launchers on forecastle, India (active 6), *Taragiri* and *Vindhyagiri* with larger hangars for Sea King and Pakistan (active 2).
● Note 2 – Redundant GWS 22 Seacat systems are being replaced by Vulcan Phalanx (in 69 and 421).

Displacement full load, tons: 3035.0, 2945.0 (Broad-beamed)
Length, feet (metres): 372.0 (113.4)
Beam, feet (metres): 41.0 (12.5), 43.0 (13.1) (Broad-beamed)
Draught, feet (metres): 18.0 (5.5)
Speed, knots: 28.0
Range, miles: 3000 at 15 kts, 5500 at 15 kts (*Wellington*)

Guns: 2 Vickers 4.5 in *(114 mm)*/45 Mk 6 (twin) (except *Southland*).
2 Bofors 40 mm/60 (*Southland*).
4 or 6 12.7 mm MGs.
Torpedoes: 6 – 324 mm US Mk 32 Mod 5 (2 triple) tubes. Honeywell/Marconi Mk 46 Mod 2.
Decoys: 2 Loral Hycor SRBOC 6-barrelled Mk 36 (except *Waikato*).
Graseby Type 182; towed torpedo decoy.
Radars:
    Air search – Marconi Type 965 AKE 1 (*Waikato*).
                Signaal LW08 (*Canterbury* and *Wellington*).
    Air/surface search – Plessey Type 993 or Plessey Type 994 (*Southland*).
    Navigation – Kelvin Hughes Type 1006.
    Fire control – Plessey Type 904.
    RCA TR 76 (*Wellington* and *Canterbury*) or Plessey 903 (*Waikato*).
Sonars: Kelvin Hughes Type 162M; hull-mounted.
Graseby Type 750 or Type 177 (*Waikato*); hull-mounted.

Helicopters: 1 Westland Wasp HAS 1.

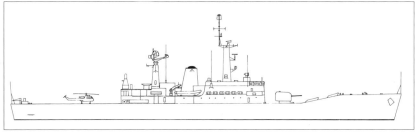

Leander Class

CANTERBURY (still with Seacat)

Maritime Photographic

Country: NORWAY
Ship type: FRIGATES
Class: OSLO
Active: 4

Name (Pennant Number): BERGEN (F 301), TRONDHEIM (F 302), STAVANGER (F 303), NARVIK (F 304)

Recognition Features:
- High bow with continuous sweeping maindeck from stem to stern.
- Long forecastle with 3 in mounting forward of A/S mortar launchers.
- High superstructure with large pedestal-mounted air search radar aerial atop.
- Unusual tripod/pole mainmast configuration at after end of forward superstructure sloping at an angle aft.
- Low, slim, black-capped funnel below angled mainmast.
- After superstructure has tall slim pedestal-mounted Mk 95 fire control radar aerial atop.
- SAM launcher at after end of after superstructure.
- 40 mm/70 mounting (Y position).
- SSM launcher right aft on quarterdeck.

Displacement full load, tons: 1745.0
Length, feet (metres): 317.0 (96.6)
Beam, feet (metres): 36.8 (11.2)
Draught, feet (metres): 18.0 (5.5) (screws)
Speed, knots: 25.0+
Range, miles: 4500 at 15 kts

Missiles:
SSM – 4 Kongsberg Penguin Mk 2.
SAM – Raytheon Sea Sparrow Mk 29 octuple launcher.
Guns: 2 US 3 in *(76 mm)*/50 Mk 33 (twin).
1 Bofors 40 mm/70.
2 Rheinmetall 20 mm/20 (not in all).

Torpedoes: 6 – 324 mm US Mk 32 (2 triple) tubes. Marconi Stingray.
A/S mortars: Kongsberg Terne III 6-tubed.
Decoys: 2 chaff launchers.
Radars:
Air search – Thomson-CSF DRBV 22.
Surface search – Racal Decca TM 1226.
Fire control – NobelTech 9LV 200 Mk 2.
Raytheon Mk 95.
Navigation – Decca.
Sonars: Thomson Sintra/Simrad TSM 2633; combined hull and VDS. Simrad Terne III.

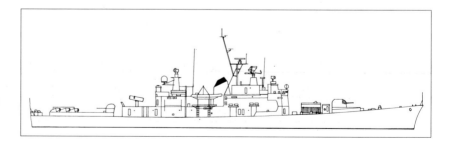

Oslo Class

TRONDHEIM

Giorgio Arra

Kaszub Class

Country: POLAND
Ship type: FRIGATES
Class: KASZUB (TYPE 620)
Active: 1
Proposed: 4

Name (Pennant Number): KASZUB (240)

Recognition Features:

● High bow, sloping forecastle.
● 3 in mounting (A position).
● A/S mortar launchers immediately forward of bridge, port and starboard.
● Smooth, slab-sided forward superstructure.
● Tall, pole mainmast tapering upwards with platform supporting lattice air/surface search radar aerial at top.
● No obvious funnel.
● SAM launcher immediately aft of mainmast.
● Long, low after superstructure with 23 mm mountings at forward and after ends.
● Short quarterdeck with dipping sonar winch equipment right aft.
● Note – Hull is often painted black from midships aft to protect hull from diesel exhaust.

Displacement full load, tons: 1183.0
Length, feet (metres): 270.0 (82.3)
Beam, feet (metres): 32.8 (10.0)
Draught, feet (metres): 10.2 (3.1)
Speed, knots: 26.0
Range, miles: 2000 at 18 kts

Missiles:

SAM – 2 SA-N-5 quad launchers.

Guns: 1 USSR 3 in *(76 mm)*/66.
6 ZU-23-2M Wrobel 23 mm/87 (3 twin).
Torpedoes: 4 – 21 in *(533 mm)* (2 twin) tubes.
A/S mortars: 2 RBU 6000 12-tubed.
Depth charges: 2 rails.
Decoys: 2 PK 16 launchers.
Radars:
    Air/surface search – Strut Curve.
    Surface search – Tamirio RN 231.
Sonars: Stern-mounted dipping type mounted on the transom.

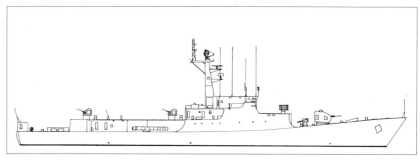

Kaszub Class

KASZUB

Guy Toremans

Country: PORTUGAL
Ship type: FRIGATES
Class: BAPTISTA DE ANDRADE
Active: 4

Name (Pennant Number): BAPTISTA DE ANDRADE (F 486), JOÃO ROBY
(F 487), AFONSO CERQUEIRA (F 488), OLIVEIRA E CARMO (F 489)

Recognition Features:
● Stepped forecastle with 3.9 in mounting (A position).
● Tall lattice mainmast just forward of midships with large distinctive air/surface search radar aerial atop.
● Large, single, black-capped funnel with sloping after end.
● 40 mm/70 mounting atop superstructure aft of funnel.
● Torpedo tubes right aft on quarterdeck.

Displacement full load, tons: 1380.0
Length, feet (metres): 277.5 (84.6)
Beam, feet (metres): 33.8 (10.3)
Draught, feet (metres): 10.2 (3.1)
Speed, knots: 22.0
Range, miles: 5900 at 18 kts

Guns: 1 Creusot Loire 3.9 in *(100 mm)*/55 Mod 1968.
2 Bofors 40 mm/70.
Torpedoes: 6 – 324 mm US Mk 32 (2 triple) tubes. Honeywell Mk 46.
Radars:
    Air/surface search – Plessey AWS 2.
    Navigation – Decca RM 316P.
    Fire control – Thomson-CSF Pollux.
Sonars: Thomson Sintra Diodon; hull-mounted.

Helicopters: Platform for 1 Lynx.

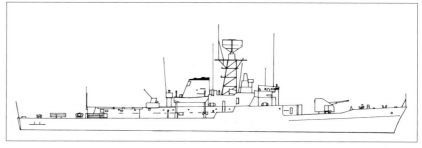

Baptista de Andrade Class

JOÃO ROBY

van Ginderen Collection

Country: PORTUGAL
Ship type: FRIGATES
Class: COMANDANTE JOÃO BELO
Active: 4

Name (Pennant Number): COMANDANTE JOÃO BELO (F 480), COMANDANTE HERMENEGILDO CAPELO (F 481), COMANDANTE ROBERTO IVENS (F 482), COMANDANTE SACADURA CABRAL (F 483)

Recognition Features:
- Long forecastle with high forward superstructure and high freeboard.
- 3.9 in turret (A position).
- A/S mortar mounting (B mounting position).
- Large lattice mainmast at after end of forward superstructure.
- Single large, black-capped funnel well aft of midships.
- Fire control director atop after superstructure.
- Two 3.9 in mountings aft (Y and X positions).
- Note – Generally similar to the French *Commandant Riviere* class.

Displacement full load, tons: 2250.0
Length, feet (metres): 336.9 (102.7)
Beam, feet (metres): 38.4 (11.7)
Draught, feet (metres): 14.4 (4.4)
Speed, knots: 25.0
Range, miles: 7500 at 15 kts

Guns: 3 Creusot Loire 3.9 in *(100 mm)*/55 Mod 1953.
2 Bofors 40 mm/60.
Torpedoes: 6 – 21.7 in *(550 mm)* (2 triple) tubes; ECAN L3.
A/S mortars: 1 Mortier 305 mm 4-barrelled.
Decoys: 2 Loral Hycor SRBOC 6-barrelled Mk 36.
SLQ-25 Nixie; towed torpedo decoy.

Radars:
Air search – Thomson-CSF DRBV 22A.
Surface search – Thomson-CSF DRBV 50.
Navigation – Kelvin Hughes KH 1007.
Fire control – Thomson-CSF DRBC 31D.
Sonars: CDC SQS 510 (after modernisation); hull-mounted.
Thomson Sintra DUBA 3A; hull-mounted.

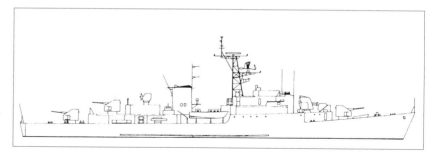

Comandante João Belo Class

COMANDANTE ROBERTO IVENS

Hartmut Ehlers

Country: PORTUGAL
Ship type: FRIGATES
Class: VASCO DA GAMA (MEKO 200)
Active: 3

Name (Pennant Number): VASCO DA GAMA (F 330), ALVARES CABRAL (F 331), CORTE REAL (F 332)

Recognition Features:

● 3.9 in mounting (A position).
● SAM VLS at raised section forward of bridge (B mounting position).
● Short lattice mainmast at after end of forward superstructure.
● Twin, vee formation, side-by-side black-capped funnels well aft from midships.
● Central superstructure forward of funnels with air/surface search aerial on legged platform and fire control radar aerial atop.
● SSM launchers aft of mainmast.
● Sea Sparrow SAM launcher aft of funnel.
● CIWS mounting atop hangar roof.
● Flight deck with open quarterdeck below.
● Note – Also operated by Turkey as the *Yavuz* class (active 4). Most obvious difference is the WM 25 fire control radar dome immediately forward of the mainmast.

Displacement full load, tons: 3300.0
Length, feet (metres): 380.3 (115.9)
Beam, feet (metres): 48 7 (14.8)
Draught, feet (metres): 20.0 (6.1)
Speed, knots: 32.0
Range, miles: 9600 at 12 kts

Missiles:

SSM – 8 McDonnell Douglas Harpoon (2 quad) launchers.
SAM – Raytheon Sea Sparrow Mk 29 octuple launcher.

Guns: 1 Creusot Loire 3.9 in *(100 mm)*/55 Mod 68 CADAM.
1 GE/GD Vulcan Phalanx 20 mm Mk 15 Mod 11.
Torpedoes: 6 – 324 mm US Mk 32 (2 triple) tubes. Honeywell Mk 46 Mod 5.
Decoys: 2 Loral Hycor SRBOC 6-barrelled Mk 36.
SLQ 25 Nixie; towed torpedo decoy.
Radars:
Air search – Signaal MW 08, 3D.
Air/surface search – Signaal DA 08.
Navigation – Kelvin Hughes Type 1007.
Fire control – 2 Signaal STIR.
Sonars: Computing Devices (Canada) SQS 510(V); hull-mounted.

Helicopters: 2 Super Sea Lynx Mk 95.

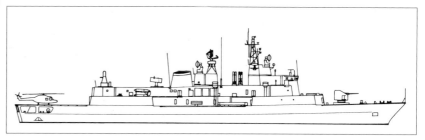

Vasco da Gama Class

ALVARES CABRAL

Guy Toremans

Country: ROMANIA
Ship type: FRIGATES
Class: TETAL
Active: 6

Name (Pennant Number): ADMIRAL PETRE BARBUNEANU (260), VICE ADMIRAL VASILE SCODREA (261), VICE ADMIRAL VASILE URSEANU (262), VICE ADMIRAL EUGENIU ROSCA (263) CONTRE ADMIRAL EUSTATIU SEBASTIAN (264), – (265)

Recognition Features:

- Regular profile hull with continuous maindeck from stem to stern.
- Very long forecastle with 3 in mounting (A position).
- A/S mortar mounting (B mounting position).
- Long superstructure centred well aft of midships.
- Large mainmast amidships, with enclosed bottom half and lattice top.
- Hawk Screech fire control radar aerial atop after end of bridge structure.
- Drum Tilt fire control radar aerial mounted atop tall pedestal towards after end of superstructure.
- 30 mm/65 mountings at after end of after superstructure, one port one starboard.
- 3 in mounting (Y position).
- Note 1 – Probably a modified Soviet Koni design.
- Note 2 – Last two of class are Improved Tetal class. Most obvious differences are large black-capped funnel at after end of superstructure and large flight deck aft.

Displacement full load, tons: 1440.0
Length, feet (metres): 303.1 (95.4)
Beam, feet (metres): 38.4 (11.7)
Draught, feet (metres): 9.8 (3.0)
Speed, knots: 24.0

Guns: 2 or 4 USSR 3 in *(76 mm)*/60 (1 or 2 twin).
4 USSR 30 mm/65 (2 twin).
2 – 14.5 mm MGs.
Torpedoes: 4 – 21 in *(533 mm)* (twin) tubes. Soviet Type 53.
A/S mortars: 2 RBU 2500 16-tubed.
Radars:
Air/surface search – Strut Curve.
Fire control – Drum Tilt.
Hawk Screech.
Sonars: Hull-mounted.

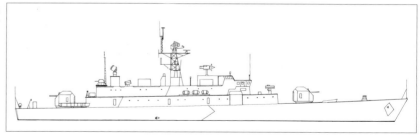

Tetal Class

VICE ADMIRAL VASILE SCODREA

Gepard Class

Country: RUSSIA AND ASSOCIATED STATES
Ship type: FRIGATES
Class: GEPARD (FFG)
Active: 1
Building: 2

Name (Pennant Number): (Not available)

Recognition Features:
● High bow, short, sloping forecastle.
● A/S mortar mounting (A mounting position).
● 3 in mounting (B position).
● CIWS mounting on raised platform forward of bridge.
● Large, forward superstructure dominated by Band Stand air/surface search radar dome atop.
● Large, pyramid mainmast with lattice top at after end of forward superstructure. Cross Dome air/surface search radar dome atop mainmast.
● Large, tapered funnel aft of mainmast.
● SSM launchers outboard of funnel, port and starboard.
● After superstructure has small tapered lattice mast at forward end and CIWS mounting aft.
● SAM launcher on lower platform immediately aft of after CIWS mounting.
● Unusual covered quarterdeck area housing VDS equipment.

Displacement full load, tons: 1900.0
Length, feet (metres): 334.6 (102.0)
Beam, feet (metres): 44.6 (13.6)
Draught, feet (metres): 14.4 (4.4)
Speed, knots: 26.0
Range, miles: 3500 at 18 kts

Missiles:
   SSM – 8 SS-N-25 (2 quad).
   SAM – 1 SA-N-4 Gecko twin launcher.
Guns: 1 – 3 in *(76 mm)*/60.
2 – 30 mm/65 ADG 630.
Torpedoes: 4 – 21 in *(533 mm)* (2 twin) tubes. Type 53.
A/S mortars: 1 RBU 6000 12-tubed.
Mines: 2 rails.
Decoys: 4 chaff launchers.
Radars:
   Air/surface search – Cross Dome.
                           Band Stand.
   Fire control – Bass Tilt.
                     Pop Group.
   Navigation – Nayada.
Sonars: Hull-mounted.
VDS.

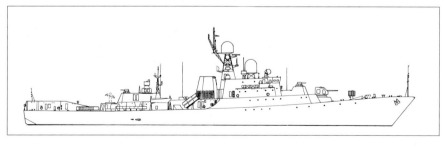

Gepard Class

GEPARD CLASS (Artist's impression)

Country: RUSSIA AND ASSOCIATED STATES
Ship type: FRIGATES
Class: GRISHA I (TYPE 1124) (ALBATROS) (FFL)
Active: 11
Class: GRISHA II (TYPE 1124P) (ALBATROS) (FFL)
Active: 12
Class: GRISHA III (TYPE 1124M) (ALBATROS) (FFL)
Active: 28
Class: GRISHA V (TYPE 1124EM) (ALBATROS) (FFL)
Active: 30
Building: 2

Name (Pennant Number): AMETYST, BRILLIANT, IZUMRUD, PREDANNY, IZMAIL, DNEPR, RESITELNY, PRIMERNY, RUBIN, SAPFIR, ZHEMCHUG, PROVORNY
(All Grisha II class (Border Guard))

Recognition Features:
Grisha I
- High bow with sweeping lines to stern.
- SAM launcher (A mounting position).
- Two A/S mortar launchers, port and starboard, (B mounting position).
- Pyramid mainmast at after end of forward superstructure.
- Small Y shaped (in profile) lattice mast at top after end of mainmast.
- Pop Group fire control radar aerial atop forward superstructure, forward of mainmast.
- Single, low profile, square shaped funnel just aft of midships.
- Small after superstructure with slender lattice mast at forward end, and Muff Cob fire control radar aerial atop after end.
- 57 mm/80 mounting (Y position).

- Note – Most obvious identification of Grisha II is 57 mm/80 mounting (A position). Grisha III same as Grisha I except for raised after superstructure with Bass Tilt fire control radar aerial atop. Grisha V is the only type with 3 in mounting (Y position).

Displacement full load, tons: 1200.0
Length, feet (metres): 236.2 (72.0)
Beam, feet (metres): 32.8 (10.0)
Draught, feet (metres): 12.1 (3.7)
Speed, knots: 30.0
Range, miles: 2500 at 14 kts

Missiles:
SAM – SA-N-4 Gecko twin launcher (Grisha I, III and V classes).
Guns: 2 – 57 mm/80 (twin) (2 twin in Grisha II class).
1 – 3 in *(76 mm)*/60 (Grisha V).
1 – 30 mm/65 (Grisha III and V classes).
Torpedoes: 4 – 21 in *(533 mm)* (2 twin) tubes. Type 53.
A/S mortars: 2 RBU 6000 12-tubed. (Only 1 in Grisha Vs).
Depth charges: 2 racks.

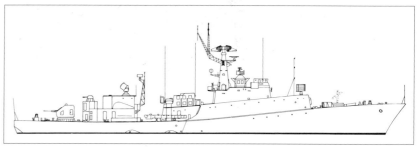

Grisha I - V Class

GRISHA V CLASS

Radars:
    Air/surface search – Strut Curve (Strut Pair in early Grisha Vs).
                Half Plate Bravo (in the later Grisha Vs).
    Navigation – Don 2. Fire control – Pop Group (Grisha I, III and V).
                Muff Cob (except in Grisha III and V).
                Bass Tilt (Grisha III and V).

Sonars: Hull-mounted.
VDS – similar to Hormone helicopter dipping sonar.

Krivak Class

Country: RUSSIA AND ASSOCIATED STATES
Ship type: FRIGATES
Class: KRIVAK I (TYPE 1135) (BUREVESTNIK) (FFG)
Active: 19

Name (Pennant Number): BDITELNY, BODRY, DRUZHNY, RAZUMNY, SILNY, STOROZHEVOY, SVIREPY, LEGKY, LETUCHY, PYLKY, RETIVY, ZADORNY, ZHARKY, BEZZAVETNY, BEZUKORIZNENNY, DOSTOYNY, DOBLESTNY, DEYATELNY, LADNY, PORYVISTY

Class: KRIVAK II (TYPE 1135M) (BUREVESTNIK) (FFG)
Active: 11

Name (Pennant Number): BESSMENNY, GORDELIVY, GROMKY, GROZYASHCHY, NEUKROTIMY (ex-*Komsomolets Litvii*), PYTLIVY, RAZITELNY, REVNOSTNY, REZKY, REZVY, RYANNY

Class: KRIVAK III (TYPE 1135MP) (BUREVESTNIK) (FF)
Active: 9

Name (Pennant Number): MENZHINSKY, DZERZHINSKY, OREL (ex-*Imeni XXVII Sezda KPSS*), IMENI LXX LETIYA VCHK-KGB, IMENI LXX LETIYA POGRANVOYSK, KEDROV, VOROVSKY, HETMAN DOROSENKO, HETMAN PETR SAGADACHNY

Recognition Features:
Krivak I
- Long forecastle with, from forward, A/S missile launcher, SAM launcher and SSM launcher.
- Forward superstructure with, at after end, complex of three lattice masts forming the mainmast structure with large air search radar aerial atop.
- Single, low profile funnel well aft of midships.

- Pop Group and Owl Screech fire control radar aerials mounted on complex structure between mainmast and funnel.
- 3 in mountings (Y and X positions).
- Note – Most obvious identification of Krivak II is A/S mortar mounting in place of SSM launcher on forecastle and Krivak III has a 3.9 mounting (A position) and a flight deck.

Displacement full load, tons: 3600.0
Length, feet (metres): 405.2 (123.5)
Beam, feet (metres): 46.9 (14.3)
Draught, feet (metres): 16.4 (5.0)
Speed, knots: 32.0
Range, miles: 4600 at 20 kts

Missiles:
    SSM – 8 SS-N-25 (2 quad); (Krivak I after modernisation).
    SAM – 2 SA-N-4 Gecko twin launchers (1 in Krivak III).
    A/S – SS-N-14 Silex quad launcher (not in Krivak III); payload nuclear or Type E53 torpedo.
Guns: 4 – 3 in *(76 mm)*/60 (2 twin) (Krivak I).
2 – 3.9 in *(100 mm)*/59 (Krivak II) (1 in Krivak III).
2 – 30 mm/65 (Krivak III).

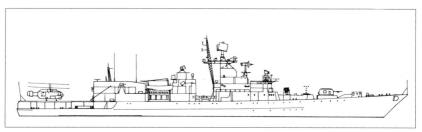

Krivak Class

VOROVSKY (KRIVAK III)

Torpedoes: 8 – 21 in *(533 mm)* (2 quad) tubes. Type 53.
A/S mortars: 2 RBU 6000 12-tubed; (not modernised Krivak I).
Decoys: 4 or 10 chaff launchers.
Towed torpedo decoy.
Radars:
  Air search – Head Net, 3D.
          Top Plate (*Orel* and later and some Krivak I after modernisation).
  Surface search – Don Kay or Palm Frond or Don 2 or Spin Trough.
          Peel Cone (Krivak III).

Fire control – 2 Eye Bowl (not in Krivak III).
          2 Pop Group (1 in Krivak III).
          Owl Screech (Krivak I).
          Kite Screech (Krivak II and III).
          Bass Tilt (Krivak III).
Sonars: Bull Nose; hull-mounted.
Mare Tail or Steer Hide (*Zharky, Bditelny, Legky,* and other Krivak Is after modernisation); VDS.

Helicopters: 1 Ka-25 Hormone or Ka-27 Helix (Krivak III).

Country: RUSSIA AND ASSOCIATED STATES
Ship type: FRIGATES
Class: NEUSTRASHIMY (FFG)
Active: 1
Building: 2

Name (Pennant Number): NEUSTRASHIMY, NEPRISTUPNY

Recognition Features:
● Elegant profile with front of long forecastle slightly depressed.
● 3.9 in mounting (A position).
● SAM VLS tubes just aft of forward mounting.
● A/S mortar mounting (B mounting position).
● Forward superstructure has short forward mast at its after end supporting Cross Dome fire control radar aerial.
● Twin funnels. Forward one aft of forward superstructure, after one aft of mainmast.
● Large, pyramid mainmast well aft of midships with distinctive air/surface radar aerial atop.
● SSM launcher between mainmast and forward funnel.
● CADS-N-1 SAM/Guns mounting at after end of after superstructure, just forward of flight deck.
● VDS towing array right aft.
● Note 1 – Class slightly larger than *Krivak*. Helicopter deck extends across the full width of the ship.
● Note 2 – After funnel is usually flush decked, therefore not obvious in profile.

Displacement full load, tons: 4100.0
Length, feet (metres): 423.2 (129.0)
Beam, feet (metres): 50.9 (15.5)
Draught, feet (metres): 15.7 (4.8)
Speed, knots: 32.0
Range, miles: 4500 at 16 kts

Missiles:
    SSM – 8 SS-N-25.
    SAM – 4 SA-N-9 Gauntlet sextuple vertical launchers.
        SAM/Guns 2 CADS-N-1; each has a twin 30 mm Gatling combined with 8 SA-N-11.
    A/S – SS-N-15 type. Type 45 torpedo or nuclear warhead; fired from torpedo tubes.
Guns: 1 – 3.9 in *(100 mm)*/70.
Torpedoes: 6 – 21 in *(533 mm)* tubes combined with A/S launcher, either SS-N-15 missiles or anti-submarine torpedoes.
A/S mortars: 1 RBU 12000; 10-tubed.
Mines: 2 rails.
Decoys: 2 – 10-barrelled launchers.
Radars:
    Air/surface search – Top Plate, 3D.
    Navigation – 2 Palm Frond.
    Fire control – Cross Dome.
        Kite Screech.
Sonars: Bull Nose; hull-mounted. Steer Hide VDS or towed sonar array.

Helicopters: 1 Ka-27 Helix.

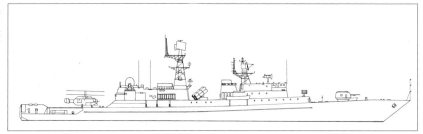

Neustrashimy Class

NEUSTRASHIMY

Country: RUSSIA AND ASSOCIATED STATES
Ship type: FRIGATES
Class: PARCHIM II (FFL)
Active: 12

Name (Pennant Number): (MPK 67), (MPK 99), (MPK 105), (MPK 192), (MPK 205), (MPK 213), (MPK 216), (MPK 219), (MPK 224), (MPK 228), (MPK 229), JUNGA (-)

Recognition Features:
- High bow, short forecastle.
- Low main superstructure with high central superstructure atop.
- CIWS mounting at forward end of main superstructure.
- A/S mortar mounting forward of bridge.
- Substantial lattice mainmast atop central superstructure. Small Y shaped (in profile) lattice mast protruding aft.
- Large air/surface search radar dome atop mainmast.
- SAM launcher at after end of forward superstructure.
- Large, enclosed aftermast supporting distinctive drum-shaped Bass Tilt radar aerial.
- 3 in mounting (Y position).
- Note – Also operated by Indonesia (active 16). Most obvious differences are conventional air/surface search radar aerial atop mainmast and much smaller enclosed aftermast supporting Muff Cob fire control radar aerial.

Displacement full load, tons: 1200.0
Length, feet (metres): 246.7 (75.2)
Beam, feet (metres): 32.2 (9.8)
Draught, feet (metres): 14.4 (4.4)
Speed, knots: 28.0

Missiles:
  SAM – 2 SA-N-5 Grail quad launchers.
Guns: 1 – 3 in *(76 mm)*/66.
1 – 30 mm/65; 6 barrels.
Torpedoes: 4 – 21 in *(533 mm)* (2 twin) tubes. Type 53.
A/S mortars: 2 RBU 6000 12-tubed.
Depth charges: 2 racks.
Mines: Rails fitted.
Decoys: 2 – 16 barrelled chaff launchers.
Radars:
  Air/surface search – Cross Dome.
  Navigation – TSR 333.
  Fire control – Bass Tilt.
Sonars: Hull-mounted.
Helicopter type VDS.

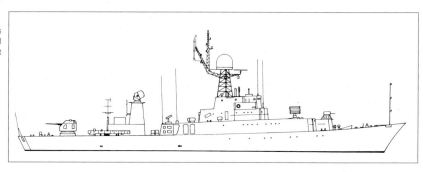

Parchim Class

PARCHIM II CLASS

Country: SAUDI ARABIA
Ship type: FRIGATES
Class: MADINA (TYPE F 2000S)
Active: 4

Name (Pennant Number): MADINA (702), HOFOUF (704), ABHA (706), TAIF (708)

Recognition Features:
- Long forecastle. Continuous maindeck profile with break down to quarterdeck.
- 3.9 mounting (A position).
- Forward superstructure has slim tripod mainmast at after end.
- Unusually large funnel with large, black, wedge shaped smoke deflector at after end, sited just aft of midships.
- SSM launchers between funnel and forward superstructure.
- SAM launcher atop after superstructure.
- Small flight deck.
- Small quarterdeck with VDS operating gear.

Displacement full load, tons: 2870.0
Length, feet (metres): 377.3 (115.0)
Beam, feet (metres): 41.0 (12.5)
Draught, feet (metres): 16.0 (4.9) (sonar)
Speed, knots: 30.0
Range, miles: 8000 at 15 kts; 6500 at 18 kts

Missiles:
SSM – 8 OTO Melara/Matra Otomat Mk 2 (2 quad).
SAM – Thomson-CSF Crotale Naval octuple launcher.
Guns: 1 Creusot Loire 3.9 in *(100 mm)*/55 compact.
4 Breda 40 mm/70 (2 twin).
Torpedoes: 4 – 21 in *(533 mm)* tubes. ECAN F17P.
Decoys: CSEE Dagaie double mounting.

Radars:
Air/surface search/IFF – Thomson-CSF Sea Tiger (DRBV 15).
Navigation – Racal Decca TM 1226.
Fire control – Thomson-CSF Castor IIB.
        Thomson-CSF DRBC 32.
Sonars: Thomson Sintra Diodon TSM 2630; hull-mounted, integrated Sorel VDS.

Helicopters: 1 SA 365F Dauphin 2.

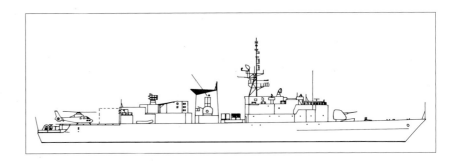

Madina Class

TAIF

G Jacobs

Country: SPAIN
Ship type: FRIGATES
Class: BALEARES (F 70)
Active: 5

Name (Pennant Number): BALEARES (F 71), ANDALUCÍA (F 72), CATALUÑA (F 73), ASTURIAS (F 74), EXTREMADURA (F 75)

Recognition Features:

● Long forecastle with 5 in mounting well forward of A/S missile launcher.
● Very unusual large cylindrical mast and funnel combined amidships;
surface search radar aerial at forward end and short lattice mast atop after end supporting large air search radar aerial.
● After superstructure with SSM launchers immediately aft of small lattice mast.
● SAM launcher (X mounting position).
● Note – Similar to US Navy's *Knox* class.

Displacement full load, tons: 4177.0
Length, feet (metres): 438.0 (133.6)
Beam, feet (metres): 46.9 (14.3)
Draught, feet (metres): 15.4 (4.7)
Speed, knots: 28.0
Range, miles: 4500 at 20 kts

Missiles:

SSM – 8 McDonnell Douglas Harpoon (4 normally carried).
SAM – 16 GDC Pomona Standard SM-1MR; Mk 22 Mod 0 launcher.
A/S – Honeywell ASROC Mk 112 octuple launcher; payload Mk 46 torpedoes.
Guns: 1 FMC 5 in *(127 mm)*/54 Mk 42 Mod 9.
2 Bazán 20 mm/120 12-barrelled Meroka.

Torpedoes: 4 – 324 mm US Mk 32 tubes (fitted internally and angled at 45°). Honeywell Mk 46 Mod 5.
2 – 484 mm US Mk 25 stern tubes. Westinghouse Mk 37.
Decoys: 4 Loral Hycor SRBOC 6-barrelled Mk 36.
Radars:
    Air search – Hughes SPS 52A, 3D.
    Surface search – Raytheon SPS 10.
    Navigation – Raytheon Marine Pathfinder.
    Fire control – Western Electric SPG 53B.
                Raytheon SPG 51C.
                Selenia RAN 12L.
                2 Sperry VPS 2.
Sonars: Raytheon SQS 56 (DE 1160); hull-mounted.
EDO SQS 35V; VDS.

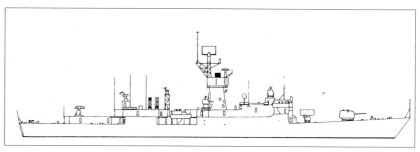

Baleares Class

EXTREMADURA

H M Steele

Country: SPAIN
Ship type: FRIGATES
Class: DESCUBIERTA
Active: 6

Name (Pennant Number): DESCUBIERTA (F 31), DIANA (F 32), INFANTA ELENA (F 33), INFANTA CRISTINA (F 34), CAZADORA (F 35), VENCEDORA (F 36)

Recognition Features:

● Short forecastle with 3 in mounting (A position).
● A/S mortar mounting forward of bridge (B mounting position).
● Short forward superstructure with pyramid mainmast at after end.
● SSM launchers between mainmast and funnels.
● Unusual, black-capped, vee formation funnels amidships with a large whip aerial atop each one.
● Short aftermast aft of funnels supporting air/surface search radar aerial.
● Two 40 mm/70 mountings, on two levels, aft of aftermast.
● SAM launcher on afterdeck, (Y mounting position).
● Note 1 – Considerably modified Portuguese *João Coutinho* design.
● Note 2 – Also operated by Egypt (active 2).

Displacement full load, tons: 1666.0
Length, feet (metres): 291.3 (88.8)
Beam, feet (metres): 34.0 (10.4)
Draught, feet (metres): 12.5 (3.8)
Speed, knots: 25.0
Range, miles: 7500 at 12 kts

Missiles:

SSM – 8 McDonnell Douglas Harpoon (2 quad) launchers. Normally 2 pairs are embarked.
SAM – Selenia Albatros octuple launcher.

Guns: 1 OTO Melara 3 in *(76 mm)*/62 compact.
1 or 2 Bofors 40 mm/70.
Torpedoes: 6 – 324 mm US Mk 32 (2 triple) tubes. Honeywell Mk 46 Mod 5.
A/S mortars: 1 Bofors 375 mm twin-barrelled.
Decoys: 2 Loral Hycor SRBOC 6-barrelled Mk 36.
US Prairie Masker; blade rate suppression.
Radars:
  Air/surface search – Signaal DA 05/2.
  Navigation – Signaal ZW 06.
  Fire control – Signaal WM 22/41 or WM 25 system.
Sonars: Raytheon 1160B; hull-mounted.

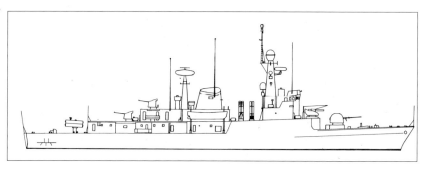

Descubierta Class

DIANA

Diego Quevedo

Country: THAILAND
Ship type: FRIGATES
Class: CHAO PHRAYA (TYPES 053 HT and 053 HT (H)) (FFG)
Active: 4
Proposed: 2

Name (Pennant Number): CHAO PHRAYA (455), BANGPAKONG (456), KRABURI (457), SAIBURI (458)

Recognition Features:
- A/S mortar mounting forward of 100 mm/56 mounting (A position).
- 37 mm/76 mounting (B position).
- High forward superstructure with Sun Visor fire control director atop.
- Pyramid mainmast at after end of forward superstructure with slim lattice mast atop its after end.
- SSM launchers forward and aft of funnel.
- Single, angular low profile funnel well aft of midships.
- Short lattice mast aft of after SSM launchers with 37 mm/76 mounting immediately astern.
- 100 mm/76 mounting (Y position).
- Note – Two of class are as described above and two are identical except for raised flight deck over open quarterdeck.

Displacement full load, tons: 1924.0
Length, feet (metres): 338.5 (103.2)
Beam, feet (metres): 37.1 (11.3)
Draught, feet (metres): 10.2 (3.1)
Speed, knots: 30.0
Range, miles: 3500 at 18 kts

Missiles:
SSM – 8 Ying Ji (Eagle Strike) (C-801).

Guns: 2 (457 and 458) or 4 China 100 mm/56 (1 or 2 twin). 8 China 37 mm/76 (4 twin) H/PJ 76 A.
A/S mortars: 2 RBU 1200 (China Type 86) 5-tubed launchers.
Depth charges: 2 BMB racks.
Decoys: 2 China Type 945 GPJ 26-barrelled launchers.
Radars:
Air/surface search – China Type 354 Eye Shield.
Surface search/fire control – China Type 352C Square Tie.
Fire control – China Type 343 Sun Visor.
China Type 341 Rice Lamp.
Navigation – Racal Decca 1290 A/D ARPA.
Sonars: China Type SJD-5A; hull-mounted.

Helicopters: Bell 212 are embarked as an interim measure.

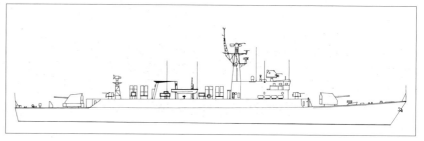

CHAO PHRAYA

Country: THAILAND
Ship type: FRIGATES
Class: NARESUAN (TYPE 25T) (FFG)
Building: 2

Name (Pennant Number): NARESUAN (621), TAKSIN (622)

Recognition Features:

● High bow, 5 in mounting (A position).
● VLS launchers below maindeck level between forward mounting and bridge.
● High forward superstructure with lattice mainmast atop at after end of bridge.
● SSM launchers aft of forward superstructure.
● Large platform amidships supporting air search radar aerial.
● Square section funnel with wedge shaped smoke deflector atop.
● After superstructure has STIR fire control radar at forward end and JM-83H fire control director aft.
● 37 mm/76 mountings, port and starboard, outboard of STIR fire control radar and one deck level down.
● Flight deck aft with open quarterdeck below.

Displacement full load, tons: 2980.0
Length, feet (metres): 393.7 (120.0)
Beam, feet (metres): 42.7 (13.0)
Draught, feet (metres): 12.5 (3.8)
Speed, knots: 32.0
Range, miles: 4000 at 18 kts

Missiles:

SSM – 8 McDonnell Douglas Harpoon (2 quad) launchers.
SAM – Mk 41 LCHR 8 cell VLS launcher.
Guns: 1 FMC 5 in *(127 mm)*/54 Mk 45 Mod 2.
4 China 37 mm/76 (2 twin) H/PJ 76 A.

Torpedoes: 6 – 324 mm Mk 32 Mod 5 (2 triple) tubes. Honeywell Mk 46.
Decoys: China Type 945 GPJ 26-barrelled launchers.
Radars:
    Air search – Signaal LW 08.
    Surface search – China Type 360.
    Navigation – Two Raytheon SPS 64(V)5.
    Fire control – Two Signaal STIR.
                China 374 G.
Sonars: China SJD-7; hull-mounted.

Helicopters: 1 Kaman SH-2F Seasprite.

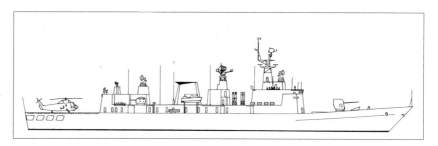

NARESUAN

Royal Thai Navy

Barbaros Class

Country: TURKEY
Ship type: FRIGATES
Class: BARBAROS
Active: 1
Building: 3

Name (Pennant Number): BARBAROS (F244), ORUCREIS (F245), SALIHREIS (F246), KEMALREIS (F247)

Recognition Features:

- Medium length forecastle with 5-in mounting (A position) and 25 mm (B position)
- High bridge superstructure with two fire control directors atop and large lattice-topped mainmast at after end
- Two four-barrelled SSM launchers abaft mainmast
- Raised central superstructure with fire control director and air search radar aerial atop
- Two small vee-formation funnels just aft of midships
- Raised after superstructure with SAM launcher atop, midway between funnel and forward end of flight deck. Fire control director at after end
- Medium-sized flight deck with open quarterdeck below

Displacement full load, tons: 3350
Length, feet (metres): 382.9 (116.7)
Beam, feet (metres): 48.6 (14.8)
Draught, feet (metres): 14.1 (4.3)
Speed, knots: 32

Missiles:
SSM - 8 McDonnell Douglas Harpoon
SAM - Raytheon Sea Sparrow Mk 29 Mod 1
Guns: 1 FMC 5-in (127 mm)/54 Mk45 Mod 2
3 Oerlikon-Contraves 25 mm Sea Zenith
Torpedoes: 6 - 324 mm Mk 32 Mod 5 (two triple) tubes. Honeywell Mk 46
Decoys: 2 Loral Hycor 6-tubed fixed Mk 36 Mod 1 SRBOC
Nixie SLQ 25; towed torpedo decoy
Radars:
Air search - Siemens/Plessey AWS 9
Air/Surface search - Plessey AWS 6 Dolphin
Navigation - Racal Decca 2690 BT ARPA
Fire control - 1 or 2 F246-247 Signaal STIR
Contraves TMX (F244-245)
2 Contraves Sea Guard
Sonars: Raytheon SQS 56 (DE1160), hull mounted

Helicopters: 1 AB 212 ASW.

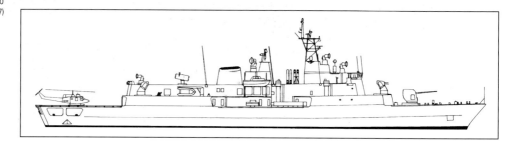

Barbaros Class

BARBAROS

H M Steele

Broadsword Class (Batch 1 and 2)

Country: UNITED KINGDOM
Ship type: FRIGATES
Class: BROADSWORD (TYPE 22) (BATCH 1 AND 2)
Active: 10

Batch 1
Name (Pennant Number): BROADSWORD (F 88), BATTLEAXE (F 89), BRILLIANT (F 90), BRAZEN (F 91)
Batch 2
Name (Pennant Number): BOXER (F 92), BEAVER (F 93), BRAVE (F 94), LONDON (ex-*Bloodhound*) (F 95), SHEFFIELD (F 96), COVENTRY (F 98)

Recognition Features:
Batch 1
- Blunt bow with short forecastle.
- SSM launcher (A mounting position).
- SAM launcher (B mounting position).
- Raised central maindeck section giving high freeboard.
- High enclosed mainmast at after end of forward superstructure.
- Large funnel, aft of midships, with sloping top and black exhausts just protruding at top.
- SATCOM dome atop superstructure just forward of funnel.
- Large enclosed aftermast aft of funnel. This mast is only slightly shorter, and similar in size, to the mainmast.
- After superstructure has fire control radar aerial atop raised forward section and SAM launcher atop hangar.
- Flight deck aft with open quarterdeck below.
- Note 1 – Easiest ways to differentiate between Batches 1 and 2 are; Batch 2 are some 15 m longer and have high sweeping bow profile.
- Note 2 – Last four Batch 2 have enlarged flight decks to take Sea King or EH 101 Merlin helicopters.

Displacement full load, tons: 4400.0 (Batch 1), 4800 (Batch 2)
Length, feet (metres): 430.0 (131.2) (Batch 1), 485.5 (145.0) (F 92-93), 480.5 (146.5) (F 94-96-98)
Beam, feet (metres): 48.5 (14.8)
Draught, feet (metres): 19.9 (6.0) (Batch 1), 21.0 (6.4) (Batch 2) (screws)
Speed, knots: 30.0
Range, miles: 4500 at 18 kts on Tynes

Missiles:
SSM – 4 Aerospatiale MM 38 Exocet.
SAM – 2 British Aerospace 6-barrelled Seawolf GWS 25 Mod 0 or Mod 4 (except F 94-96 and 98).
2 British Aerospace Seawolf GWS 25 Mod 3 (F 94-96 and 98).
Guns: 4 Oerlikon/BMARC GCM-A03 30 mm/75 (2 twin).
2 Oerlikon/BMARC 20 mm GAM-BO1.
Torpedoes: 6 – 324 mm Plessey STWS Mk 2 (2 triple) tubes. Marconi Stingray.
Decoys: 2 Plessey Shield launchers.

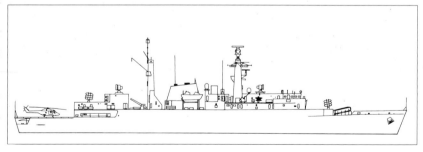

Broadsword Class (Batch 1 and 2)

BATTLEAXE

4 Marconi Sea Gnat 6-barrelled launchers. Graseby Type 182; towed torpedo decoy.
Radars:
  Air/surface search – Marconi Type 967/968 (Type 967M in F 94).
  Navigation – Kelvin Hughes Type 1006 or Type 1007.
  Fire control – 2 Marconi Type 911 or Type 910 (in Mod 0 ships).

Sonars: Plessey Type 2016 or Ferranti/Thomson Sintra Type 2050; hull-mounted. Dowty Type 2031Z (Batch 2 only); towed array.

Helicopters: 2 Westland Lynx HAS 3 (in all); or 1 Westland Sea King HAS 5 (or EH 101 Merlin) (F 94-96 and 98).

Broadsword Class (Batch 3)

Country: UNITED KINGDOM
Ship type: FRIGATES
Class: BROADSWORD (TYPE 22) (BATCH 3)
Active: 4

Name (Pennant Number): CORNWALL (F 99), CUMBERLAND (F 85), CAMPBELTOWN (F 86), CHATHAM (F 87)

Recognition Features:
● Similar in profile to Batch 2. Major identification differences are as follows -
● Steeper angle stern profile.
● 4.5 mounting (A position).
● SSM launchers forward of mainmast.

Displacement full load, tons: 4900.0
Length, feet (metres): 485.9 (148.1)
Beam, feet (metres): 48.5 (14.8)
Draught, feet (metres): 21.0 (6.4)
Speed, knots: 30.0
Range, miles: 4500 at 18 kts

Missiles:
SSM – 8 McDonnell Douglas Harpoon Block 1C (2 quad) launchers.
SAM – 2 British Aerospace Seawolf GWS 25 Mod 3.
Guns: 1 Vickers 4.5 in *(114 mm)*/55 Mk 8.
1 Signaal/General Electric 30 mm 7-barrelled Goalkeeper.
2 DES/Oerlikon 30 mm/75.
Torpedoes: 6 – 324 mm Plessey STWS Mk 2 (2 triple) tubes. Marconi Stingray.
Decoys: 4 Marconi Sea Gnat 6-barrelled launchers.
Graseby Type 182; towed torpedo decoy.

Radars:
Air/surface search – Marconi Type 967/968.
Navigation – Kelvin Hughes Type 1006 or Type 1007.
Fire control – Two Marconi Type 911.
Sonars: Plessey Type 2016; hull-mounted.
Dowty Type 2031; towed array.

Helicopters: 2 Westland Lynx HAS 3; or 1 Westland Sea King HAS 5 (or EH 101 Merlin).

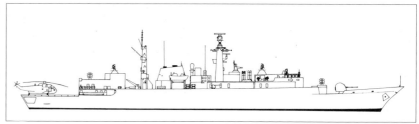

CORNWALL

92 Wing RAAF

Duke Class

Country: UNITED KINGDOM
Ship type: FRIGATES
Class: DUKE (TYPE 23)
Active: 9
Building: 4
Proposed: 3

Name (Pennant Number): NORFOLK (F 230), ARGYLL (F 231), LANCASTER (F 229 (ex-F 232)), MARLBOROUGH (F 233), IRON DUKE (F 234), MONMOUTH (F 235), MONTROSE (F 236), WESTMINSTER (F 237), NORTHUMBERLAND (F 238), RICHMOND (F 239), SOMERSET (F 240), GRAFTON (F 241), SUTHERLAND (F 242)

Recognition Features:
● High bow with continuous maindeck through to stern.
● Three major weapons sited on forecastle; from the bow aft, 4.5 in mounting, SAM VLS launchers, SSM launchers.
● Forward superstructure has large enclosed mainmast at after end with distinctive SATCOM domes, port and starboard, on wing platforms at its base.
● Unusual square section funnel amidships with two large black exhausts protruding from the top forward edge.
● Square profile after superstructure with short pyramid mast at forward end.
● Flight deck right aft.
● Note – All vertical surfaces have a 7° slope and rounded edges to reduce IR emissions.

Displacement full load, tons: 4200.0
Length, feet (metres): 436.2 (133.0)
Beam, feet (metres): 52.8 (16.1)
Draught, feet (metres): 18.0 (5.5) (screws)
Speed, knots: 28.0
Range, miles: 7800 miles at 15 kts

Missiles:
SSM – 8 McDonnell Douglas Harpoon (2 quad) launchers.
SAM – British Aerospace Seawolf GWS 26 Mod 1 VLS.
Guns: 1 Vickers 4.5 in *(114 mm)*/55 Mk 8.
2 Oerlikon/DES 30 mm/75 Mk 1.
Torpedoes: 4 Cray Marine 324 mm (2 twin) tubes. Marconi Stingray.
Decoys: 4 Marconi Sea Gnat 6-barrelled launchers.
Type 182; towed torpedo decoy.
Radars:
Air/surface search – Plessey Type 996(I), 3D.
Navigation – Kelvin Hughes Type 1007.
Fire control – 2 Marconi Type 911.
Sonars: Ferranti/Thomson Sintra Type 2050; bow-mounted.
Dowty Type 2031Z; towed array.

Helicopters: 1 Westland Lynx HAS 3 or EH 101 Merlin.

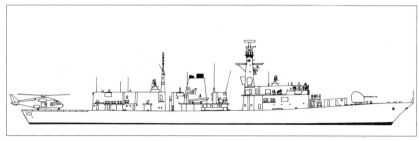

Duke Class

NORFOLK

H M Steele

Country: UNITED STATES OF AMERICA
Ship type: FRIGATES
Class: OLIVER HAZARD PERRY (FFG)
Active: 51

Name (Pennant Number): OLIVER HAZARD PERRY (FFG 7 (ex-PF 109)), McINERNEY (FFG 8), WADSWORTH (FFG 9), DUNCAN (FFG 10), CLARK (FFG 11), GEORGE PHILIP (FFG 12), SAMUEL ELIOT MORISON (FFG 13), JOHN H SIDES (FFG 14), ESTOCIN (FFG 15), CLIFTON SPRAGUE (FFG 16), JOHN A MOORE (FFG 19), ANTRIM (FFG 20), FLATLEY (FFG 21), FAHRION (FFG 22), LEWIS B PULLER (FFG 23), JACK WILLIAMS (FFG 24), COPELAND (FFG 25), GALLERY (FFG 26), MAHLON S TISDALE (FFG 27), BOONE (FFG 28), STEPHEN W GROVES (FFG 29), REID (FFG 30), STARK (FFG 31), JOHN L HALL (FFG 32), JARRETT (FFG 33), AUBREY FITCH (FFG 34), UNDERWOOD (FFG 36), CROMMELIN (FFG 37), CURTS (FFG 38), DOYLE (FFG 39), HALYBURTON (FFG 40), McCLUSKY (FFG 41), KLAKRING (FFG 42), THACH (FFG 43), De WERT (FFG 45), RENTZ (FFG 46), NICHOLAS (FFG 47), VANDEGRIFT (FFG 48), ROBERT G BRADLEY (FFG 49), TAYLOR (FFG 50), GARY (FFG 51), CARR (FFG 52), HAWES (FFG 53), FORD (FFG 54), ELROD (FFG 55), SIMPSON (FFG 56), REUBEN JAMES (FFG 57), SAMUEL B ROBERTS (FFG 58), KAUFFMAN (FFG 59), RODNEY M DAVIS (FFG 60), INGRAHAM (FFG 61)

Recognition Features:
- Raised bow protection with a break down in the forecastle profile at its after end.
- SAM launcher (A mounting positon).
- High, square profile, upper deck superstructure.
- Fire control radar dome on pedestal atop bridge roof.
- Twin, lattice masts. Mainmast, after one of two, is taller and has sloping forward edge.
- Smaller foremast supports large lattice air search radar aerial.
- Squat funnel protruding from superstructure well aft of midships.
- 3 in mounting atop superstructue forward of funnel.
- CIWS mounting aft on hangar roof.
- Flight deck aft.

- Note – Also operated by Australia (active 6) (see Australia, Adelaide entry), Spain (active 5, building 1), Taiwan (active 2, building 4).
Displacement full load, tons: 3638.0, 4100 (FFG 8, 36-61)
Length, feet (metres): 445.0 (135.6), 453 (138.1) (FFG 8, 36-61)
Beam, feet (metres): 45.0 (13.7)
Draught, feet (metres): 14.8 (4.5)
Speed, knots: 29.0
Range, miles: 4500 at 20 kts

Missiles:
    SSM – 4 McDonnell Douglas Harpoon.
    SAM – 36 GDC Standard SM-1MR.
1 Mk 13 Mod 4 launcher for both SSM and SAM missiles.
Guns: 1 OTO Melara 3 in *(76 mm)*/62 Mk 75.
1 GE/GD 20 mm/76 6-barrelled Mk 15 Vulcan Phalanx.
4 – 12.7 mm MGs.
Torpedoes: 6 – 324 mm Mk 32 (2 triple) tubes. Honeywell Mk 46.
Decoys: 2 Loral Hycor SRBOC 6-barrelled Mk 36.
T – Mk-6 Fanfare/SLQ-25 Nixie; torpedo decoy.

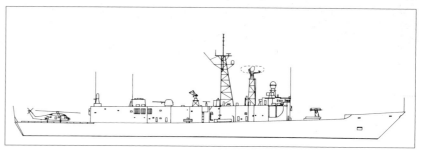

NICHOLAS

Radars:
    Air search – Raytheon SPS 49(V)4 or 5 (FFG 61 and during modernisation of others).
    Surface search – ISC Cardion SPS 55. Fire control – Lockheed STIR (modified SPG 60).
    Sperry Mk 92 (Signaal WM 28).
Sonars: Raytheon SQS 56 or SQS 53B; hull-mounted.

Gould SQR 19; towed array.
SQQ 89(V)2 (SQS 53B and SQR 19) (in FFG 36-61 and retrofitted in all except 14 of the class).

Helicopters: 2 SH-2F LAMPS I or 2 SH-60B LAMPS III (FFG 8, 36-61).

Country: BAHRAIN
Ship type: CORVETTES
Class: AL MANAMA (LÜRSSEN FPB 62 TYPE)
Active: 2

Name (Pennant Number): AL MANAMA (50), AL MUHARRAQ (51)

Recognition Features:
- Continuous maindeck from stem to stern.
- Low freeboard.
- Forward superstructure has enclosed mainmast centrally sited atop.
- 3 in mounting (A position).
- Flat-topped after superstructure with helicopter platform atop.
- 40 mm/70 mountings (Y position).
- Note 1 – This class operated as Corvettes by the United Arab Emirates and Fast Attack Craft by Bahrain.
- Note 2 – Also operated by United Arab Emirates (active 2). Most obvious difference is tall lattice mast atop superstructure aft of bridge.
- Note 3 – Similar to Abu Dhabi and Singapore designs.

Displacement full load, tons: 632.0
Length, feet (metres): 206.7 (63.0)
Beam, feet (metres): 30.5 (9.3)
Draught, feet (metres): 9.5 (2.9)
Speed, knots: 32.0
Range, miles: 4000 at 16 kts

Missiles:
   SSM – 4 Aerospatiale MM 38 Exocet (2 twin) launchers.
Guns: 1 OTO Melara 3 in *(76 mm)*/62 compact.
2 Breda 40 mm/70 (twin).
2 Oerlikon GAM-BO1 20 mm/93.
Decoys: CSEE Dagaie.

Radars:
   Air/surface search – Philips Sea Giraffe 50 HC.
   Navigation – Racal Decca 1226.
   Fire control – Philips 9LV 331.

Helicopters: SA 365F Dauphin 2 (planned).

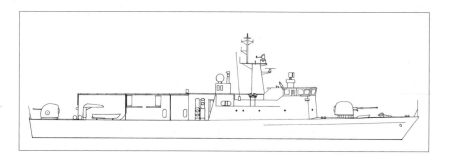

Al Manama Class

AL MUHARRAQ

Country: CROATIA
Ship type: CORVETTES
Class: KRALJ (TYPE 400)
Active: 1
Building: 1
Proposed: 2

Radars:
 Surface search – Racal BT 502.
 Fire control – BEAB 9LV 249 Mk 2.
 Navigation – Racal 1290 A.
Sonars: RIZ PP10M; hull mounted.

Name (Pennant Number): KRALJ PETAR KRESIMIR IV (11), – (12)

Recognition Features:
● Smooth, rounded hull with low forecastle and continuous maindeck from stem to stern.
● 57 mm/70 mounting (A position).
● Long, centrally sited superstructure, raised in bridge area.
● Pyramid shaped, lattice mainmast aft of bridge.
● SSM launchers on afterdeck, port and starboard, trained forward.
● Note – Derived from the Koncar class with a stretched hull and a new superstructure. Mine rails may be removed in favour of increasing SSM capability.

Displacement full load, tons: 385.0
Length, feet (metres): 175.9 (53.6)
Beam, feet (metres): 27.9 (8.5)
Draught, feet (metres): 7.5 (2.3)
Speed, knots: 36.0
Range, miles: 1500 at 20 kts

Missiles:
 SSM – 4 or 8 Saab RBS 15.
Guns: 1 Bofors 57 mm/70. Launchers for illuminants on side of mounting.
1 – 30 mm/65 AK 630; 6 barrels.
2 Oerlikon 20 mm or 2 – 12.7 mm MGs.
Decoys: Wallop Barricade launcher.

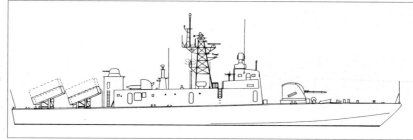

Kralj Class

KRALJ PETAR KRASIMIR IV

L Poggiali

Country: ECUADOR
Ship type: CORVETTES
Class: ESMERALDAS
Active: 6

Name (Pennant Number): ESMERALDAS (CM 11), MANABI (CM 12), LOS RIOS (CM 13), EL ORO (CM 14), LOS GALAPAGOS (CM 15), LOJA (CM 16)

Recognition Features:

- High bow with sweeping continuous maindeck aft to stern.
- 3 in mounting (A position).
- Square profile main superstructure with raised bridge area.
- Pyramid mainmast atop centre of main superstructure.
- SAM launcher atop after end of main superstructure.
- Two SSM launchers immediately aft of forward superstructure.
- Raised helicopter landing platform aft of SSM launchers.
- 40 mm/70 mounting (Y position).
- Note – Similar to Libyan and Iraqi corvettes, with a helicopter deck.

Displacement full load, tons: 685.0
Length, feet (metres): 204.4 (62.3)
Beam, feet (metres): 30.5 (9.3)
Draught, feet (metres): 8.0 (2.5)
Speed, knots: 37.0
Range, miles: 4400 at 14 kts

Missiles:
    SSM – 6 Aerospatiale MM 40 Exocet (2 triple) launchers.
    SAM – Selenia Elsag Albatros quad launcher.
Guns: 1 OTO Melara 3 in *(76 mm)*/62 compact.
2 Breda 40 mm/70 (twin).

Torpedoes: 6 – 324 mm ILAS-3 (2 triple) tubes; Whitehead Motofides A244.
Decoys: 1 Breda 105 mm SCLAR launcher.
Radars:
    Air/surface search – Selenia RAN 10S.
    Navigation – SMA 3 RM 20.
    Fire control – 2 Selenia Orion 10X.
Sonars: Thomson Sintra Diodon; hull-mounted.

Helicopters: 1 Bell 206B can be embarked (platform only).

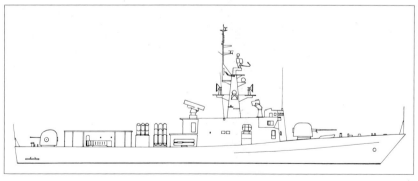

ESMERELDAS

Country: FINLAND
Ship type: CORVETTES
Class: TURUNMAA
Active: 2

Name (Pennant Number): TURUNMAA (03), KARJALA (04)

Recognition Features:
● Long forecastle with 4.7 in mounting (A position).
● High superstructure running from after end of forecastle to quarterdeck.
● Distinctive fire control radar dome mounted atop superstructure aft of bridge.
● Slim, tapered pole mainmast amidships.
● Small tapered, pole mast just forward of mainmast.
● 2 – 40 mm/70 mountings, one central after superstructure, second right aft.
● A/S mortars mounted inside maindeck superstructure abaft the pennant number.
● Note – The exhaust system is trunked on either side of the quarterdeck.

Displacement full load, tons: 770.0
Length, feet (metres): 243.1 (74.1)
Beam, feet (metres): 25.6 (7.8)
Draught, feet (metres): 7.9 (2.4)
Speed, knots: 35.0
Range, miles: 2500 at 14 kts

Guns: 1 Bofors 4.7 in *(120 mm)*/46.
6 – 103 mm rails for illuminants are fitted on the side of the mounting.
2 Bofors 40 mm/70.
4 USSR 23 mm/87 (2 twin).
A/S mortars: 2 RBU 1200 5-tubed launchers.
Depth charges: 2 racks.
Decoys: Wallop Barricade double launcher.

Radars:
Surface search – Terma 20T 48 Super.
Fire control – Signaal WM 22.
Navigation – Raytheon ARPA.
Sonars: Hull-mounted.

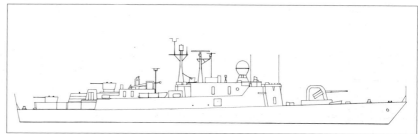

Turunmaa Class

TURUNMAA

Country: GREECE
Ship type: CORVETTES
Class: NIKI (THETIS) (TYPE 420)
Active: 5

Name (Pennant Number): NIKI (ex-*Thetis*) (P 62 (ex-P 6052)), DOXA (ex-*Najade*) (P 63 (ex-P 6054)), ELEFTHERIA (ex-*Triton*) (P 64 (ex-P 6055)), CARTERIA (ex-*Hermes*) (P 65 (ex-P 6053)), AGON (ex-*Andreia*, ex-*Theseus*) (P 66 (ex-P 6056))

Recognition Features:
● A/S mortar mounting (A mounting position).
● High, smooth, forward superstructure with tripod mainmast at after end.
● Black-capped, sloping-topped funnel amidships.
● Torpedo tubes, port and starboard, on maindeck outboard of after superstructure.
● 40 mm/70 mounting at after end of after superstructure.
● Note – *Doxa* has a deckhouse forward of bridge for sick bay.

Displacement full load, tons: 732.0
Length, feet (metres): 229.7 (70.0)
Beam, feet (metres): 26.9 (8.2)
Draught, feet (metres): 8.6 (2.7)
Speed, knots: 19.5
Range, miles: 2760 at 15 kts

Guns: 2 Breda 40 mm/70 (twin)
Torpedoes: 4 – 324 mm single tubes. 4 Honeywell Mk 46.
A/S mortars: 1 Bofors 375 mm 4-barrelled launcher.
Depth charges: 2 rails.
Radars:
    Surface search – Thomson-CSF TRS 3001.
    Navigation – Kelvin Hughes 14/9.
Sonars: Atlas Elektronik ELAC 1 BV; hull-mounted.

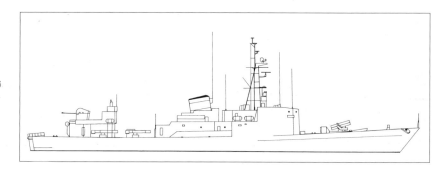

Niki Class

ELEFTHERIA (with German pennant number)

Horst Dehnst

Khukri Class

Country: INDIA
Ship type: CORVETTES
Class: KHUKRI (PROJECTS 25 and 25A)
Active: 4
Building: 4
Proposed: 4

Name (Pennant Number): KHUKRI (P 49), KUTHAR (P 46), KIRPAN (P 44), KHANJAR (P 47), KORA (-), KIRCH (-)

Recognition Features:
- High bow with sloping forecastle.
- 3 in mounting mid-forecastle.
- SSM launchers forward of bridge, port and starboard.
- Unusual curved sloping front up to bridge windows.
- Midships superstructure has large lattice mainmast at after end.
- Distinctive air search radar dome atop mainmast.
- Low funnel aft of mainmast.
- 30 mm/65 mounting immediately aft of funnel.
- Raised flight deck forward of short quarterdeck.

Displacement full load, tons: 1350.0
Length, feet (metres): 298.6 (91.0)
Beam, feet (metres): 34.4 (10.5)
Draught, feet (metres): 8.2 (2.5)
Speed, knots: 25.0
Range, miles: 4000 at 16 kts

Missiles:
    SSM – 2 or 4 SS-N-2D Styx (1 or 2 twin) launchers.
    SAM – SA-N-5 Grail.
Guns: 1 USSR AK 176 3 in *(76 mm)*/60.
2 – 30 mm/65 (twin) AK 630.

Decoys: 2 – 16-barrelled launchers.
NPOL (Cochin); towed torpedo decoy.
Radars:
    Air search – Positive E/Cross Sword.
    Air/surface search – Plank Shave.
    Fire control – Bass Tilt.
    Navigation – Bharat 1245.

Helicopters: Platform only for Chetak.

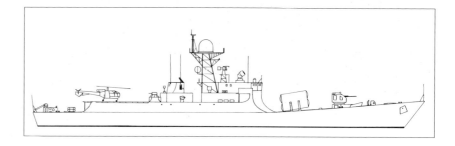

Khukri Class

KIRPAN

Royal Australian Navy

Country: IRAN
Ship type: CORVETTES
Class: BAYANDOR (ex-US PF 103)
Active: 2

Name (Pennant Number): BAYANDOR (ex-US PF 103) (81), NAGHDI (ex-US PF 104) (82)

Recognition Features:
- Unusual curved bow.
- Sloping forecastle with 3 in mounting (A position).
- 20 mm mounting (B position).
- High, complex midships superstructure with sloping pole mainmast atop.
- Large air/surface search radar aerial on forward platform halfway up mainmast.
- Tall, sloping, black-capped funnel with curved after profile.
- 3 in mounting (Y position).
- 40 mm/60 mounting (X position).
- 20 mm mounting after end of quarterdeck.
- Note – Also operated by Thailand (active 2). Most obvious differences are straight after end to funnel profile and torpedo tubes on quarterdeck.

Displacement full load, tons: 1135.0
Length, feet (metres): 275.6 (84.0)
Beam, feet (metres): 33.1 (10.1)
Draught, feet (metres): 10.2 (3.1)
Speed, knots: 20.0
Range, miles: 4800 at 12 kts

Guns: 2 US 3 in *(76 mm)*/50 Mk 3/4.
2 Bofors 40 mm/60 (twin).
2 Oerlikon GAM-B01 20 mm.
2 – 12.7 mm MGs.

Radars:
Air/surface search – Westinghouse SPS 6C.
Surface search – Racal Decca.
Navigation – Raytheon 1650.
Fire control – Western Electric Mk 36.
Sonars: EDO SQS 17A; hull-mounted.

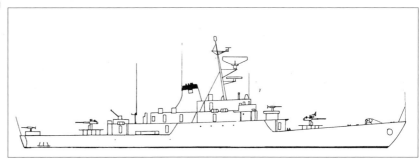

Bayandor Class

BAYANDOR

Eithne Class

Country: IRELAND
Ship type: CORVETTES
Class: EITHNE
Active: 1
Proposed: 1

Name (Pennant Number): EITHNE (P 31)

Recognition Features:
- High freeboard with high central superstructure.
- Short forecastle with 57 mm/70 mounting (B position).
- Large, solid based lattice mainmast atop superstructure aft of bridge.
- Tall tapered funnel at after end of superstructure.
- Long flight deck with break down to short quarterdeck.
- Distinctive flight deck overhang.
- Ship's boats in davits high up superstructure, amidships.

Displacement full load, tons: 1910.0
Length, feet (metres): 265.0 (80.8)
Beam, feet (metres): 39.4 (12.0)
Draught, feet (metres): 14.1 (4.3)
Speed, knots: 20.0
Range, miles: 7000 at 15 kts

Guns: 1 Bofors 57 mm/70 Mk 1.
2 Rheinmetall 20 mm/20
2 Wallop 57 mm launchers for illuminants.
Radars:
    Air/surface search – Signaal DA 05 Mk 4.
    Navigation – Two Racal Decca.
Sonars: Plessey PMS 26; hull-mounted.

Helicopters: 1 SA 365F Dauphin 2.

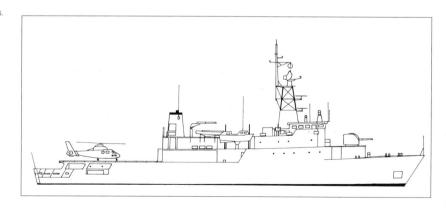

Eithne Class

EITHNE

T Smith

Country: ISRAEL
Ship type: CORVETTES
Class: EILAT (SAAR 5)
Active: 2
Building: 1

Name (Pennant Number): EILAT (501), LAHAV (502), HANIT (503)

Recognition Features:
- High bow, short sloping forecastle.
- 3 in mounting or Vulcan Phalanx on raised forecastle position.
- High, bulky forward superstructure with tall pole mainmast atop.
- Harpoon SSM launchers immediately aft of forward superstructure.
- Gabriel II SSM launchers, four port, four starboard atop central superstructure outboard of funnel.
- Squat, black-capped funnel with unusual sloping forward edge.
- SAM VLS launcher immediately aft of funnel.
- Substantial after superstructure with after pole mast atop.
- Large air search radar aerial atop after superstructure.
- Flight deck right aft.

Displacement full load, tons: 1227.0
Length, feet (metres): 280.8 (85.6)
Beam, feet (metres): 39.0 (11.9)
Draught, feet (metres): 10.5 (3.2)
Speed, knots: 33.0
Range, miles: 3500 at 17 kts

Missiles:
SSM – 8 McDonnell Douglas Harpoon (2 quad) launchers.
8 IAI Gabriel II.
SAM – 2 Israeli Industries Barak I (vertical launch).

Guns: OTO Melara 3 in *(76 mm)*/62 compact. Interchangeable with a Bofors 57 mm gun or Vulcan Phalanx CIWS.
2 Sea Vulcan 25 mm CIWS.
Torpedoes: 6 – 324 mm Mk 32 (2 triple) tubes. Honeywell Mk 46.
Decoys: 4 chaff launchers.
Nixie SLQ 25 towed torpedo decoy.
Radars:
Air search – Elta EL/M 2218S.
Surface search – Cardion SPS 55.
Navigation – I band.
Fire control – 3 Elta EL/M 2221 GM STGR.
Sonars: EDO Type 796 Mod 1; hull-mounted.
VDS or towed array.

Helicopters: 1 Dauphin SA 366G.

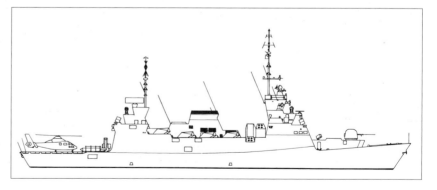

Eilat Class

EILAT (with Vulcan Phalanx)

Ingalls

Country: ITALY
Ship type: CORVETTES
Class: MINERVA
Active: 8

Name (Pennant Number): MINERVA (F 551), URANIA (F 552), DANAIDE (F 553), SFINGE (F 554), DRIADE (F 555), CHIMERA (F 556), FENICE (F 557), SIBILLA (F 558)

Recognition Features:

- Continuous maindeck from bow to break down to quarterdeck.
- Long forecastle with 3 in mounting at mid-point.
- Isolated forward superstructure with short pole mast at after end.
- Midships enclosed mainmast supporting distinctive air/surface search radar aerial.
- Tapered funnel atop central after superstructure with unusual forward sloping top.
- SAM launcher at after end of after superstructure.
- Low freeboard quarterdeck.

Displacement full load, tons: 1285.0
Length, feet (metres): 284.1 (86.6)
Beam, feet (metres): 34.5 (10.5)
Draught, feet (metres): 10.5 (3.2)
Speed, knots: 24.0
Range, miles: 3500 at 18 kts

Missiles:

SSM – Fitted for but not with 4 or 6 Teseo Otomat between the masts.
SAM – Selenia Elsag Albatros octuple launcher.
Guns: 1 OTO Melara 3 in *(76 mm)*/62 compact.
Torpedoes: 6 – 324 mm Whitehead B 515 (2 triple) tubes. Honeywell Mk 46.
Decoys: 2 Wallop Barricade double layer launchers.
SLQ 25 Nixie; towed torpedo decoy.

Radars:
Air/surface search – Selenia SPS 774 (RAN 10S).
Navigation – SMA SPN 728(V)2.
Fire control – Selenia SPG 76 (RTN 30X).
Sonars: Raytheon/Elsag DE 1167; hull-mounted.

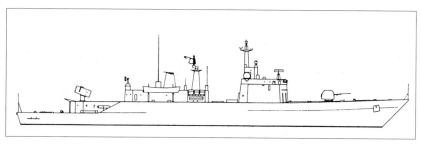

Minerva Class

DANAIDE

H M Steele

Qahir (FSG)

Country: OMAN
Ship type: CORVETTES
Class: QAHIR (FSG)
Active: 0
Building: 2

Name (Pennant Number): QAHIR AL AMWAJ (Q31), AL MUA'ZZER (Q32)

Recognition Features:

● Sloping straight-edged bow with long, gently sloping forecastle
● Two 4-barrelled SSM launchers immediately forward of bridge, after one trained to port, forward one to starboard
● 3 in gun mounting forward of SSM launchers
● Large, smooth midships superstructure with angle surfaces for low reflective radar signature
● Squat black-capped funnel immediately abaft mainmast
● SAM launcher at after end of superstructure immediately forward of flight deck
● Long flight deck at after end of ship

Displacement full load, tons: 1450
Length, feet (metres): 274.6 (83.7)
Beam, feet (metres): 37.7 (11.5)
Draught, feet (metres): 11.8 (3.6)
Speed, knots: 25

Missiles:
  SSM - 8 Aerospatiale MM40 Exocet
  SAM - Thomson-CSF Crotale NG, octupal launcher
Guns: 1 OTO Melara 3 in (76mm)/62 Super Rapid
2 Oerlikon/Royal Ordnance 20 mm GAM-BO1
Decoys: 2 Barricade 12-barrelled launchers
Radars:
  Air/Surface search - Signaal MW 08
  Fire control - Signaal STING, Thomson -CSF DRBV51C

Helicopters: Platform for one medium helicopter

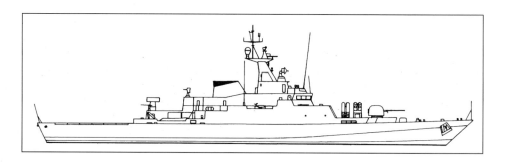

Qahir (FSG)

QAHIR AL AMWAJ

H M Steele

Po Hang Class# Po Hang Class

Country: KOREA, SOUTH
Ship type: CORVETTES
Class: PO HANG
Active: 23
Building: 1

Name (Pennant Number): PO HANG (756), KUN SAN (757), KYONG JU (758), MOK PO (759), KIM CHON (761), CHUNG JU (762), JIN JU (763), YO SU (765), AN DONG (766), SUN CHON (767), YEE REE (768), WON JU (769), JE CHON (771), CHON AN (772), SONG NAM (773), BU CHON (775), DAE CHON (776), JIN HAE (777), SOK CHO (778), YONG JU (779), NAM WON (781), KWAN MYONG (782), – (783)

Recognition Features:

Po Hang

- 3 in mounting (A position).
- High forward superstructure with enclosed mainmast at after end.
- WM 28 fire control radar dome atop mainmast.
- Large funnel well aft of midships with gas turbine air intakes immediately forward.
- Ship's boats in davits at funnel level outboard of air intakes.
- SSM launchers at after end of after superstructure.
- 30 mm mounting on afterdeck.
- Note – There are two versions of this class. Most obvious difference is that the second version has 40 mm/70 mounting in place of SSM launcher.

Displacement full load, tons: 1220.0
Length, feet (metres): 289.7 (88.3)
Beam, feet (metres): 32.8 (10.0)
Draught, feet (metres): 9.5 (2.9)
Speed, knots: 32.0
Range, miles: 4000 at 15 kts

Missiles:
SSM – 2 Aerospatiale MM 38 Exocet (756-759). Not in all.
Guns: 1 or 2 OTO Melara 3 in *(76 mm)*/62 compact.
4 Emerson Electric 30 mm (2 twin) (756-759).
4 Breda 40 mm/70 (761 onwards).
Torpedoes: 6 – 324 mm Mk 32 (2 triple) tubes (761 onwards). Honeywell Mk 46.
Depth charges: 12 (761 onwards).
Decoys: 4 MEL Protean fixed launchers.
2 Loral Hycor SRBOC 6-barrelled Mk 36 (in some).
Radars:
Surface search – Marconi 1810 and/or Raytheon SPS 64.
Fire control – Signaal WM 28; or Marconi 1802.
Sonars: Signaal PHS 32 (761 onwards); hull-mounted.

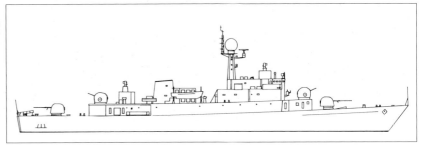

290 Corvettes – Korea, South

Po Hang Class

NAM WON

Ships of the World

Country: RUSSIA AND ASSOCIATED STATES
Ship type: CORVETTES
Class: NANUCHKA
Active: 14 NANUCHKA I (BURYA) (TYPE 1234), 18 NANUCHKA III (VETER) (TYPE 1234.1), 1 NANUCHKA IV (NAKAT) (TYPE 1234.1)

Name (Pennant Number): NANUCHKA I – GRAD, RADUGA, SKVAL, STORM, TAIFUN, ZYKLON, METL, ZARNITSA, GROM, MOLNIJA, MUSSON, VICHR, BORA, BRIZ
NANUCHKA III – METEOR, ZYB, TUCHA, PRILIV BURUN, URAGAN, LIVEN, PASSAT, PRIBOY ZARUA, SMERCH, MIRAS, GROSA, SHTYL, VETER + 3
NANUCHKA IV – NAKAT

Recognition Features:
● Continuous maindeck from stem to stern.
● SAM launcher (A mounting position).
● Fire control radar forward of bridge.
● High central superstructure with lattice mainmast at after end.
● Large, distinctive air/surface search radar dome atop bridge, forward of mainmast.
● Forward pointing SSM launchers on maindeck adjacent to bridge, port and starboard.
● 57 mm/80 mounting (Y position).
● Note 1 – Obvious differences between I and III; larger lattice mainmast on III, 30 mm/65 mounting (X position) on III, 3 in mounting (Y position) on III, air/surface search radar dome atop bridge III.
● Note 2 – Nanuchka IV similar to III except she is trials vehicle for possible 300 km range version of SS-N-9 or its successor.
● Note 3 – Also operated by India (active 3).

Displacement full load, tons: 850.0
Length, feet (metres): 194.5 (59.3)
Beam, feet (metres): 38.7 (11.8)

Draught, feet (metres): 8.5 (2.6)
Speed, knots: 36.0
Range, miles: 2500 at 12 kts

Missiles:
SSM – 6 SS-N-9 Siren (2 triple) launchers.
SAM – SA-N-4 Gecko twin launcher.
Guns: 2 – 57 mm/80 (Nanuchka I).
1 – 3 in (76 mm/60) (Nanuchka III and IV).
1 – 30 mm/65 (Nanuchka III and IV).
Decoys: 2 – 16 or 10 (Nanuchka III) barrelled launchers.
Radars:
Air/surface search – Band Stand.
Plank Shave in later Nanuchka III units.
Surface search – Peel Pair (in early units).
Fire control – Muff Cob (Nanuchka I).
Bass Tilt (Nanuchka III).
Pop Group.

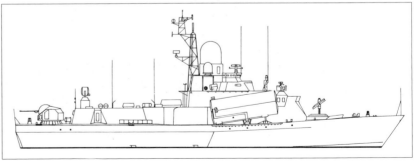

Nanuchka Class

NANUCHKA III

Country: RUSSIA AND ASSOCIATED STATES
Ship type: CORVETTES
Class: TARANTUL (MOLNIYA)
Active: 2 TARANTUL I (TYPE 1241.1), 18 TARANTUL II (TYPE 1241.1M), 27 + 2 TARANTUL III (TYPE 1241.1MP)

Name (Pennant Number): (Not available)

Recognition Features:

● Continuous maindeck from stem to stern with sweeping lines down from high bow to midships, then gently sloping up to slightly higher stern.
● 3 in mounting mid-forecastle.
● High central superstructure with mainmast atop.
● Distinctive, forward pointing SSM launchers, two port two starboard, on maindeck adjacent mainmast
● 2 – 30 mm/65 mountings, port and starboard, on after end of after superstructure.
● Note 1 – The above features generally apply to all three types.
● Note 2 – Obvious differences between I, II and III are; lattice mainmast only on III, air/surface search radar dome atop bridge II and III only.
● Note 3 – Also operated by Bulgaria (II) (active 1), India (I) (active 9, building 3), Poland (I) (active 4), Romania (I) (active 3), Yemen (active 2).

Displacement full load, tons: 455.0
Length, feet (metres): 184.1 (56.1)
Beam, feet (metres): 37.7 (11.5)
Draught, feet (metres): 8.2 (2.5)
Speed, knots: 36.0
Range, miles: 1650 at 14 kts

Missiles:
SSM – 4 SS-N-2C/D Styx (2 twin) launchers.
4 SS-N-22 Sunburn (2 twin) launchers (Tarantul III).
SAM – SA-N-5 Grail quad launcher.
SAM/Guns – CADS-N-1 30 mm Gatling/SA-N-11 mounting.
Guns: 1 – 3 in *(76 mm)*/60.
2 – 30 mm/65.
Decoys: 2 – 16 or 10 (Tarantul III) barrelled launchers.
Radars:
Air/surface search – Plank Shave (Tarantul I), Band Stand (with Plank Shave) (Tarantul II and III).
Navigation – Spin Trough or Krivach II.
Fire control – Bass Tilt.

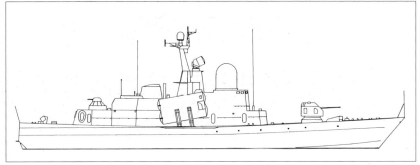

Tarantul Class

TARANTUL I

Jürg Kürsener

Badr Class

Country: SAUDI ARABIA
Ship type: CORVETTES
Class: BADR
Active: 4

Name (Pennant Number): BADR (612), AL YARMOOK (614), HITTEEN (616), TABUK (618)

Recognition Features:
● Long forecastle with 3 in mounting midpoint between bows and bridge.
● Centrally sited superstructure with central lattice mainmast.
● Fire control radar dome atop bridge roof.
● Short, black-capped funnel at after end of superstructure.
● Torpedo tubes on maindeck level at after end of superstructure.
● SSM launchers on afterdeck.
● CIWS mounting right aft.

Displacement full load, tons: 1038.0
Length, feet (metres): 245.0 (74.7)
Beam, feet (metres): 31.5 (9.6)
Draught, feet (metres): 8.9 (2.7)
Speed, knots: 30.0
Range, miles: 4000 at 20 kts

Missiles:
   SSM – 8 McDonnell Douglas Harpoon (2 quad) launchers.
Guns: 1 FMC/OTO Melara 3 in *(76 mm)*/62 Mk 75.
1 GE/GD 20 mm 6-barrelled Vulcan Phalanx.
2 Oerlikon 20 mm/80.
1 – 81 mm mortar.
2 – 40 mm Mk 19 grenade launchers.
Torpedoes: 6 – 324 mm US Mk 32 (2 triple) tubes. Honeywell Mk 46.
Decoys: 2 Loral Hycor SRBOC 6-barrelled Mk 36.

Radars:
   Air search – Lockheed SPS 40B.
   Surface search – ISC Cardion SPS 55.
   Fire control – Sperry Mk 92.
Sonars: Raytheon SQS 56 (DE 1164); hull-mounted.

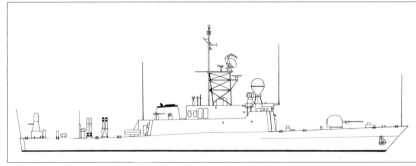

Badr Class

BADR

van Ginderen Collection

Country: SINGAPORE
Ship type: CORVETTES
Class: VICTORY
Active: 6

Name (Pennant Number): VICTORY (P 88), VALOUR (P 89), VIGILANCE (P 90), VALIANT (P 91), VIGOUR (P 92), VENGEANCE (P 93)

Recognition Features:
- Sloping forecastle with 3 in mounting (A position).
- Short forward superstructure with large, distinctive, enclosed mainmast at after end.
- Unusual forward sloping pole mast atop mainmast.
- SSM launchers on maindeck aft of superstructure.
- Torpedo tubes, port and starboard, on maindeck well aft of midships.
- Note – Built to a Lürssen MGB 62 design similar to Bahrain and UAE vessels.

Displacement full load, tons: 550.0
Length, feet (metres): 204.7 (62.4)
Beam, feet (metres): 27.9 (8.5)
Draught, feet (metres): 10.2 (3.1)
Speed, knots: 35.0
Range, miles: 4000 at 18 kts

Missiles:
    SSM – 8 McDonnell Douglas Harpoon.
    SAM – Rafael Barak I.
Guns: 1 OTO Melara 3 in *(76 mm)*/62 Super Rapid.
Torpedoes: 6 – 324 mm Whitehead B 515 (2 triple) tubes. Whitehead A 244S.
Decoys: 2 Plessey Shield launchers.

Radars:
    Surface search – Ericsson/Radamec Sea Giraffe 150HC.
    Navigation – Racal Decca.
    Fire control – Bofors Electronic 9LV 200.
Sonars: Thomson Sintra TSM 2064.

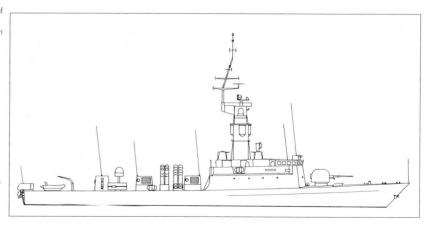

Victory Class

VIGOUR

A M Nixon, RAN

Country: SWEDEN
Ship type: CORVETTES
Class: GÖTEBORG
Active: 4

Name (Pennant Number): GÖTEBORG (K 21), GÄLVE (K 22), KALMAR (K 23), SUNDSVALL (K 24)

Recognition Features:
- Continuous maindeck lines from stem to stern.
- 57 mm/70 mounting (A position).
- A/S mortar launchers (B mounting position).
- Long central superstructure with, midships, large enclosed mainmast atop.
- Torpedo tubes, on maindeck outboard of bridge.
- SSM launchers, two port two starboard, on maindeck at after end of superstructure.
- 40 mm/70 mounting on afterdeck.
- VDS towing equipment right aft.

Displacement full load, tons: 399.0
Length, feet (metres): 187.0 (57.0)
Beam, feet (metres): 26.2 (8.0)
Draught, feet (metres): 6.6 (2.0)
Speed, knots: 32.0

Missiles:
SSM – 8 Saab RBS 15 (4 twin) launchers.
Guns: 1 Bofors 57 mm/70 Mk 2.
1 Bofors 40 mm/70 (or Bofors Sea Trinity).
Torpedoes: 4 – 15.75 in *(400 mm)* tubes. Swedish Ordnance Type 43/45 or Whitehead Type 442.
A/S mortars: 4 Saab Elma LLS-920 9-tubed launchers.
Depth charges: On mine rails.
Decoys: 4 Philips Philax launchers.

Radars:
Air/surface search – Ericsson Sea Giraffe 150 HC.
Navigation – Terma PN 612.
Fire control – Two Bofors Electronics 9GR 400.
Sonars: Thomson Sintra TSM 2643 Salmon; VDS.
Simrad SA 950; hull-mounted.

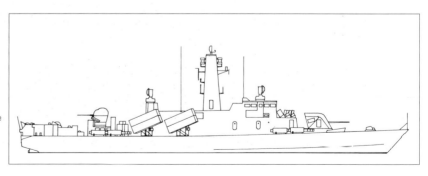

Göteborg Class

KALMAR

Erik Laursen

Country: SWEDEN
Ship type: CORVETTES
Class: STOCKHOLM
Active: 2

Name (Pennant Number): STOCKHOLM (K 11), MALMÖ (K 12)

Recognition Features:

● Long forecastle with A/S mortar launcher at forward end and 57 mm/70 mounting midpoint between bows and bridge.
● Short, high, central superstructure with lattice mainmast at after end.
● Distinctive SSM launchers, two port two starboard, on maindeck at after end of superstructure.
● 40 mm/70 mounting right aft.
● Note – Developed from Spica II class.

Displacement full load, tons: 335.0
Length, feet (metres): 164.0 (50.0)
Beam, feet (metres): 22.3 (6.8)
Draught, feet (metres): 6.2 (1.9)
Speed, knots: 32.0

Missiles:

SSM – 8 Saab RBS 15 (4 twin) launchers.
Guns: 1 Bofors 57 mm/70 Mk 2.
1 Bofors 40 mm/70.
Torpedoes: 2 – 21 in *(533 mm)* tubes. FFV Type 613.
4 – 15.75 in *(400 mm)* tubes. Swedish Ordnance Type 43 or Whitehead A 244/S Mod 2.
A/S mortars: 4 Saab Elma LLS-920 9-tubed launchers.
Depth charges: On mine rails.
Decoys: 2 Philips Philax launchers. A/S mortars have also been adapted to fire decoys.

Radars:
Air/surface search – Ericsson Sea Giraffe 50HC.
Navigation – Terma PN 612.
Fire control – Philips 9LV 200 Mk 3.
Sonars: Simrad SA 950; hull-mounted.
Thomson Sintra TSM 2642 Salmon; VDS.

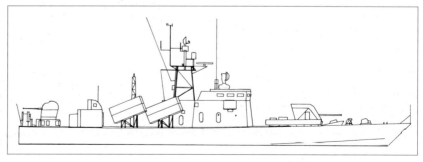

Stockholm Class

STOCKHOLM

Antonio Moreno

Country: THAILAND
Ship type: CORVETTES
Class: KHAMRONSIN (ASW CORVETTES)
Active: 3

Name (Pennant Number): KHAMRONSIN (1), THAYANCHON (2), LONGLOM (3)

Recognition Features:
- Short forecastle with 76 mm/62 mounting (A position).
- High freeboard, slab sided superstructure running from forecastle to afterdeck.
- Lattice mainmast amidships, atop central superstructure.
- Squat, black-capped funnel with sloping top aft of mainmast.
- 30 mm/70 mounting (X position).
- Break down from maindeck to short quarterdeck.
- Note 1 – Based on a Vosper Thornycroft *Province* class 56 m design stretched by increasing the frame spacing along the whole length of the hull.
- Note 2 – Lightly armed version active with marine police.

Displacement, half load (tons): 475.0
Length, feet (metres): 203.4 (62.0)
Beam, feet (metres): 26.9 (8.2)
Draught, feet (metres): 8.2 (2.5)
Speed, knots: 25.0
Range, miles: 2500 at 15 kts

Guns: 1 OTO Melara 76 mm/62 Mod 7.
2 Breda 30 mm/70 (twin).
Torpedoes: 6 Plessey PMW 49A (2 triple) launchers. MUSL Stingray.

Radars:
   Air/surface search – Plessey AWS 4.
Sonars: Atlas Elektronik DSQS-21C; hull-mounted.

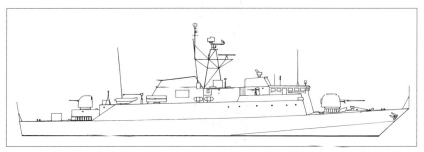

KHAMRONSIN

Royal Thai Navy

Country: THAILAND
Ship type: CORVETTES
Class: RATTANAKOSIN (MISSILE CORVETTES)
Active: 2

Name (Pennant Number): RATTANAKOSIN (1), SUKHOTHAI (2)

Recognition Features:
- High bow, short forecastle.
- 3 in mounting (A position).
- 40 mm/70 mounting (B position).
- Slab sided high superstructure running from forecastle to afterdeck.
- Large, solid pyramid mainmast atop forward superstructure supporting fire control radar dome.
- Low, tapered funnel well aft of midships with curved after profile and twin exhaust protruding from top.
- Short, enclosed aftermast, immediately aft of funnel, supporting air/surface search radar aerial.
- SSM launchers atop after end of superstructure.
- SAM launcher right aft on quarterdeck.
- Note – Similar design to missile corvettes built for Saudi Arabia.

Displacement full load, tons: 960.0
Length, feet (metres): 252.0 (76.8)
Beam, feet (metres): 31.5 (9.6)
Draught, feet (metres): 8.0 (2.4)
Speed, knots: 26.0
Range, miles: 3000 at 16 kts

Missiles:
　　SSM – 8 McDonnell Douglas Harpoon (2 quad) launchers.
　　SAM – Selenia Elsag Albatros octuple launcher.

Guns: 1 OTO Melara 3 in *(76 mm)*/62.
2 Breda 40 mm/70 (twin).
2 Oerlikon 20 mm.
Torpedoes: 6 – 324 mm US Mk 32 (2 triple) tubes. MUSL Stingray.
Decoys: CSEE Dagaie 6 or 10-tubed.
Radars:
　　Air/surface search – Signaal DA 05.
　　Surface search – Signaal ZW 06.
　　Navigation – Decca 1226.
　　Fire control – Signaal WM 25/41.
Sonars: Atlas Elektronik DSQS 21C; hull-mounted.

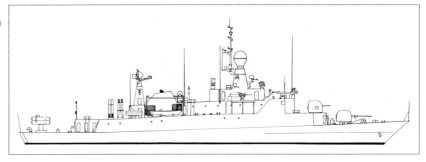

RATTANAKOSIN

Ships of the World

Country: AUSTRALIA
Ship type: PATROL FORCES
Class: FREMANTLE (LARGE PATROL CRAFT)
Active: 15

Name (Pennant Number): FREMANTLE (203), WARRNAMBOOL (204), TOWNSVILLE (205), WOLLONGONG (206), LAUNCESTON (207), WHYALLA (208), IPSWICH (209), CESSNOCK (210), BENDIGO (211), GAWLER (212), GERALDTON (213), DUBBO (214), GEELONG (215), GLADSTONE (216), BUNBURY (217)

Recognition Features:
● Continuous maindeck from stem to stern.
● 40 mm/60 mounting (A position).
● Stepped, central superstructure.
● Sloping top to forward end of superstructure with bridge set back.
● Open bridge atop after end of enclosed bridge.
● Large whip aerial either side of forward end of superstructure.
● Pole mainmast amidships with small lattice structure supporting radar aerial just forward.
● Small ships boat stowed at after end of superstructure.

Displacement full load, tons: 245.0
Length, feet (metres): 137.1 (41.8)
Beam, feet (metres): 23.3 (7.1)
Draught, feet (metres): 5.9 (1.8)
Speed, knots: 30.0
Range, miles: 4800

Guns: 1 Bofors AN 4 – 40 mm/60.
1 – 81 mm mortar.
2 – 12.7 mm MGs.
Radars:
　Navigation – Kelvin Hughes Type 1006.

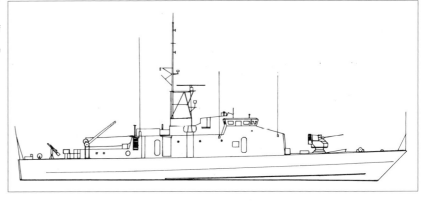

GERALDTON

J Mortimer

Country: BAHRAIN
Ship type: PATROL FORCES
Class: AHMAD EL FATEH (FPB 45) (FAST ATTACK CRAFT – MISSILE)
Active: 4

Name (Pennant Number): AHMAD EL FATEH (20), AL JABIRI (21), ABDUL RAHMAN AL FADEL (22), AL TAWEELAH (23)

Recognition Features:
● Sweeping bow, low freeboard.
● Continuous maindeck from stem to stern.
● 3 in mounting (A position).
● High superstructure forward of midships.
● Open bridge atop enclosed bridge.
● Lattice mainmast aft of bridge with short pole mast at after end.
● 4 SSM launchers, two trained to port two to starboard in crossover configuration aft of superstructure.
● 40 mm/70 mounting right aft.
● Note 1 – Also operated by Ecuador (active 3), Ghana (active 2), Malaysia (active 6 (Jerong class)), Singapore (active 6).
● Note 2 – The basic outline of these craft are similar, the weapon fit differences are too numerous to list.
● Note 3 – Classified as corvettes in Bahrain.

Displacement full load, tons: 259.0
Length, feet (metres): 147.3 (44.9)
Beam, feet (metres): 22.9 (7.0)
Draught, feet (metres): 8.2 (2.5)
Speed, knots: 40.0
Range, miles: 1600 at 16 kts

Missiles:
  SSM – 4 Aerospatiale MM 40 Exocet (2 twin) launchers.

Guns: 1 OTO Melara 3 in *(76 mm)*/62.
2 Breda 40 mm/70 (twin).
3 – 7.62 mm MGs.
Decoys: CSEE Dagaie launcher.
Radars:
  Surface search/fire control – Philips LV223.
  Navigation – Racal Decca 1226.

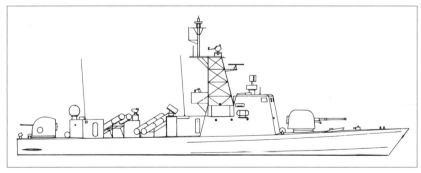

Ahmad El Fateh Class

ABDUL RAHMAN AL FADEL

Grajaú Class

Country: BRAZIL
Ship type: PATROL FORCES
Class: GRAJAÚ (LARGE PATROL CRAFT)
Active: 2
Building: 4
Proposed: 2

Name (Pennant Number): GRAJAÚ (P 40), GUAIBA (P 41), GRAÚNA (P 42), GOIANA (P 43),
GUAJARÁ (P 44), GUAPORÉ (P 45), GURUPÁ (P 46), GURUPI (P 47)

Recognition Features:
- Smooth, uncluttered lines from bow to stern.
- Small, flat fronted, central superstructure stepped down at after end.
- 40 mm/70 mounting (A position).
- Tall, lattice mainmast atop central superstructure.
- Large, distinctive surface search radar dome atop mainmast.
- 20 mm mounting on afterdeck.

Displacement full load, tons: 410.0
Length, feet (metres): 152.6 (46.5)
Beam, feet (metres): 24.6 (7.5)
Draught, feet (metres): 7.5 (2.3)
Speed, knots: 22.0
Range, miles: 2000 at 12 kts

Guns: 1 Bofors 40 mm/70.
2 Oerlikon 20 mm.
Radars:
    Surface search – Racal Decca 1290A.

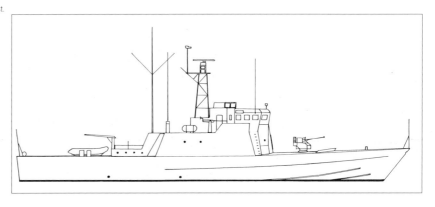

Grajaú Class

GRAJAÚ

Country: CHINA
Ship type: PATROL FORCES
Class: HAINAN (TYPE 037) (FAST ATTACK CRAFT – PATROL)
Active: 95
Building: 3

Name (Pennant Number): (267-285), (290), (302), (305), (609), (610), (622), (628), (636-687), (689-692), (695), (696), (698), (699), (701), (707), (723-730)

Recognition Features:
● High bow, long sloping forecastle, low freeboard.
● A/S mortars towards forward end of forecastle.
● 57 mm/70 mounting (A position).
● 25 mm/60 mounting (B position).
● Tall, angular midships superstructure.
● Small lattice mainmast atop after end of bridge.
● 57 mm/70 mounting (Y position).
● 25 mm/60 mounting (X position).
● Note 1 – A larger Chinese-built version of Soviet SO 1.
● Note 2 – Missile launchers can be fitted in lieu of the after 57 mm mounting. Later ships have a tripod foremast and a short stub mainmast.
● Note 3 – Also operated by Bangladesh (active 2), Burma (active 10), Egypt (active 8), North Korea (active 6), Pakistan (active 1).

Displacement full load, tons: 392.0
Length, feet (metres): 192.8 (58.8)
Beam, feet (metres): 23.6 (7.2)
Draught, feet (metres): 7.2 (2.2)
Speed, knots: 30.5
Range, miles: 1300 at 15 kts

Guns: 4 China 57 mm/70 (2 twin).
4 USSR 25 mm/60 (2 twin).
A/S mortars: 4 RBU 1200.
Depth charges: 2 BMB-2 projectors; 2 racks.
Mines: Rails fitted.
Radars:
   Surface search – Pot Head or Skin Head.
Sonars: Stag Ear; hull-mounted.
Thomson Sintra SS 12 VDS on at least two of the class.

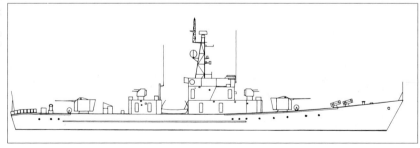

Hainan Class

HAINAN 686

Country: CHINA
Ship type: PATROL FORCES
Class: HEGU or HOKU (TYPE 024) (FAST ATTACK CRAFT – MISSILE)
Active: 70
Reserve: 25

Name (Pennant Number): (1100) and (3100) series

Recognition Features:
- Low freeboard.
- 25 mm/60 mounting (A position).
- Very small and low central superstructure.
- Stout, pole mainmast atop central superstructure.
- Surface search radar aerial atop mainmast.
- Two large, distinctive SSM launchers on quarterdeck, both raised at forward end and angled slightly outboard.
- Note 1 – Also operated by Bangladesh (active 4), Egypt (active 6), Iran (active 0, on order 10), Pakistan (active 4).
- Note 2 – A hydrofoil variant, the Hema class, has a semi-submerged foil fwd and has a length of 95.3 feet. The extra 6 ft length allows for the mounting of a second twin 25 mm abaft the missile launchers.

Displacement full load, tons: 79.2
Length, feet (metres): 88.6 (27)
Beam, feet (metres): 20.7 (6.3)
Draught, feet (metres): 4.3 (1.3)
Speed, knots: 37.5
Range, miles: 400 at 30 kts

Missiles:
  SSM – 2 SY-1.

Guns: 2 USSR 25 mm/60 (twin).
Radars:
  Surface search – Square Tie.

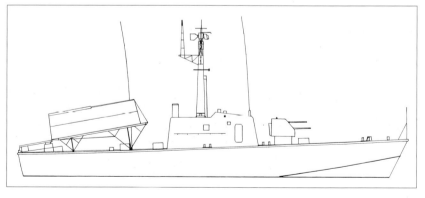

HEGU

A Sheldon Duplaix

Country: CHINA
Ship type: PATROL FORCES
Class: HOUJIAN (OR HUANG) (TYPE 520) (FAST ATTACK CRAFT – MISSILE)
Active: 1

Name (Pennant Number): (770)

Recognition Features:
- High bow, sloping forecastle.
- 37 mm/63 mounting (A position).
- Main superstructure stepped down at after end.
- Tall, lattice mainmast at after end of bridge superstructure.
- Distinctive fire control director atop bridge roof.
- Boxlike SSM launchers aft of forward superstructure; port and starboard, trained forward and slightly outboard.
- Two 30 mm/65 mountings (Y and X positions).

Displacement standard, tons: 520
Length, feet (metres): 214.6 (65.4)
Beam, feet (metres): 27.6 (8.4)
Draught, feet (metres): 7.9 (2.4)
Speed, knots: 32.0
Range, miles: 1800 at 18 kts

Missiles:
SSM: 6 YJ-1 (Eagle Strike) (C-801) (2 triple).
Guns: 2 – 37 mm/63 (twin) Type 76A.
4 – 30 mm/65 (2 twin) Type 69.
Radars:
Surface search – Square Tie.
Fire control – Rice Lamp.

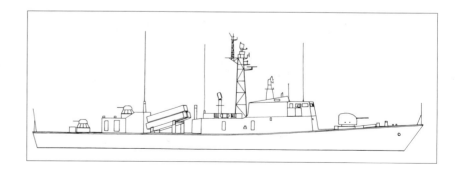

Houjian Class

HOUJIAN 770

Country: CHINA
Ship type: PATROL FORCES
Class: HOUXIN (FAST ATTACK CRAFT – MISSILE)
Active: 8
Building: 3

Name (Pennant Number): (751-758)

Recognition Features:
- High bow, long forecastle.
- 37 mm/63 mounting (A position).
- Long, central superstructure, stepped down at after end.
- Two 14.5 mm mountings, port and starboard, (B mounting position).
- Large lattice mainmast amidships with surface search radar aerial atop.
- Small gap between forward and low after superstructure.
- 37 mm/63 mounting atop after superstructure (X position).
- Two forward pointing (twin) SSM launchers, port and starboard, on quarterdeck. Both launchers angled up and slightly outboard.

Displacement full load, tons: 480.0
Length, feet (metres): 213.3 (65.0)
Beam, feet (metres): 23.6 (7.2)
Draught, feet (metres): 7.5 (2.3)
Speed, knots: 32.0
Range, miles: 750 at 18 kts

Missiles:
　SSM – 4 YJ-1 (Eagle Strike) (C-801) (2 twin).
Guns: 4 – 37 mm/63 (2 twin).
4 – 14.5 mm (2 twin).
Radars:
　Surface search – Square Tie.
　Fire control – Rice Lamp.

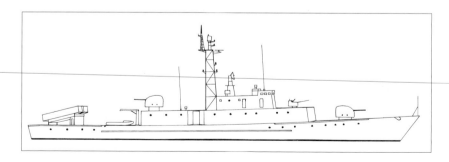

Houxin Class

HOUXIN   *CSSC*

Country: DENMARK
Ship type: PATROL FORCES
Class: FLYVEFISKEN (LARGE PATROL CRAFT AND MINEHUNTERS/LAYERS)
Active: 11
Building: 3

Name (Pennant Number): FLYVEFISKEN (P 550), HAJEN (P 551), HAVKATTEN (P 552), LAXEN (P 553), MAKRELEN (P 554), STØREN (P 555), SVAERDFISKEN (P 556), GLENTEN (P 557), GRIBBEN (P 558), LOMMEN (P 559), RAUNEN (P 560), SKADEN (P 561), VIBEN (P 562), SØLØVEN (P 563)

Recognition Features:
- 3 in mounting (A position).
- High freeboard with break down to afterdeck adjacent to funnel.
- High, angular central superstructure flush with ships side.
- Tall enclosed mainmast amidships with air/surface search radar aerial atop.
- Very low profile, black-capped funnel aft of mainmast with sloping after end.
- Two SSM launchers, athwartships in crossover configuration, aft of funnel adjacent to break in maindeck.
- Two torpedo tubes, one port one starboard, outboard of SSM launchers.
- Note – The overall design allows ships to change as required to the attack, patrol, MCMV or minelayer roles. Requirement is to be able to change within 48 hours.

Displacement full load, tons: 450.0
Length, feet (metres): 177.2 (54.0)
Beam, feet (metres): 29.5 (9.0)
Draught, feet (metres): 8.2 (2.5)
Speed, knots: 30.0
Range, miles: 2400 at 18 kts

Missiles:
SSM – 8 McDonnell Douglas Harpoon.
Guns: 1 OTO Melara 3 in *(76 mm)*/62 Super Rapid.
2 – 12.7 mm MGs.
Torpedoes: 2 – 21 in *(533 mm)* tubes.
Decoys: 2 Sea Gnat 6-barrelled launcher.
Radars:
Air/surface search – Plessey AWS 6 (P 550-P 556).
Telefunken SystemTechnik TRS-3D (P 557-P 563).
Navigation – Furuno.
Fire control – CelsiusTech 9LV 200.
Sonars: Thomson Sintra TSM 2640; hull-mounted and VDS.
CelsiusTech CTS-36; hull-mounted.

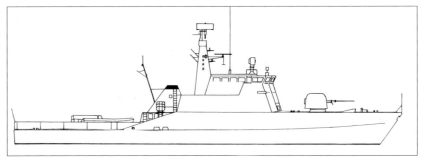

HAJEN (Attack Version)

Royal Danish Navy

Country: DENMARK
Ship type: PATROL FORCES
Class: WILLEMOES (FAST ATTACK CRAFT - MISSILE)
Active: 10

Name (Pennant Number): BILLE (P 540), BREDAL (P 541), HAMMER (P 542), HUITFELD (P 543), KRIEGER (P 544), NORBY (P 545), RODSTEEN (P 546), SEHESTED (P 547), SUENSON (P 548), WILLEMOES (P 549)

Recogniton Features:

- Long forecastle with visible breakwater just forward of 3 in mounting (A position).
- Low rounded superstructure from midships aft to quarterdeck.
- Torpedo tubes, port and starboard, adjacent to A mounting.
- Short lattice mainmast mid-superstructure with taller tripod mast immediately aft supporting air/surface search radar aerial.
- Fire control radar aerial on pedestal immediately aft of bridge.
- SSM launchers mounted right aft on quarterdeck pointing forward and angled upwards and outboard.

Displacement full load, tons: 260.0
Length, feet (metres): 151.0 (46.0)
Beam, feet (metres): 24.0 (7.4)
Draught, feet (metres): 8.2 (2.5)
Speed, knots: 38.0

Missiles:

SSM – 4 or 8 McDonnell Douglas Harpoon.
Guns: 1 OTO Melara 3 in *(76 mm)*/62 compact.
2 triple 103 mm illumination rocket launchers.
Torpedoes: 2 or 4 - 21 in *(533 mm)* tubes. FFV Type 61.
Decoys: Sea Gnat dispensers.

Radars:

Air/surface search – 9GA 208.
Navigation – Terma Elektronik 20T 48 Super.
Fire control – Philips 9LV 200.

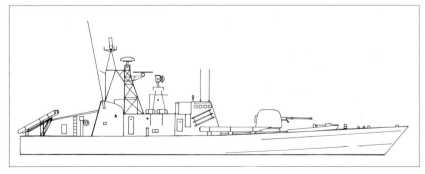

Willemoes Class

HUITFELD

Royal Danish Navy

Country: EGYPT
Ship type: PATROL FORCES
Class: OCTOBER (FAST ATTACK CRAFT – MISSILE)
Active: 6

Name (Pennant Number): (781), (783), (785), (787), (789), (791)

Recognition Features:
- Long forecastle with 30 mm/75 (A position).
- Low profile, rounded superstructure well aft of midships.
- Distinctive pyramid platform atop superstructure aft of bridge supporting fire control radar aerial.
- Very large, lattice mainmast at after end of superstructure with air/surface search radar dome atop.
- SSM launchers outboard, port and starboard at after end of superstructure.
- 30 mm/75 mounting (Y position).
- Note 1 – Same hull design and basic craft as Komar class.
- Note 2 – Also operated as Komar class by North Korea (active 10), Syria (active 5).

Displacement full load, tons: 82.0
Length, feet (metres): 84.0 (25.5)
Beam, feet (metres): 20.0 (6.1)
Draught, feet (metres): 5.0 (1.3)
Speed, knots: 40.0
Range, miles: 400 at 30 kts

Missiles:
  SSM – 2 OTO Melara/Matra Otomat Mk 1.
Guns: 4 BMARC/Oerlikon 30 mm//5 (2 twin).
Decoys: 2 Protean launchers.

Radars:
  Air/surface search – Marconi S 810.
  Fire control – Marconi/ST 802.

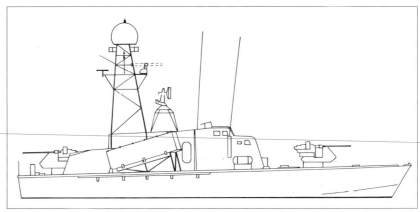

October Class

OCTOBER

Country: EGYPT
Ship type: PATROL FORCES
Class: RAMADAN (FAST ATTACK CRAFT – MISSILE)
Active: 6

Name (Pennant Number): RAMADAN (670), KHYBER (672), EL KADESSAYA (674), EL YARMOUK (676), BADR (678), HETTEIN (680)

Recognition Features:
- Short forecastle with 3 in mounting (A position).
- Main superstructure well forward of midships.
- Large, pyramid mainmast at after end of superstructure with pole mast atop the after end.
- Distinctive air/surface search radar dome atop mainmast.
- Small after superstructure supporting short enclosed mast with radome atop.
- SSM launchers sited between superstructures. Forward two trained to port, after two starboard. All launchers angled towards the bow.
- 40 mm/70 mounting (Y position).

Displacement full load, tons: 307.0
Length, feet (metres): 170.6 (52.0)
Beam, feet (metres): 25.0 (7.6)
Draught, foot (metres): 7.5 (2.3)
Speed, knots: 40.0
Range, miles: 1600 at 18 kts

Missiles:
  SSM – 4 OTO Melara/Matra Otomat Mk 1.
Guns: 1 OTO Melara 3 in *(76 mm)* compact.
2 Breda 40 mm/70 (twin).
Decoys: 4 Protean launchers.

Radars:
  Air/surface search – Marconi S 820.
  Navigation – Marconi S 810.
  Fire control – Two Marconi ST 802.

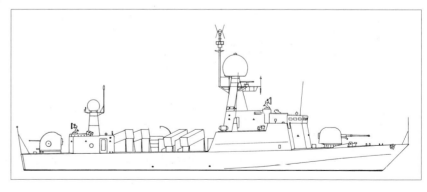

Ramadan Class

RAMADAN

Country: FINLAND
Ship type: PATROL FORCES
Class: HELSINKI (FAST ATTACK CRAFT – MISSILE)
Active: 4

Name (Pennant Number): HELSINKI (60), TURKU (61), OULU (62), KOTKA (63)

Recognition Features:
- Short forecastle with 57 mm/70 mounting (A position).
- High, rounded superstructure forward of midships.
- Tall, slender, enclosed mainmast atop superstructure aft of bridge.
- Two 23 mm/87 mountings on wings at after end of superstructure.
- Four twin SSM launchers on afterdeck. Two port two starboard, trained forward and angled outboard.

Displacement full load, tons: 300.0
Length, feet (metres): 147.6 (45.0)
Beam, feet (metres): 29.2 (8.9)
Draught, feet (metres): 9.9 (3.0)
Speed, knots: 30.0

Missiles:
   SSM – 8 Saab RBS 15.
Guns: 1 Bofors 57 mm/70.
4 USSR 23 mm/87 (2 twin).
Decoys: Philax launcher.
Radars:
   Surface search – 9GA 208.
   Fire control – Philips 9LV 225.
Sonars: Simrad Marine SS 304.

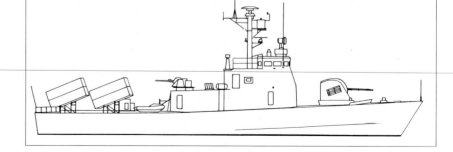

HELSINKI

Finnish Navy

Country: FINLAND
Ship type: PATROL FORCES
Class: RAUMA (FAST ATTACK CRAFT – MISSILE)
Active: 4

Name (Pennant Number): RAUMA (70), RAAHE (71), PORVOO (72), NAANTALI (73)

Recognition Features:
- High bow with long forecastle.
- 57 mm/70 mounting mid-forecastle.
- A/S mortar between mounting and forward superstructure.
- Central, angular, stepped superstructure.
- Fire control radar aerial atop bridge roof.
- Short, robust pole mainmast amidships.
- Surface search radar aerial atop mainmast.
- Two SSM launchers outboard of after end of superstructure with second two right aft on the port and starboard quarter.
- Note – SAM and 23 mm guns are interchangeable within the same barbette.

Displacement full load, tons: 248.0
Length, feet (metres): 157.5 (48.0)
Beam, feet (metres): 26.2 (8.0)
Draught, feet (metres): 4.5 (1.5)
Speed, knots: 30.0

Missiles:
SSM – 6 Saab RBS 15SF.
SAM – Matra Sadral sextuple launcher; Mistral.
Guns: Bofors 40 mm/70.
6 – 103 mm rails for rocket illuminants.
2 USSR 23 mm/87 (twin); can be fitted instead of Sadral.
A/S mortars: 4 Saab Elma LLS-920 9-tubed launchers.
Decoys: Philax launcher.

Radars:
Surface search – 9GA 208.
Fire control – Bofors Electronic 9LV 225.
Navigation – Raytheon ARPA.
Sonars: Simrad Subsea toadfish sonar.

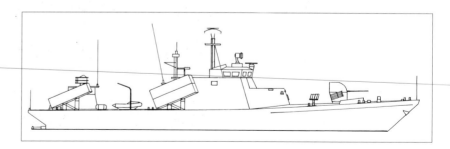

Rauma Class

RAUMA

Finnish Navy

Country: FRANCE
Ship type: PATROL FORCES
Class: P 400 (FAST ATTACK CRAFT – PATROL)
Active: 10

Name (Pennant Number): L'AUDACIEUSE (P 682), LA BOUDEUSE (P 683), LA CAPRICIEUSE (P 684), LA FOUGUEUSE (P 685), LA GLORIEUSE (P 686), LA GRACIEUSE (P 687), LA MOQUEUSE (P 688), LA RAILLEUSE (P 689), LA RIEUSE (P 690), LA TAPAGEUSE (P 691)

Recognition Features:
- 40 mm/60 mounting (A position).
- High, angular, midships superstructure.
- Pole mainmast, angled aft, atop superstructure amidships.
- Very unusual twin funnels aft of superstructure at outboard extremities of hull. Funnels are of square section, black-capped, and angled aft.
- Note – Also operated by Gabon (active 2) and Oman (building 3).

Displacement full load, tons: 454.0
Length, feet (metres): 178.6 (54.5)
Beam, feet (metres): 26.2 (8.0)
Draught, feet (metres): 8.5 (2.5)
Speed, knots: 24.5
Range, miles: 4200 at 15 kts

Guns: 1 Bofors 40 mm/60.
1 Giat 20F2 20 mm.
2 – 12.7 mm MGs.
Radars:
Surface search – Racal Decca 1226.

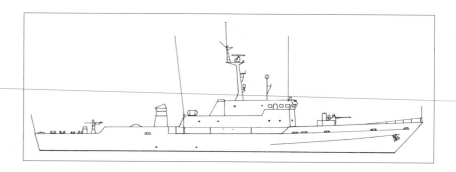

L'AUDACIEUSE

Guy Toremans

Albatros Class

Country: GERMANY
Ship type: PATROL FORCES
Class: ALBATROS (TYPE 143B) (FAST ATTACK-CRAFT – MISSILE)
Active: 10

Name (Pennant Number): ALBATROS (P 6111), FALKE (P 6112), GEIER (P 6113), BUSSARD (P 6114), SPERBER (P 6115), GREIF (P 6116), KONDOR (P 6117), SEEADLER (P 6118), HABICHT (P 6119), KORMORAN (P 6120)

Recognition Features:
- Long forecastle, prominent breakwater forward of 3 in mounting (A position).
- Narrow central superstructure, stepped down aft of bridge.
- Lattice structure aft of bridge supporting distinctive surface search/fire control radar dome.
- Tall tripod mainmast at after end of superstructure.
- Two SSM launchers aft of superstructure, one trained forward and to port and one immediately aft trained forward and to starboard.
- 3 in mounting aft of SSM launchers (Y position).
- Two torpedo tubes outboard of after mounting, trained aft.
- Note – SAM launcher has been fitted in Y mounting position for trials (*Habicht*).

Displacement full load, tons: 398.0
Length, feet (metres): 189.0 (57.6)
Beam, feet (metres): 25.6 (7.8)
Draught, feet (metres): 8.5 (2.6)
Speed, knots: 40.0
Range, miles: 1300 at 30 kts

Missiles:
SSM – 4 Aerospatiale MM 38 Exocet (2 twin) launchers.
Guns: 2 OTO Melara 3 in *(76 mm)*/62 compact.
Torpedoes: 2 – 21 in *(533 mm)* aft tubes. AEG Seeal.
Decoys: Buck-Wegmann Hot Dog/Silver Dog.

Radars:
Surface search/fire control – Signaal WM 27.
Navigation – SMA 3 RM 20.

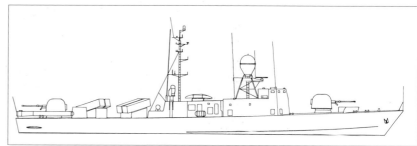

KORMORAN

Per Kornefeldt

Country: GERMANY
Ship type: PATROL FORCES
Class: GEPARD (TYPE 143 A) (FAST ATTACK CRAFT – MISSILE)
Active: 10

Name (Pennant Number): GEPARD (P 6121), PUMA (P 6122), HERMELIN (P 6123), NERZ (P 6124), ZOBEL (P 6125), FRETTCHEN (P 6126), DACHS (P 6127), OZELOT (P 6128), WIESEL (P 6129), HYÄNE (P 6130)

Recognition Features:
● Long forecastle with 3 in mounting (A position).
● Central superstructure with high forward end, stepped down aft of bridge.
● Distinctive surface search/fire control radar dome atop after end of bridge.
● Tall tripod mainmast at after end of superstructure.
● Two SSM launchers aft of superstructure trained forward and to port and two further aft trained forward and to starboard.

Displacement full load, tons: 391.0
Length, feet (metres): 190.0 (57.6)
Beam, feet (metres): 25.6 (7.8)
Draught, feet (metres): 8.5 (2.6)
Speed, knots: 40.0
Range, miles: 2600 at 16 kts
Missiles:
    SSM – 4 Aerospatiale MM 38 Exocet.
    SAM – GDC RAM 21 cell point defence system (being fitted behind Exocet 1992-95).
Guns: 1 OTO Melara 3 in *(76 mm)*/62 compact.
Decoys: Buck-Wegmann Hot Dog/Silver Dog.
Radars:
    Surface search/fire control – Signaal WM 27.
    Navigation – SMA 3 RM 20.

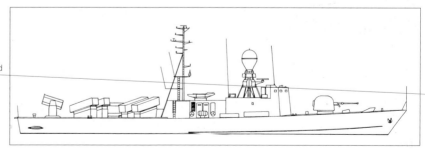

GEPARD

Giorgio Ghiglione

Country: GREECE
Ship type: PATROL FORCES
Class: LA COMBATTANTE II (FAST ATTACK CRAFT – MISSILE)
Active: 4

Name (Pennant Number): ANTHIPOPLOIARHOS ANNINOS (ex-*Navsithoi*) (P 14), IPOPLOIARHOS ARLIOTIS (ex-*Evniki*) (P 15), IPOPLOIARHOS KONIDIS (ex-*Kymothoi*) (P 16), IPOPLOIARHOS BATSIS (ex-*Calypso*) (P 17)

Recognition Features:
● Small bridge superstructure forward of midships.
● 35 mm/90 mounting (A position).
● Tall lattice mainmast at after end of superstructure.
● Fire control radar aerial atop bridge roof.
● Four SSM launchers aft of superstructure, forward two immediately aft of superstructure trained forward and to starboard, after two trained forward and to port.
● 35 mm/90 mounting aft (Y position).
● Single torpedo tube each side of after mounting, trained aft.
● Note – Also operated by Iran (active 10) (most obvious differences are tubular SSM launchers and surface search/ fire control radar dome atop mainmast), Malaysia (active 4 as Perdana class), and Libya (active 9-IIG).

Displacement full load, tons: 255.0
Length, feet (metres): 154.2 (47.0)
Beam, feet (metres): 23.3 (7.1)
Draught, feet (metres): 8.2 (2.5)
Speed, knots: 36.5
Range, miles: 850 at 25 kts

Missiles:
SSM – 4 Aerospatiale MM 38 Exocet.
Guns: 4 Oerlikon 35 mm/90 (2 twin).

Torpedoes: 2 – 21 in *(533 mm)* tubes. AEG SST-4.
Radars:
Surface search – Thomson-CSF Triton.
Navigation – Decca 1226C.
Fire Control – Thomson-CSF Pollux.

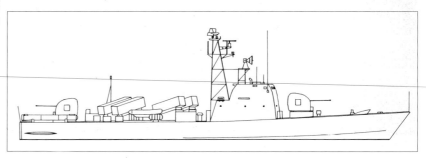

IPOPLOIARHOS BATSIS

Hellenic Navy

Country: GREECE
Ship type: PATROL FORCES
Class: LA COMBATTANTE III (FAST ATTACK CRAFT – MISSILE)
Active: 10

Name (Pennant Number): ANTHIPLOIARHOS LASKOS (P 20), PLOTARHIS BLESSAS (P 21), IPOPLOIARHOS MIKONIOS (P 22), IPOPLOIARHOS TROUPAKIS (P 23), SIMEOFOROS KAVALOUDIS (P 24), ANTHIPOPLOIARHOS KOSTAKOS (P 25), IPOPLOIARHOS DEYIANNIS (P 26), SIMEOFOROS XENOS (P 27), SIMEOFOROS SIMITZOPOULOS (P 28), SIMEOFOROS STARAKIS (P 29)

Recognition Features:
● Low freeboard craft with 3 in mounting (A position).
● Low profile, rounded superstructure well forward of midships.
● Fire control radar aerial mounted on lattice structure atop bridge roof.
● Tall lattice mainmast atop mid-superstructure.
● Surface search radar aerial atop mainmast.
● Two 30 mm mountings, one port one starboard, atop after end of superstructure.
● Low profile after superstructure forward of 3 in mounting (Y position).
● SSM launchers between forward and after superstructures.
● Two single torpedo tubes trained aft and sited outboard either side of after mounting.
● Note – Also operated by Nigeria (active 3-IIIB), Qatar (active 3- IIIM), Tunisia (active 3-IIIM).

Displacement full load, tons: 425.0 (P 20-23), 429.0 (P 24-29)
Length, feet (metres): 184.0 (56.2)
Beam, feet (metres): 26.2 (8.0)
Draught, feet (metres): 7.0 (2.1)
Speed, knots: 36 (P 20-23); 32.5 (P 24-29)

Range, miles: 2700 at 15 kts

Missiles:
SSM – 4 Aerospatiale MM 38 Exocet (P 20-P 23).
6 Kongsberg Penguin Mk 2 (P 24-P 29).
Guns: 2 OTO Melara 3 in *(76 mm)*/62 compact.
4 Emerson Electric 30 mm (2 twin).
Torpedoes: 2 – 21 in *(533 mm)* aft tubes. AEG SST-4.
Decoys: Wegmann launchers.
Radars:
Surface search – Thomson-CSF Triton.
Navigation – Decca 1226C.
Fire control – Thomson-CSF Castor II.
Thomson-CSF Pollux.

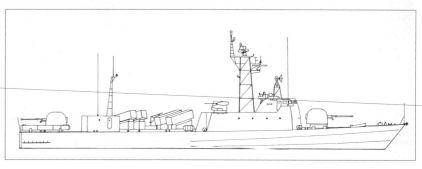

La Combattante III Class

IPOPLOIARHOS DEYIANNIS

Hellenic Navy

Country: INDIA
Ship type: PATROL FORCES
Class: SUKANYA (OFFSHORE PATROL SHIPS)
Active: 7
Building: 3

Name (Pennant Number): SUKANYA (P 50), SUBHADRA (P 51), SUVARNA (P 52), SAVITRI (P 53), SARYU (P 54), SHARADA (P 55), SUJATA (P 56), – (P 57-59)

Recognition Features:
- High freeboard forward.
- Break down to maindeck level adjacent to funnel.
- Angular forward superstructure with bridge set well aft from its forward end.
- 20 mm mounting forward of bridge (B position).
- Pyramid mainmast at after end of forward superstructure supporting surface search and navigation radar aerials.
- Tall, tapered, black-capped funnel just aft of midships.
- Ship's boats in davits outboard of funnel.
- Square profile superstructure aft of funnel.
- Raised flight deck right aft.
- Note – 6 building for coastguard.

Displacement full load, tons: 1890.0
Length, feet (metres): 334.6 (102.0)
Beam, feet (metres): 37.7 (11.5)
Draught, feet (metres): 11.2 (3.4)
Speed, knots: 21.0
Range, miles: 7000 at 15 kts

Guns: 1 Oerlikon 20 mm.

Radars:
Surface search – Selenia.
Navigation – Racal Decca.

Helicopters: 1 Chetak.

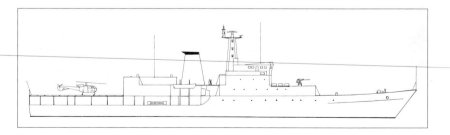

SUBHADRA

Country: INDONESIA
Ship type: PATROL FORCES
Class: DAGGER (FAST ATTACK CRAFT – MISSILE)
Active: 4

Radars:
  Surface search – Racal Decca 1226.
  Fire control – Signaal WM 28.

Name (Pennant Number): MANDAU (621), RENCONG (622), BADIK (623), KERIS (624)

Recognition Features:
- 57 mm/70 mounting (A position).
- Superstructure amidships stepped down at the after end.
- Short lattice structure aft of bridge with radar dome atop.
- Tripod mainmast at after end of superstructure.
- Short, black-capped funnel aft of mainmast.
- Four SSM launchers aft of superstructure, forward two trained to starboard, after two trained to port.
- 40 mm/70 mounting (Y position).
- Note – *Mandau* has a different shaped mainmast with a tripod base.

Displacement full load, tons: 270.0
Length, feet (metres): 164.7 (50.2)
Beam, feet (metres): 23.9 (7.3)
Draught, feet (metres): 7.5 (2.3)
Speed, knots: 41.0
Range, miles: 2000 at 17 kts

Missiles:
  SSM – 4 Aerospatiale MM 38 Exocet.
Guns: 1 Bofors 57 mm/70 Mk 1. Launchers for illuminants on each side.
1 Bofors 40 mm/70.
2 Rheinmetall 20 mm.

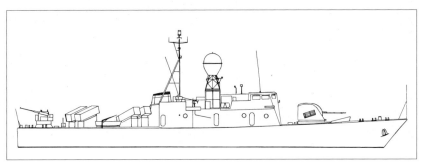

Dagger Class

KERIS

Hetz Class

Country: ISRAEL
Ship type: PATROL FORCES
Class: HETZ (SAAR 4.5) (FAST ATTACK CRAFT – MISSILE)
Active: 3

Name (Pennant Number): ROMAT, KESHET, HETZ (ex-*Nirit*)

Recognition Features:
- Long sleek hull, low freeboard.
- CIWS mounting (A position) with distinctive domed top.
- Short superstructure well forward of midships.
- Large enclosed mainmast at after end of superstructure.
- Air/surface search radar aerial atop mainmast.
- SSM launchers aft of superstructure and forward of after mounting.
- 3 in mounting (B position).
- Note 1 – Easily confused with the Saar 4 class.
- Note 2 – Two Aliya Class (Saar 4.5) operated by Israel. Of same basic hull design with substantially different weapons fits.

Displacement full load, tons: 488.0
Length, feet (metres): 202.4 (61 7)
Beam, feet (metres): 24.9 (7.6)
Draught, feet (metres): 8.2 (2.5)
Speed, knots: 31.0
Range, miles: 3000 at 17 kts

Missiles:
  SSM – 8 Harpoon (2 quad) plus 6 or 8 Gabriel.
  SAM – Israeli Industries Barak I (vertical launch).
Guns: 1 OTO Melara 3 in *(76 mm)*/62.
2 Oerlikon 20 mm.
1 GE/GD Vulcan Phalanx.
2 or 4 – 12.7 mm (twin or quad) MGs.

Decoys: 1 – 45 tube, 4 – 24 tube, 4 single tube launchers.
Radars:
  Air/surface search – Thomson-CSF TH-D 1040 Neptune.
  Fire control – Selenia Orion RTN-10X.
      Elta EL/M-2221 GM STGR (*Hetz*).

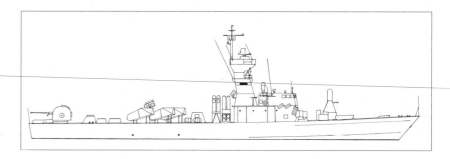

Hetz Class

HETZ

Israel Shipyards

Reshef Class

Country: ISRAEL
Ship type: PATROL FORCES
Class: RESHEF (SAAR 4) (FAST ATTACK CRAFT – MISSILE)
Active: 8

Name (Pennant Number): RESHEF, KIDON, TARSHISH, YAFFO, NITZHON, ATSMOUT, MOLEDET, KOMEMIUT

Recognition Features:
● Long sleek hull, low freeboard.
● CIWS mounting (A position) with distinctive domed top.
● Short superstructure well forward of midships.
● Large complex lattice mainmast at after end of superstructure.
● Air/surface search radar aerial atop mainmast.
● Combination of Harpoon and Gabriel SSM launchers aft of superstructure and forward of after mounting.
● 3 in mounting (Y position).
● Note 1 – Also operated by Chile (active 2 as Casma class), main difference is 3 in mounting in place of CIWS (A position).
● Note 2 – Very similar to Minister class, South Africa.
● Note 3 – Easily confused with the Saar 4.5 class.
● Note 4 – Photograph and line diagram have slightly different weapons fits illustrating different modification states.

Displacement full load, tons: 450.0
Length, feet (metres): 190.6 (58.0)
Beam, feet (metres): 25.0 (7.8)
Draught, feet (metres): 8.0 (2.4)
Speed, knots: 32.0
Range, miles: 4000 at 17.5 kts

Missiles:
  SSM – 2-4 McDonnell Douglas Harpoon (twin or quad) launchers.
    4-6 Gabriel II or III.
Guns: 1 or 2 OTO Melara 3 in *(76 mm)*/62 compact.
2 Oerlikon 20 mm.
1 GE/GD Vulcan Phalanx Mk 15.
2 – 12.7 mm MGs.
Decoys: 1 – 45 tube, 4 or 6 – 24 tube, 4 single tube launchers.
Radars:
  Air/surface search – Thomson-CSF TH-D 1040 Neptune.
  Fire control – Selenia Orion RTN 10X.
Sonars: EDO 780; VDS; occasionally fitted in some of the class.

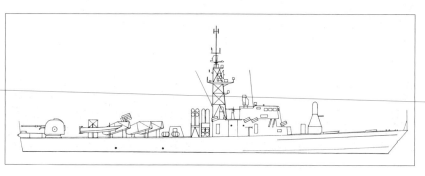

Reshef Class

RESHEF

Country: ITALY
Ship type: PATROL FORCES
Class: SPARVIERO (HYDROFOIL – MISSILE)
Active: 6

Name (Pennant Number): NIBBIO (P 421), FALCONE (P 422), ASTORE (P 423), GRIFONE (P 424), GHEPPIO (P 425), CONDOR (P 426)

Recognition Features:
● Compact craft with blunt bow and long forecastle.
● Small bridge superstructure well aft of midships.
● 3 in mounting (A position) dominating the forecastle.
● Fire control radar aerial atop bridge roof.
● Short tripod mainmast at after end of bridge supporting surface search radar aerial.
● Two SSM launchers, right aft, trained forward and steeply raised at forward end.
● Note 1 – When hullborne, hydrofoils stow vertically either side adjacent to mainmast.
● Note 2 – Six of class being built under licence in Japan, substantially modified, particularly armament.

Displacement full load, tons: 60.6
Length, feet (metres): 80.7 (24.6)
Beam, feet (metres): 23.1 (7.0)
Draught, feet (metres): 14.4 (4.4)
Speed, knots: 48 foilborne
Range, miles: 400 at 45 kts

Missiles:
SSM – 2 OTO Melara/Matra Otomat Teseo Mk 2 (IG 1).
Guns: 1 OTO Melara 3 in (76 mm)/62 compact.

Radars:
Surface search – SMA SPQ 701.
Fire control – Selenia SPG 70 (RTN 10X).

GHEPPIO

Camil Busquets i Vilanova

Chaho Class

Country: KOREA, NORTH
Ship type: PATROL FORCES
Class: CHAHO (FAST ATTACK CRAFT – GUN)
Active: 62

Name (Pennant Number): (Not available)

Recognition Features:
● 23 mm/87 mounting just forward of midway between bows and bridge.
● Low freeboard.
● Very low profile bridge, well forward of midships.
● Pole mainmast amidships.
● Large, distinctive multiple rocket launcher immediately aft of bridge and raised above bridge level.
● 14.5 mm mounting on afterdeck.
● Note – Also operated by Iran (active 3).

Displacement full load, tons: 82.0
Length, feet (metres): 85.3 (26.0)
Beam, feet (metres): 19.0 (5.8)
Draught, feet (metres): 6.6 (2.0)
Speed, knots: 40.0

Guns: 1 BM 21 multiple rocket launcher.
2 USSR 23 mm/87 (twin).
2 – 14.5 mm (twin) MGs.
Radars:
    Surface search – Pot Head.

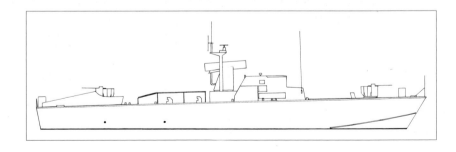

Chaho Class

CHAHO

Pae Ku Class

Country: KOREA, SOUTH
Ship type: PATROL FORCES
Class: PAE KU (PSMM 5) (FAST ATTACK CRAFT – MISSILE)
Active: 8

Name (Pennant Number): PAE KU 52 (PGM 582 (ex-PGM 352)), PAE KU 53 (PGM 583 (ex-PGM 353)), PAE KU 55 (PGM 585 (ex-PGM 355)), PAE KU 56 (PGM 586 (ex-PGM 356)), PAE KU 57 (PGM 587 (ex-PGM 357)), PAE KU 58 (PGM 588 (ex-PGM 358)), PAE KU 59 (PGM 589 (ex-PGM 359)), PAE KU 61 (PGM 591 (ex-PGM 361))

Recognition Features:
● High bow with OTO Melara 3 in mounting (A position) (PGM 586-591) or USN 3 in mounting (A position) (PGM 582-585).
● High angular central superstructure.
● Pole mainmast atop mid-superstructure.
● Two long whip aerials at after end of superstructure.
● Harpoon SSM launchers immediately aft of superstructure (PGM 586-591) or Standard SSM launchers right aft (PGM 582-585).
● 30 mm mounting right aft (PGM 586-591).
● Note – Based on the US Navy's Asheville (PG 84) design, but appearance of Korean-built ships' superstructure differs.

Displacement full load, tons: 268.0
Length, feet (metres): 176.2 (53.7)
Beam, feet (metres): 23.9 (7.3)
Draught, feet (metres): 9.5 (2.9)
Speed, knots: 40.0+
Range, miles: 2400 at 18 kts

Missiles:
SSM – 2 GDC Standard ARM launchers (PGM 582-585).
4 McDonnell Douglas Harpoon (PGM 586-591).

Guns: 1 OTO Melara 3 in *(76 mm)*/62 compact (PGM 586-591).
1 USN 3 in *(76 mm)*/50 Mk 34 (PGM 582-585).
2 Emerson Electric 30 mm (twin).
Browning 12.7 mm MGs.
Decoys: Loral RBOC 4-barrelled Mk 33 launchers.
Radar:
Air search – SPS 58.
Surface search – Marconi Canada HC 75.
Fire control – Western Electric SPG 50 or Westinghouse W-120.

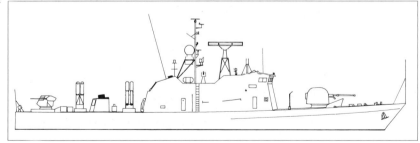

Pae Ku Class

PAE KU 53

G Jacobs

# Handalan Class

Country: MALAYSIA
Ship type: PATROL FORCES
Class: HANDALAN (SPICA-M) (FAST ATTACK CRAFT – MISSILE)
Active: 4

Name (Pennant Number): HANDALAN (3511), PERKASA (3512), PENDEKAR (3513), GEMPITA (3514)

Sonars: Simrad; hull-mounted.

Recognition Features:
● 57 mm/70 mounting (A position).
● Main superstructure just forward of midships with tall lattice mainmast at after end.
● Fire control radar aerial atop bridge.
● Surface search radar aerial atop mainmast.
● Two, twin SSM launchers aft of bridge pointing forward and outboard in crossover formation forward pair to port after pair to starboard.
● 40 mm/70 mounting aft of SSM launchers on afterdeck.
● Note – Bridge further forward than in similar Swedish class to accommodate SSM.

Displacement full load, tons: 240.0
Length, feet (metres): 142.6 (43.6)
Beam, feet (metres): 23.3 (7.1)
Draught, feet (metres): 7.4 (2.4) (screws)
Speed, knots: 34.5
Range, miles: 1850 at 14 kts

Missiles:
    SSM – 4 Aerospatiale MM 38 Exocet.
Guns: 1 Bofors 57 mm/70.
1 Bofors 40 mm/70.
Radars:
    Surface search – Philips 9GR 600.
    Navigation – Decca 616.
    Fire control – Philips 9LV 212.

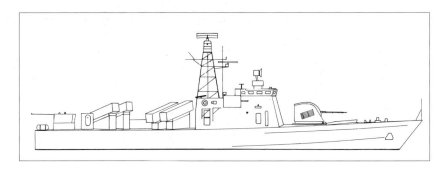

Handalan Class

PENDEKAR

J Mortimer

Country: MALAYSIA
Ship type: PATROL FORCES
Class: PERDANA (LA COMBATTANTE II) (FAST ATTACK CRAFT – MISSILE)
Active: 4

Name (Pennant Number): PERDANA (3501), SERANG (3502), GANAS (3503), GANYANG (3504)

Recognition Features:

- 50 mm/70 mounting (A position).
- Main superstructure forward of midships extends full width of craft.
- Open bridge atop enclosed bridge structure.
- Fire control radar aerial atop bridge.
- Tall lattice mainmast at after end of superstructure.
- Forward pointing SSM launchers aft of superstructure angled outboardforward one to starboard after one to port.
- 40 mm/70 mounting on afterdeck (Y position).
- Note 1 – All of basic La Combattante IID design.
- Note 2 – Same basic hull and design as Perdana class (Malaysia), but with significantly different weapons fits.

Displacement full load, tons: 265.0
Length, feet (metres): 154.2 (47.0)
Beam, feet (metres): 23.1 (7.0)
Draught, feet (metres): 12.8 (3.9)
Speed, knots: 36.5
Range, miles: 1800 at 15 kts

Missiles:

SSM – 2 Aerospatiale MM 38 Exocet.
Guns: 1 Bofors 57 mm/70.
1 Bofors 40 mm/70.
Decoys: 4 – 57 mm launchers.

Radars:
Air/surface search – Thomson-CSF TH-D 1040 Triton.
Navigation – Racal Decca 616.
Fire control – Thomson-CSF Pollux.

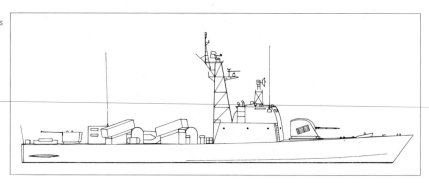

GANAS

Country: MEXICO
Ship type: PATROL FORCES
Class: AZTECA (LARGE PATROL CRAFT)
Active: 31

Name (Pennant Number): AZETCA (P 01), GUAYCURA (P 02), NAHUATL (P 03), TOTORAN (P 04), PAPAGO (P 05), TARAHUMARA (P 06), TEPEHUAN (P 07), MEXICA (P 08), ZAPOTECA (P 09), HUASTECA (P 10), MAZAHUA (P 11), HUICHOL (P 12), SERI (P 13), UAQUI (P 14), TLAPANECO (P 15), TARASCO (P 16), ACOLHUA (P 17), OTOMI (P 18), MAYO (P 19), PIMAS (P 20), CHICHIMECA (P 21), CHONTAZ (P 22), MAZATECO (P 23), TOLTECA (P 24), MAYA (P 25), COCHIMIE (P 26), CORA (P 27), TOTONACA (P 28), MIXTECO (P 29), OLMECA (P 30), TLAHUICA (P 31)

Recognition Features:
- Continuous maindeck from stem to stern, high freeboard.
- 40 mm/70 mounting (A position).
- Rounded, low profile central superstructure.
- Small mast and funnel combined at after end of superstructure with radar aerial at its forward end.
- 20 mm mounting on afterdeck.

Displacement full load, tons: 148.0
Length, feet (metres): 111.8 (34.1)
Beam, foot (metres): 28.1 (8.6)
Draught, feet (metres): 6.8 (2.0)
Speed, knots: 24.0
Range, miles: 2500 at 12 kts

Guns: 1 Bofors 40 mm/70.
1 Oerlikon 20 mm.

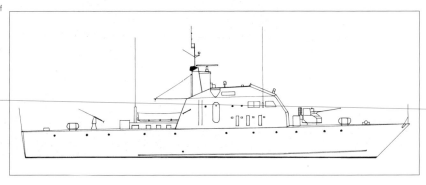

Azteca Class

TOTORAN

Mexican Navy

Country: NORWAY
Ship type: PATROL FORCES
Class: HAUK (FAST ATTACK CRAFT – MISSILE)
Active: 14

Name (Pennant Number): HAUK (P 986), ØRN (P 987), TERNE (P 988), TJELD (P 989), SKARV (P 990), TEIST (P 991), JO (P 992), LOM (P 993), STEGG (P 994), FALK (P 995), RAVN (P 996), GRIBB (P 997), GEIR (P 998), ERLE (P 999).

Recognition Features:
- Low profile, compact craft.
- 40 mm/70 mounting (A position).
- Low superstructure centred just forward of midships.
- Forward pointing single torpedo tubes outboard of A mounting, port and starboard.
- Short lattice mainmast atop after end of superstructure.
- 20 mm/20 mounting immediately aft of superstructure surrounded by high circular armoured breakwater.
- Distinctive SSM launchers mounted on afterdeck, two port two starboard, angled outboard.
- Note – Can be confused with Snögg class.

Displacement full load, tons: 148.0
Length, feet (metres): 120.0 (36.5)
Beam, feet (metres): 20.0 (6.1)
Draught, feet (metres): 5.0 (1.5)
Speed, knots: 32.0
Range, miles: 440 at 30 kts

Missiles:
SSM – 6 Kongsberg Penguin Mk 2 Mod 5.
SAM – Twin Simbad launcher for Matra Mistral.
Guns: 1 Bofors 40 mm/70.
1 Rheinmetall 20 mm/20.
Torpedoes: 2 – 21 in *(533 mm)* tubes. FFV Type 613.

Radars:
Surface search/navigation – Two Racal Decca TM 1226.
Sonars: Simrad; active search.

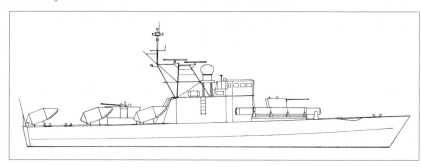

SKARV

Antonio Moreno

Snögg Class

Country: NORWAY
Ship type: PATROL FORCES
Class: SNÖGG (FAST ATTACK CRAFT – MISSILE)
Active: 6

Name (Pennant Number): SNÖGG (ex-*Lyr*) (P 980), RAPP (P 981), SNAR (P 982), RASK (P 983), KVIKK (P 984), KJAPP (P 985)

Recognition Features:

- 40 mm/70 mounting (A position).
- Central superstructure stepped down at after end.
- Short lattice mainmast atop centre of superstructure supporting surface search radar aerial.
- One torpedo tube outboard either side of 40 mm/70 mounting.
- One torpedo tube outboard either side of afterdeck.
- SSM launchers, port and starboard quarters.
- Note – Hull profile is similar to that of the Storm class.

Displacement full load, tons: 135.0
Length, feet (metres): 120.0 (36.5)
Beam, feet (metres): 20.0 (6.1)
Draught, feet (metres): 5.0 (1.5)
Speed, knots: 32.0

Missiles:
    SSM – Up to 4 Kongsberg Penguin Mk 1.
Guns: 1 Bofors 40 mm/70.
Torpedoes: 4 – 21 in *(533 mm)* tubes.
Radars:
    Surface search – Racal Decca 1626.

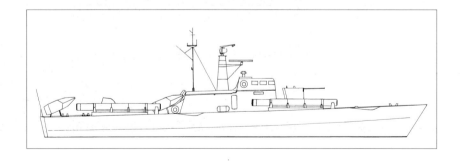

KJAPP

Country: NORWAY
Ship type: PATROL FORCES
Class: STORM (FAST ATTACK CRAFT – MISSILE)
Active: 10

Name (Pennant Number): BLINK (P 961), SKJOLD (P 963), TRYGG (P 964), KJEKK (P 965), DJERV (P 966), SKUDD (P 967), STEIL (P 969), HVASS (P 972), BRASK (P 977), GNIST (P 979)

Recognition Features:
- Low profile, compact craft.
- 3 in mounting (A position).
- Low, rounded central superstructure.
- Central tripod mainmast supporting distinctive semi-spherical radar dome.
- 40 mm/70 mounting aft of superstructure.
- Distinctive SSM launchers mounted on afterdeck, two port two starboard, angled outboard.

Displacement full load, tons: 135.0
Length, feet (metres): 120.0 (36.5)
Beam, feet (metres): 20.0 (6.1)
Draught, feet (metres): 5.0 (1.5)
Speed, knots: 32.0

Missiles:
  SSM – Up to 6 Kongsberg Penguin Mk 1 Mod 7.
Guns: 1 Bofors 3 in *(76 mm)*/50.
1 Bofors 40 mm/70.
Radars:
  Surface search – Racal Decca TM 1226.
  Fire control – Signaal WM 26.

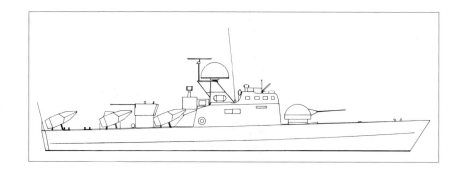

Storm Class

TRYGG

Antonio Moreno

Al Bushra (OPV)

Country: OMAN
Ship type: PATROL FORCES
Class: AL BUSHRA (OPV)
Active: 2
Building: 1

Name (Pennant Number): AL BUSHRA (B1), AL MANSOOR (B2), NAJAH (B3)

Recognition Features:
● High bow with long forecastle
● 3-in (76mm)/62 mounting (A position)
● High, central flush-sided superstructure with lattice mainmast atop
● Distinctive tapered funnel at after end of superstructure with tall whip aerial at forward end
● Long afterdeck with low freeboard
● Towed array sonar winching gear right aft on quarterdeck

Displacement full load, tons: 475
Length, feet (metres): 187.6 (54.5)
Beam, feet (metres): 26.2 (8.0)
Draught, feet (metres): 8.9 (2.7)
Speed, knots: 24.5

Guns: 1 OTO Melara 3 in (76mm)/62 Compact or DCN 40mm/60
Torpedoes: 2 - 16 in (406mm) (twin tubes)
Decoys: Plessey Barricade Chaff
Radars:
 Air/Surface search - E/F band
 Surface search: I band
Sonars: Thomson Sintra/BAe Sema ATAS towed array

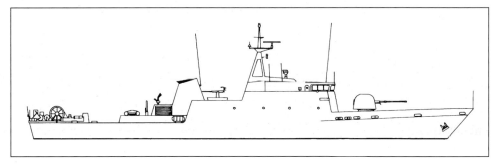

Al Bushra (OPV)

AL BUSHRA AND AL MANSOOR

CMN Cherbourg

Country: OMAN
Ship type: PATROL FORCES
Class: DHOFAR (PROVINCE) (FAST ATTACK CRAFT – MISSILE)
Active: 4
Name (Pennant Number): DHOFAR (B 10), AL SHARQIYAH (B 11), AL BAT'NAH (B 12), MUSSANDAM (B 14)

Recognition Features:

● Short forecastle, 3 in mounting (A position).
● High superstructure forward of midships. Superstructure is flush with craft's sides.
● Lattice mainmast centrally sited atop superstructure supporting air/surface search radar aerial.
● Two quadruple SSM launchers on maindeck aft of superstructure. Both launchers angled slightly forward. Forward launcher port side and after one starboard.
● 40 mm/70 mounting right aft.
● Note – Similar to Kenyan Nyayo class.

Displacement full load, tons: 394.0
Length, feet (metres): 186.0 (56.7)
Beam, feet (metres): 26.9 (8.2)
Draught, feet (metres): 7.9 (2.4)
Speed, knots: 38.0
Range, miles: 2000 at 18 kts

Missiles:

SSM – 8 or 6 (B´10) Aerospatiale MM 40 Exocet.
Guns: 1 OTO Melara 3 in *(76 mm)*/62 compact.
2 Breda 40 mm/70 (twin).
2 – 12.7 mm MGs.
Decoys: 2 Wallop Barricade triple barrels.

Radars:

Air/surface search – Plessey AWS 4 (B 10) or AWS 6 (remainder).
Navigation – Racal Decca TM 1226C.

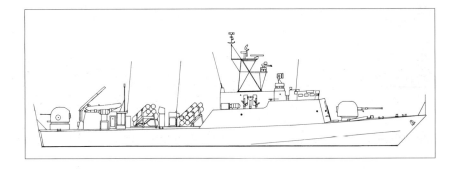

Dhofar Class

AL SHARQIYAH

Hartmut Ehlers

Country: PERU
Ship type: PATROL FORCES
Class: VELARDE (PR-72P) (FAST ATTACK CRAFT – MISSILE)
Active: 6

Name (Pennant Number): VELARDE (CM 21), SANTILLANA (CM 22), DE LOS HEROS (CM 23), HERRERA (CM 24), LARREA (CM 25), SANCHEZ CARRILLON (CM 26)

Recognition Features:
● Unusual, downturned forward end of forecastle.
● 3 in mounting (A position).
● High, rounded main superstructure forward of midships.
● Large lattice mainmast atop central superstructure supporting surface search radar aerial.
● Fire control radar aerial atop bridge.
● Two, twin SSM launchers aft of superstructure. Forward pair angled to starboard, after pair to port.
● 40 mm/70 mounting right aft.

Displacement full load, tons: 560.0
Length, feet (metres): 210.0 (64.0)
Beam, feet (metres): 27.4 (8.4)
Draught, feet (metres): 5.2 (1.6)
Speed, knots: 37.0
Range, miles: 2500 at 16 kts

Missiles:
 SSM – 4 Aerospatiale MM 38 Exocet.
Guns: 1 OTO Melara 3 in *(76 mm)*/62.
2 Breda 40 mm/70 (twin).
Radars:
 Surface search – Thomson-CSF Triton.
 Navigation – Racal Decca 1226.
 Fire control – Thomson-CSF/Castor II.

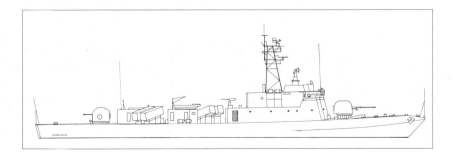

Velarde Class

HERRERA

Peruvian Navy

Osa I, Osa II, Class

Country: RUSSIA AND ASSOCIATED STATES
Ship type: PATROL FORCES
Class: OSA I (TYPE 205), OSA II (TYPE 205M) (FAST ATTACK CRAFT – MISSILE)
Active: 6 OSA I and 12 OSA II

Name (Pennant Number): (Not available)

Recognition Features:
- 30 mm/65 mounting (A position).
- Low profile, rounded superstructure running from the forecastle almost to the stern.
- Pole mainmast just forward of midships with surface search radar aerial atop.
- Prominent, raised pedestal aft supporting fire control radar aerial.
- Four large distinctive SSM launchers, two outboard of mainmast (one port one starboard) and two outboard of fire control director (aft), (one port one starboard). Launchers tilted up at forward end and lying forward and aft.
- 30 mm/65 mounting right aft.
- Note – Also operated by Algeria (active 9-II and 2-I), Bangladesh (active 4-I), Bulgaria (active 4-II and 2-I), China (active 79-I (Huangfen class)), Croatia (active 2-I), Cuba (active 13-II and 5-I), Egypt (active 6- I), Ethiopia (active 1-II), India (active 8-II), Iran (active 4-II), Iraq (active 1-I), North Korea (active 8-I), Latvia (active 3-I), Libya (active 12-II), Poland (active 7-I, 4-I Maritime frontier guard), Romania (active 6-I), Syria (active 10-II and 4-I), Vietnam (active 8-II), Yemen (active 5-II) Yugoslavia (active 5-I).

Displacement full load, tons: 210.0 (Osa I), 245.0 (Osa II)
Length, feet (metres): 126.6 (38.6)
Beam, feet (metres): 24.9 (7.6)
Draught, feet (metres): 8.8 (2.7)
Speed, knots: 35.0 (Osa I), 37.0 (Osa II)
Range, miles: 400 at 34 kts (Osa I), 500 at 35 kts (Osa II)

Missiles:
 SSM – 4 SS-N-2A/B (Osa I), 4 SS-N-2B/C (Osa II).
 SAM – SA-N-5 Grail (some Osa II).
Guns: 4 – 30 mm/65 (2 twin).
Radars:
 Surface search/fire control – Square Tie.
 Fire control – Drum Tilt.

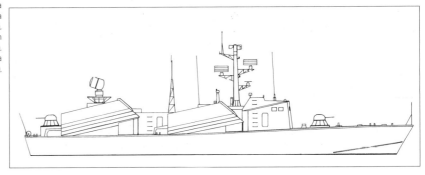

OSA II

Pauk I Class

Country: RUSSIA AND ASSOCIATED STATES
Ship type: PATROL FORCES
Class: PAUK I (TYPE 1241P) (FAST ATTACK CRAFT – PATROL)
Active: 32

Name (Pennant Number): (Not available)

Recognition Features:

● High angled bow with long forecastle.
● 3 in mounting (A position).
● Large, central, stepped superstructure extending from forecastle to afterdeck.
● Prominent, raised pedestal supporting fire control radar aerial sited amidships atop superstructure.
● Tall lattice mainmast well aft of midships with small lattice mast atop at after end.
● Torpedo tubes mounted on maindeck, two port two starboard. One pair adjacent bridge, second pair adjacent mainmast.
● A/S mortars on maindeck, either side of forward superstructure.
● 30 mm/65 AK 630 mounting right aft (X position).
● Note 1 – This appears to be an ASW version of the Tarantul class.
● Note 2 – First three of class have a lower bridge than successors.
● Note 3 – Also operated by Bulgaria (active 2), Cuba (active 1), India (active 4 (Pauk II, Abhay class)).

Displacement full load, tons: 440.0
Length, feet (metres): 195.2 (59.5)
Beam, feet (metres): 33.5 (10.2)
Draught, feet (metres): 10.8 (3.3)
Speed, knots: 32.0
Range, miles: 2200 at 18 kts

Missiles:
    SAM – SA-N-5 Grail quad launcher.
Guns: 1 – 3 in *(76 mm)*/60.
1 – 30 mm/65 AK 630.
Torpedoes: 4 – 16 in *(406 mm)* tubes. Type 40.
A/S mortars: 2 RBU 1200 5-tubed.
Depth charges: 2 racks.
Decoys: 2 – 16-barrelled launchers.
Radars:
    Air/surface search – Peel Cone.
    Surface search – Kivach.
    Fire control – Bass Tilt.
Sonars: Rat Tail; VDS (mounted on transom).

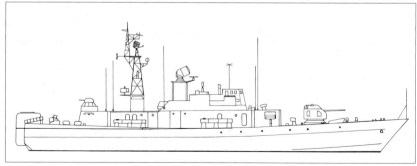

Pauk I Class

PAUK I

Stenka Class

Country: RUSSIA AND ASSOCIATED STATES
Ship type: PATROL FORCES
Class: STENKA (TYPE 205P) (FAST ATTACK CRAFT – PATROL)
Active: 98

Name (Pennant Number): (Not available)

Recognition Features:
- Short high freeboard forecastle with 30 mm/65 mounting (A position).
- Large superstructure, higher at forward end, extending to quarterdeck. Superstructure has vertical ribbed appearance.
- Complex tripod mainmast atop after end of bridge supporting surface search radar aerial.
- Distinctive fire control radar aerial on pedestal at after end of superstructure.
- 30 mm/65 mounting on quarterdeck (X position).
- Note – Also operated by Azerbaijan (active 10), Cambodia (active 4 (Mod)) Cuba (active 3).

Displacement full load, tons: 253.0
Length, feet (metres): 129.3 (39.4)
Beam, feet (metres): 25.9 (7.9)
Draught, feet (metres): 8.2 (2.5)
Speed, knots: 37.0
Range, miles: 800 at 24 kts

Guns: 4 – 30 mm/65 (2 twin).
Torpedoes: 4 – 16 in (*406 mm*) tubes.
Depth charges: 2 racks.
Radars:
 Surface search – Pot Drum or Peel Cone.
 Fire control – Drum Tilt.
Sonars: VDS.

Stenka Class

STENKA

G Jacobs

Turya Class

Country: RUSSIA AND ASSOCIATED STATES
Ship type: PATROL FORCES
Class: TURYA (TYPE 206M) (FAST ATTACK CRAFT – TORPEDO HYDROFOIL)
Active: 29

Name (Pennant Number): (Not available)

Recognition Features:
- Blunt bow, short forecastle with 25 mm/80 mounting (A position).
- Angular central superstructure with raised open bridge just aft of enclosed bridge.
- Lattice mainmast aft of bridge with surface search radar aerial atop.
- Two torpedo tubes on maindeck each side of central superstructure, angled outboard.
- Pedestal supporting fire control radar aerial atop after end of superstructure.
- Prominent 57 mm/80 mounting right aft (Y position).
- Note – Also operated by Cambodia (active 2), Cuba (active 9), Lithuania (active 2), Seychelles (active 1), Vietnam (active 5).

Displacement full load, tons: 250.0
Length, feet (metres): 129.9 (39.6)
Beam, feet (metres): 24.9 (7.6), (41.0 (12.5) over foils)
Draught, feet (metres): 5.9 (1.8), (13.1 (4.0) over foils)
Speed, knots: 40 foilborne
Range, miles: 600 at 35 kts foilborne, 1450 at 14 kts hullborne

Guns: 2 – 57 mm/80 (twin, aft).
2 – 25 mm/80 (twin, fwd).
1 – 14.5 mm MG.
Torpedoes: 4 – 21 in *(533 mm)* tubes. Type 53.
Depth charges: 1 rack.

Radars:
  Surface search – Pot Drum.
  Fire control – Muff Cob.
Sonars: VDS.

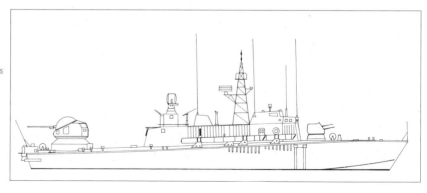

TURYA

Country: SAUDI ARABIA
Ship type: PATROL FORCES
Class: AL SIDDIQ (FAST ATTACK CRAFT – MISSILE)
Active: 9

Name (Pennant Number): AL SIDDIQ (511), AL FAROUQ (513), ABDUL AZIZ (515), FAISAL (517), KAHLID (519), AMYR (521), TARIQ (523), OQBAH (525), ABU OBAIDAH (527)

Radars:
  Surface search – ISC Cardion SPS 55.
  Fire control – Sperry Mk 92.

Recognition Features:
● High bow with sloping forecastle.
● 3 in mounting (A position).
● High central superstructure flush with ship's side.
● Large distinctive radar dome atop bridge roof.
● Slim tripod mainmast amidships.
● Angular, black-capped funnel with exhausts protruding at top aft of mainmast.
● Crossover SSM launchers on afterdeck, after two trained to port forward two to starboard.
● CIWS mounting with distinctive white dome right aft.

Displacement full load, tons: 478.0
Length, feet (metres): 190.5 (58.1)
Beam, feet (metres): 26.5 (8.1)
Draught, feet (metres): 6.6 (2.0)
Speed, knots: 38.0
Range, miles: 2900 at 14 kts

Missiles:
  SSM – 4 McDonnell Douglas Harpoon (2 twin) launchers.
Guns: 1 FMC/OTO Melara 3 in *(76 mm)*/62 Mk 75 Mod 0.
1 GE/GD 20 mm 6-barrelled Vulcan Phalanx.
2 Oerlikon 20 mm/80.
2 – 81 mm mortars.
2 – 40 mm Mk 19 grenade launchers.
Decoys: 2 Loral Hycor SRBOC 6-barrelled Mk 36.

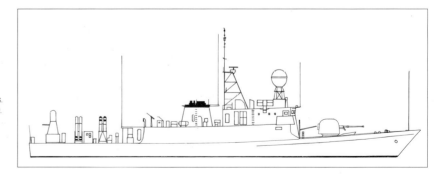

Al Siddiq Class

AL SIDDIQ

Guy Toremans

Minister Class

Country: SOUTH AFRICA
Ship type: PATROL FORCES
Class: MINISTER (FAST ATTACK CRAFT – MISSILE)
Active: 9

Name (Pennant Number): JAN SMUTS (P 1561), P W BOTHA (P 1562), FREDERIC CRESSWELL (P 1563), JIM FOUCHÉ (P 1564), FRANS ERASMUS (P 1565), OSWALD PIROW (P 1566), HENDRIK MENTZ (P 1567), KOBIE COETSEE (P 1568), MAGNUS MALAN (P 1569)

Recognition Features:
- Low freeboard with continuous maindeck from stem to stern.
- 3 in mounting (A position).
- Cluttered forward superstructure with large lattice mainmast at after end.
- Air/surface search radar aerial atop mainmast.
- Four forward facing SSM launchers aft of mainmast, two port and two starboard, angled outboard.
- 3 in mounting (Y position).
- Note – Similar to Israeli Saar 4 class.

Displacement full load, tons: 430.0
Length, feet (metres): 204.0 (62.2)
Beam, feet (metres): 25.0 (7.8)
Draught, feet (metres): 8.0 (2.4)
Speed, knots: 32.0
Range, miles: 3600

Missiles:
SSM – 8 Skerpioen.
Guns: 2 OTO Melara 3 in *(76 mm)*/62 compact.
2 Oerlikon 20 mm.
2 – 12.7 mm MGs.
Decoys: 4 launchers for chaff.

Radars:
Air/surface search – Thomson-CSF Triton.
Fire control – Selenia RTN 10X.

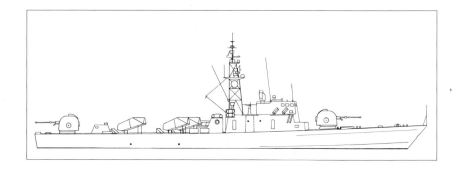

Minister Class

P W BOTHA

Peter Humphries

Country: SPAIN
Ship type: PATROL FORCES
Class: SERVIOLA (OFFSHORE PATROL VESSELS)
Active: 4

Name (Pennant Number): SERVIOLA (P 71), CENTINELA (P 72), VIGIA (P 73), ATALAYA (P 74)

Recognition Features:
● High bow with break in profile forward of superstructure.
● High central freeboard adjacent to superstructure.
● 3 in mounting (B position).
● Tall, angular central superstructure.
● High, wide bridge set well aft from forward end of superstructure.
● Lattice mainmast atop after end of bridge.
● Large angular funnel at after end of superstructure, with wedge shaped, black smoke deflector atop.
● Large flight deck aft of superstructure.
● Note 1 – A modified Halcon class design.
● Note 2 – Other equipment fits could include four Harpoon SSM, Meroka CIWS, Sea Sparrow SAM or a Bofors 375 mm ASW rocket launcher.

Displacement full load, tons: 1106.0
Length, feet (metres): 225.4 (68.7)
Beam, feet (metres): 34.0 (10.4)
Draught, feet (metres): 11.0 (3.4)
Speed, knots: 19.0
Range, miles: 8000 at 12 kts

Guns: 1 US 3 in (*76 mm*)/50 Mk 27.
2 – 12.7 mm MGs.

Radars:
  Surface search – Racal Decca 2459.
  Navigation – Racal Decca ARPA 2690 BT.

Helicopters: 1 AB-212.

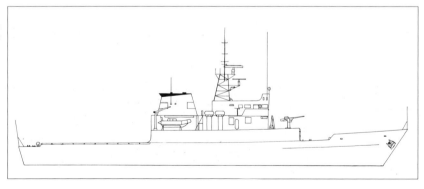

Serviola Class

SERVIOLA

Giorgio Arra

Country: SWEDEN
Ship type: PATROL FORCES
Class: HUGIN (FAST ATTACK CRAFT – MISSILE)
Active: 16

Name (Pennant Number): HUGIN (P 151), MUNIN (P 152), MAGNE (P 153), MODE (P 154), VALE (P 155), VIDAR (P 156), MJÖLNER (P 157), MYSING (P 158), KAPAREN (P 159), VÄKTAREN (P 160), SNAPPHANEN (P 161), SPEJAREN (P 162), STYRBJÖRN (P 163), STARKODDER (P 164), TORDÖN (P 165), TIRFING (P 166)

Recognition Features:
● Long forecastle with 57 mm/70 mounting (A position).
● Low profile, rounded midships superstructure.
● Short, tripod mainmast aft of bridge.
● Surface search radar aerial atop mainmast.
● Fire control radar aerial atop after end of bridge.
● Forward pointing SSM launchers on afterdeck, angled outboard, port and starboard.
● Short lattice aftermast with pole mast atop.
● Mine rails running from after end of bridge superstructure with an extension over the stern. (Cannot be used with missiles in place.)

Displacement full load, tons: 150.0 (170.0 after modernisation)
Length, feet (metres): 120.0 (36.6)
Beam, feet (metres): 20.7 (6.3)
Draught, feet (metres): 5.6 (1.7)
Speed, knots: 36.0

Missiles:
SSM – 6 Kongsberg Penguin Mk 2.

Guns: 1 Bofors 57 mm/70 Mk 1. 57 mm illuminant launchers on either side of mounting.
A/S mortars: 4 Saab Elma 9-tubed launchers.
Depth charges: 2 racks.
Mines: 24.
Decoys: A/S mortars can fire decoys.
Radars:
Surface search – Skanter 16 in Mk 009.
Fire control – Philips 9LV 200 Mk 2.
Sonars: Simrad SA 950 (after modernisation) or SQ 3D/SF; hull-mounted. Simrad ST 570 VDS (in some).

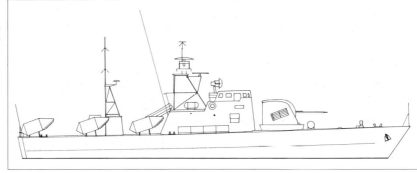

Hugin Class

SNAPPHANEN

Hartmut Ehlers

Country: SWEDEN
Ship type: PATROL FORCES
Class: NORRKÖPING (FAST ATTACK CRAFT – MISSILE)
Active: 12

Name (Pennant Number): NORRKÖPING (R 131), NYNÄSHAMN (R 132), NORRTÄLJE (R 133), VARBERG (R 134), VÄSTERÅS (R 135), VASTERVIK (R 136), UMEÅ (R 137), PITEÅ (R 138), LULEÅ (R 139), HALMSTAD (R 140), STRÖMSTAD (R 141), YSTAD (R 142)

Recognition Features:

- Exceptionally long forecastle with 57 mm/70 mounting just aft of midway between bows and bridge.
- Narrow superstructure centred well aft of midships.
- Complex lattice mainmast atop mid-superstructure.
- Air/surface search radar aerial atop mainmast.
- Fire control radar aerial atop bridge roof.
- Single torpedo tubes outboard of mounting, port and starboard.
- Afterdeck can be fitted with any one of several combinations of torpedo tubes and SSM launchers.
- Note – Similar to the original Spica class from which they were developed.

Displacement full load, tons: 230.0
Length, feet (metres): 143.0 (43.6)
Beam, feet (metres): 23.3 (7.1)
Draught, feet (metres): 7.4 (2.4)
Speed, knots: 40.5

Missiles:

SSM – 8 Saab RBS 15.

Guns: 1 Bofors 57 mm/70 Mk 1, launchers for 57 mm illuminants on side of mounting.

Torpedoes: 6 – 21 in *(533 mm)* tubes (2-6 can be fitted at the expense of missile armament); Swedish Ordnance Type 613.
Mines: Minelaying capability.
Decoys: 2 Philips Philax launchers.
A/S mortars can also fire decoys.

Radars:

Air/surface search – Ericsson Sea Giraffe 50HC.
Fire control – Philips 9LV 200 Mk 1.

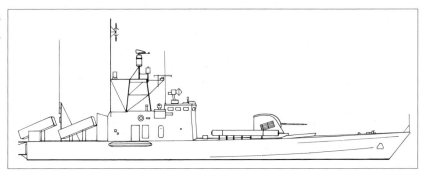

Norrköping Class

UMEÅ

Antonio Moreno

Hai Ou Class

Country: TAIWAN
Ship type: PATROL FORCES
Class: HAI OU (FAST ATTACK CRAFT – MISSILE)
Active: 50

Name (Pennant Number): FABG 1-3, 5-51

Recognition Features:
- Low, rounded bridge structure with square profile lattice mainmast at after end.
- Surface search and fire control radar aerials atop mainmast.
- SSM launcher athwartships immediately aft of mainmast.
- 20 mm mounting right aft.
- Note – The first series had an enclosed mainmast and the missiles were nearer the stern. Second series changed to a lattice mainmast and moved the missiles further forward allowing room for 20 mm mounting.

Displacement full load, tons: 47.0
Length, feet (metres): 70.8 (21.6)
Beam, feet (metres): 18.0 (5.5)
Draught, feet (metres): 3.3 (1.0)
Speed, knots: 36.0
Range, miles: 700

Missiles:
SSM – 2 Hsiung Feng I.
Guns: 1 Oerlikon 20 mm.
2 – 12.7 mm MGs.
Decoys: 4 Israeli AV2 launchers.
Radars:
Surface search – Marconi LN 66.
Fire control – RCA R76 C5.

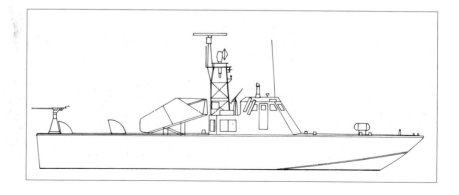

FABG 17

Chien Chung

Country: TURKEY
Ship type: PATROL FORCES
Class: DOĞAN (FAST ATTACK CRAFT – MISSILE)
Active: 8

Name (Pennant Number): DOĞAN (P 340), MARTI (P 341), TAYFUN (P 342), VOLKAN (P 343), RUZGAR (P 344), POYRAZ (P 345), GURBET (P 346), FIRTINA (P 347)

Recognition Features:
- Long forecastle with 3 in mounting (A position).
- Low freeboard.
- Rounded, short superstructure forward of midships stepped down at after end.
- Short, square profile lattice mainmast at after end of superstructure.
- Surface search radar dome atop mainmast.
- SSM launchers in vee formation on afterdeck.
- 35 mm/70 mounting right aft (Y position).
- Note 1 – Similar to Lürssen FPB 57.
- Note 2 – The new Yildiz class are based on the Doğan class hull.

Displacement full load, tons: 436.0
Length, feet (metres): 190.6 (58.1)
Beam, feet (metres): 25.0 (7.6)
Draught, feet (metres): 8.8 (2.7)
Speed, knots: 38.0
Range, miles: 1050

Missiles:
 SSM – 8 McDonnell Douglas Harpoon (2 quad) launchers.
Guns: 1 OTO Melara 3 in *(76 mm)*/62 compact.
2 Oerlikon 35 mm/90 (twin).
Decoys: 2 multi-barrelled launchers.

Radars:
 Surface search – Racal Decca 1226.
 Fire control – Signaal WM 28/41.

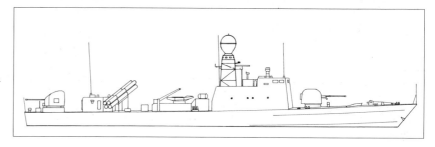

Doğan Class

POYRAZ

Selim San

Country: TURKEY
Ship type: PATROL FORCES
Class: KARTAL (FAST ATTACK CRAFT – MISSILE)
Active: 8

Name (Pennant Number): DENIZKUSU (P 321 (ex-P 336)), ATMACA (P 322 (ex-P 335)), SAHIN (P 323 (ex-P 334)), KARTAL (P 324 (ex-P 333)), PELIKAN (P 326), ALBATROS (P 327 (ex-P 325)), ŞIMŞEK (P 328 (ex-P 332)), KASIRGA (P 329 (ex-P 338))

Recognition Features:
- Long forecastle with 40 mm/70 mounting (A position).
- Very low profile central superstructure with rounded forward end.
- One torpedo tube at maindeck level either side of forward end of superstructure.
- Very short mainmast supporting surface search radar aerial atop centre of superstructure.
- 40 mm/70 mounting at forward end of afterdeck.
- SSM launcher right aft.
- Note – Similar design to the Jaguar class.

Displacement full load, tons: 190.0
Length, feet (metres): 139.4 (42.5)
Beam, feet (metres): 23.0 (7.0)
Draught, feet (metres): 7.9 (2.4)
Speed, knots: 42.0
Range, miles: 500 at 40 kts

Missiles:
SSM – 2 or 4 Kongsberg Penguin Mk 2.
Guns: 2 Bofors 40 mm/70.
Torpedoes: 2 – 21 in *(533 mm)* tubes.
Radars:
Surface search – Racal Decca 1226.

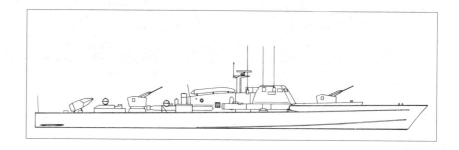

Kartal Class

ALBATROS

Hartmut Ehlers

Country: UNITED KINGDOM
Ship type: PATROL FORCES
Class: CASTLE (OFFSHORE PATROL VESSELS Mk 2)
Active: 2

Name (Pennant Number): LEEDS CASTLE (P 258), DUMBARTON CASTLE (P 265)

Recognition Features:
- High bow, long sweeping forecastle, high freeboard.
- 30 mm/75 mounting forward of bridge (B position).
- Prominent, angular midships superstructure, lower at forward end.
- High bridge set well aft from bows.
- Substantial enclosed mainmast, topped by pole mast, amidships supporting surface search and navigation radar aerials.
- Large flight deck aft.

Displacement full load, tons: 1427.0
Length, feet (metres): 265.7 (81.0)
Beam, feet (metres): 37.7 (11.5)
Draught, feet (metres): 11.8 (3.6)
Speed, knots: 19.5
Range, miles: 10,000 at 12 kts

Guns: 1 DES/Lawrence Scott Mk 1 30 mm/75.
Decoys: 2 Plessey Shield launchers.
Radars:
    Surface search – Plessey Type 944 (P 265).
    Navigation – Kelvin Hughes Type 1006.

Helicopters: Platform for operating Westland Sea King or Lynx.

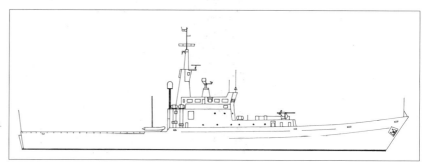

Castle Class

LEEDS CASTLE

H M Steele

Island Class

Country: UNITED KINGDOM
Ship type: PATROL FORCES
Class: ISLAND (OFFSHORE PATROL VESSELS)
Active: 6

Name (Pennant Number): ANGLESEY (P 277), ALDERNEY (P 278), GUERNSEY (P 297), SHETLAND (P 298), ORKNEY (P 299), LINDISFARNE (P 300)

Recognition Features:
● High bow profile with break down to lower level forward of bridge, high freeboard.
● Tall, substantial superstructure just aft of midships.
● 40 mm mounting on unusual raised barbette at after end of forecastle (B mounting position).
● Short, tripod mainmast atop mid-superstructure.
● Prominent funnel, with sloping after end, atop superstructure aft of mainmast.
● Two small crane jibs at after end of superstructure, port and starboard.
● Note – also operated by Bangladesh (active 1).

Displacement full load, tons: 1260.0
Length, feet (metres): 195.3 (59.5)
Beam, feet (metres): 36.0 (11.0)
Draught, feet (metres): 15.0 (4.5)
Speed, knots: 16.5
Range, miles: 7000 at 12 kts

Guns: 1 Bofors 40 mm Mk 3.
1 DES/Oerlikon 30 mm/75 Mk 1 (P 297).
2 FN 7.62 mm MGs.
Radars:
   Navigation – Kelvin Hughes Type 1006.

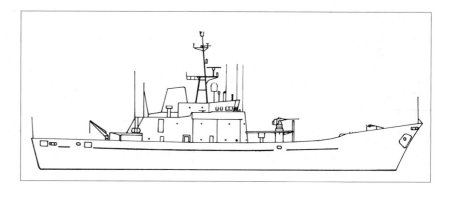

Island Class

GUERNSEY

H M Steele

Peacock Class

Country: UNITED KINGDOM
Ship type: PATROL FORCES
Class: PEACOCK (LARGE PATROL CRAFT)
Active: 3

Name (Pennant Number): PEACOCK (P 239), PLOVER (P 240), STARLING (P 241)

Recognition Features:
- Low bow, low freeboard.
- 3 in mounting (A position).
- Superstructure amidships, stepped down aft of bridge.
- Lattice mainmast atop mid-superstructure.
- Squat, square-section funnel with sloping top atop after end of superstructure.
- Slender crane jib aft of funnel.
- Note – Also operated by Ireland (active 2).

Displacement full load, tons: 690.0
Length, feet (metres): 204.1 (62.6)
Beam, feet (metres): 32.8 (10.0)
Draught, feet (metres): 8.9 (2.7)
Speed, knots: 25.0
Range, miles: 2500 at 17 kts

Guns: 1 – 3 in (76 mm)/62 OTO Melara compact.
4 FN 7.62 mm MGs.
Radars:
Navigation – Kelvin Hughes Type 1006.

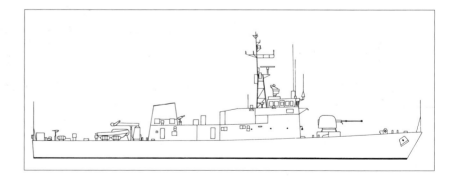

PLOVER

van Ginderen Collection

Cyclone Class

Country: UNITED STATES OF AMERICA
Ship type: PATROL FORCES
Class: CYCLONE (COASTAL PATROL CRAFT) (PC)
Active: 6
Building: 7

Name (Pennant Number): CYCLONE (PC 1), TEMPEST (PC 2), HURRICANE (PC 3), MONSOON (PC 4), TYPHOON (PC 5), SIROCCO (PC 6), SQUALL (PC 7), ZEPHYR (PC 8), CHINOOK (PC 9), FIREBOLT (PC 10), WHIRLWIND (PC 11), THUNDERBOLT (PC 12), SHAMAR (PC 13)

Recognition Features:
● Short forecastle with sloping forward edge to main superstructure.
● 25 mm mounting (A position).
● Raised bridge set well aft from bows.
● Continuous maindeck from stem to stern.
● Superstructure built in three distinct sections with catwalks between the tops of each section.
● Large lattice mainmast at after end of bridge supporting surface search radar aerial atop.
● 25 mm mounting atop after section of superstructure (X position).
● Note – The design is based on the Vosper Thornycroft Ramadan class, modified to meet US Navy requirements.

Displacement full load, tons: 328.0
Length, feet (metres): 170.6 (52.0)
Beam, feet (metres): 24.9 (7.6)
Draught, feet (metres): 7.2 (2.2)
Speed, knots: 35.0
Range, miles: 2500

Guns: 2 – 25 mm Mk 38.
2 – 12.7 mm MGs.
2 – 40 mm Mk 19 grenade launchers (interchangeable with MG).
Decoys: 2 Mk 52 launchers.

Radars:
Surface search – Sperry RASCAR.
Navigation – Raytheon SPS 64(V)8.
Sonars: Wesmar; hull-mounted.

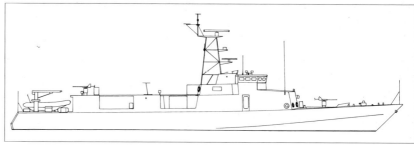

CYCLONE

Bollinger

Country: VIETNAM
Ship type: PATROL FORCES
Class: SHERSHEN (FAST ATTACK CRAFT – TORPEDO)
Active: 16

Name (Pennant Number): (Not available)

Recognition Features:
- Blunt bow, short forecastle.
- 30 mm/65 mounting (A position).
- Long, low rounded superstructure running from forecastle to afterdeck.
- Dip in upper deck profile adjacent to forward edge of superstructure.
- Short tripod mainmast atop bridge supporting distinctive, semi-spherical, surface search radar dome.
- Fire control radar aerial on platform aft of mainmast.
- Two torpedo tubes each side of superstructure at maindeck level. Tubes trained forward and angled slightly outboard. After tubes extend beyond after end of superstructure.
- 30 mm/65 mounting on raised platform immediately aft of superstructure (X position).
- Note 1 – Also operated by Cape Verde (active 2), Croatia (active 1), Egypt (active 6), Yugoslavia (active 4).
- Note 2 – Not all are fitted with torpedo tubes.

Displacement full load, tons: 170.0
Length, feet (metres): 113.8 (34.7)
Beam, feet (metres): 22.0 (6.7)
Draught, feet (metres): 4.9 (1.5)
Speed, knots: 45.0
Range, miles: 850 at 30 kts

Missiles:
SAM – 1 SA-N-5 Grail quad launcher.
Guns: 4 USSR 30 mm/65 (2 twin).
Torpedoes: 4 – 21 in (533 mm) tubes (not in all).

Depth charges: 2 racks.
Radars:
Surface search – Pot Drum.
Fire control – Drum Tilt.

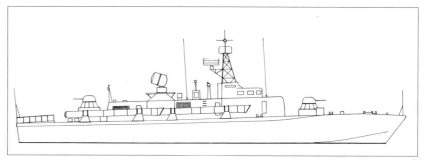

Shershen Class

SHERSHEN

Country: CHINA
Ship type: AMPHIBIOUS FORCES
Class: QIONSHA (7 AP + 2 AH)
Active: 9

Name (Pennant Number): (Y 830), (Y 831), (Y 832), (Y 833) + 5

Recognition Features:
● High bow with sloping deck aft to high, long main superstructure.
● Two 14.5 mm/93 mountings atop bridge roof.
● Short, tapered mast atop forward end of superstructure.
● Unusually high twin funnels at after end of superstructure.
● Short, tapered mast atop funnels.
● Four large sets of davits, two port two starboard, forward of funnel.
● Two 14.5 mm/93 mountings on small raised deck right aft.
● Light cargo booms forward and aft.
● Note 1 – No helicopter pad.
● Note 2 – Two converted to Hospital Ships (AH) and painted white.

Displacement full load, tons: 2150.0
Length, feet (metres): 282.1 (86.0)
Beam, feet (metres): 44.3 (13.5)
Draught, feet (metres): 13.1 (4.0)
Speed, knots: 16.0

Guns: 8 China 14.5/93 mm (4 twin).

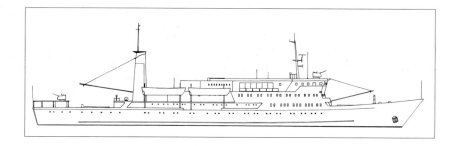

Qionsha Class

QIONSHA

G Jacobs

Country: FRANCE
Ship type: AMPHIBIOUS FORCES
Class: BOUGAINVILLE (BTS)
Active: 1

Name (Pennant Number): BOUGAINVILLE (L 9077)

Recognition Features:
- Ship has clean lines with very high freeboard.
- Short forecastle, high forward superstructure.
- Enclosed mainmast atop after end of forward superstructure.
- Flight deck aft of forward superstructure.
- Large crane derrick aft of flight deck.
- Squat funnel starboard side adjacent crane.
- Note – Well size 78 x 10.2 m (256 x 33.5 ft) which can receive tugs and one BSR or two CTMs, a supply tender of the Chamois class, containers, mixed bulk cargo. Can dock a 400 ton ship.

Displacement full load, tons: 5100.0
Length, feet (metres): 372.3 (113.5)
Beam, feet (metres): 55.8 (17.0)
Draught, feet (metres): 14.1 (4.3)
Flight deck, feet (metres): 85.3 x 55.8 (26 x 17)
Speed, knots: 15.0
Range, miles: 6000 at 12 kts

Guns: 2 – 12.7 mm MGs.
Radars:
 Navigation – 2 Decca 1226.

Helicopters: Platform for 2 AS 332B Super Puma.

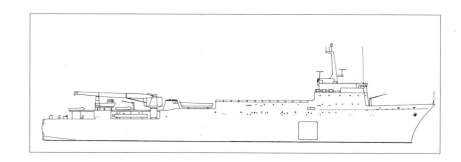

Bougainville Class

BOUGAINVILLE

Alsthom

Foudre Class

Country: FRANCE
Ship type: AMPHIBIOUS FORCES
Class: FOUDRE (LANDING SHIPS (DOCK)) (TYPE TCD 90)
Active: 1
Building: 1
Proposed: 2

Name (Pennant Number): FOUDRE (L 9011), SIROCO (L 9012)

Recognition Features:
● Short forecastle with high, distinctive superstructure set well forward.
● High freeboard.
● 40 mm/60 mounting immediately forward of bridge.
● Large complex mainmast atop main superstructure supporting air/surface search and surface search radar aerials.
● Two SATCOM domes, on pedestals, on after outboard edges of superstructure.
● Two SAM launchers at base of mainmast.
● Long flight deck aft of superstructure.
● Large crane derrick at after end of well deck.
● Two 20 mm mountings, port and starboard, aft of crane.
● Note 1 – Designed to take a mechanised regiment and act as a logistic support ship.
● Note 2 – Well dock 122 x 14.2 x 7.7 m, can dock a 400 ton ship.

Displacement full load, tons: 11,900.0
Length, feet (metres): 551.0 (168.0)
Beam, feet (metres): 77.1 (23.5)
Draught, feet (metres): 17.0 (5.2), (30.2 (9.2) flooded)
Speed, knots: 21.0
Range, miles: 11,000 at 15 kts

Missiles:
    SAM – 2 Matra Simbad twin launchers.
Guns: 1 Bofors 40 mm/60.
2 Giat 20F2 20 mm.
2 – 12.7 mm MGs.
Radars:
    Air/surface search – Thomson-CSF DRBV 21A Mars.
    Surface search – Racal Decca 2459.
    Navigation – 2 Racal Decca RM 1229.

Helicopters: 4 AS 332F Super Puma or 2 Super Frelon.

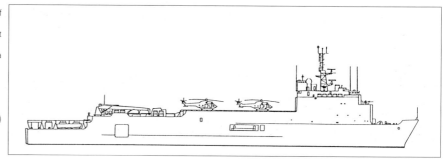

Foudre Class

FOUDRE

B Sullivan

Country: FRANCE
Ship type: AMPHIBIOUS FORCES
Class: OURAGAN (LANDING SHIPS (DOCK) (TCDs))
Active: 2

Name (Pennant Number): OURAGAN (L 9021), ORAGE (L 9022)

Recognition Features:
- Very high freeboard section forward of midships.
- High distinctive bridge structure on starboard side of ship, well forward of midships.
- Large pole mainmast supporting radar aerials atop bridge roof.
- Flight deck aft of bridge.
- Two medium-sized crane derricks aft at well deck.
- Small, black-capped funnel adjacent forward crane.
- Note 1 – Three LCVPs can be carried.
- Note 2 – Typical loads; 18 Super Frelon or 80 Alouette III helicopters or 120 AMX 13 tanks or 84 DUKWs or 340 Jeeps or 12 – 50 ton barges.
- Note 3 – A 400 ton ship can be docked.

Displacement full load, tons: 8500.0
Length, feet (metres): 488.9 (149.0)
Beam, feet (metres): 75.4 (23.0)
Draught, feet (metres): 17.7 (5.4) (28.5 (8.7) flooded)
Speed, knots: 17.0
Range, miles: 9000 at 15 kts

Guns: 2 – 4.7 in *(120 mm)* mortars.
4 Bofors 40 mm/70.
Radars:
    Air/surface search – Thomson-CSF DRBV 51A.
    Navigation – 2 Racal Decca 1226.

Sonars: EDO SQS-17 (*Ouragan*).

Helicopters: 4 SA 321G Super Frelon or Super Pumas or 10 SA 319B Alouette III.

OURAGAN

Albert Campanera i Rovira

Jason Class

Country: GREECE
Ship type: AMPHIBIOUS FORCES
Class: JASON (LST)
Active: 1
Building: 4

Name (Pennant Number): CHIOS (L 173), SAMOS (L 174), LESBOS (L 176), IKARIA (L 175), RODOS (L 177)

Recognition Features:
- High forecastle with 76 mm/62 mounting at mid-point on raised platform and two 40mm/70 mountings, port and starboard at after end..
- Break, down from forecastle, to extensive well deck.
- High superstructure aft of well deck.
- Large tripod mainmast atop bridge roof supporting radar aerials.
- Distinctive twin funnels, side-by-side, at after end of superstructure. Funnels of square section, black-capped, with sloping tops.
- 20 mm mountings, port and starboard, outboard of funnels.
- Large raised helicopter platform aft.
- Note – Bow and stern ramps, drive through design.

Displacement full load, tons: 4400.0
Length, feet (metres): 380.5 (116.0)
Beam, feet (metres): 50.2 (15.3)
Draught, feet (metres): 11.3 (3.4)
Speed, knots: 16.0

Guns: 1 OTO Melara 76 mm/62 Mod 9 compact.
4 Breda 40 mm/70 (2 twin) compact.
4 Rheinmetall 20 mm (2 twin).

Radars:
Surface search – CSF Triton.
Fire control – Thomson-CSF Pollux.
Navigation – Kelvin Hughes Type 1007.

Helicopters: Platform for one.

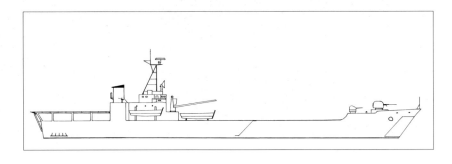

Jason Class

CHIOS (Artist's Impression)

Eleusis Shipyard

Country: INDONESIA
Ship type: AMPHIBIOUS FORCES
Class: FROSCH I (TYPE 108) (LSM)
Active: 12

Name (Pennant Number): TELUK GILIMANUK (ex-*Hoyerswerda* 611) (531), TELUK CELUKAN BAWANG (ex-*Hagenow* 632) (532), TELUK CENDRAWASIH (ex-*Frankfurt/Oder* 613) (533), TELUK BERAU (ex-*Eberswalde-Finow* 634) (534), TELUK PELENG (ex-*Lübben* 631) (535), TELUK SIBOLGA (ex-*Schwerin* 612) (536), TELUK MANADO (ex-*Neubrandenburg* 633) (537), TELUK HADING (ex-*Cottbus* 614) (538), TELUK PARIGI (ex-*Anklam* 635) (539), TELUK LAMPUNG (ex-*Schwedt* 636) (540), TELUK JAKARTA (ex-*Eisenhüttenstadt* 615) (541), TELUK SANGKULIRANG (ex-*Grimmen* 616) (542)

Recognition Features:
● Wide bow ramp at forward end of forecastle with very distinctive wide, flat-topped bows.
● Crane at mid-foredeck.
● Large, stepped, slab-sided superstructure well aft of midships giving very high freeboard.
● Distinctive vertical-ribbed appearance to main superstructure.
● Large double-pole mainmast atop mid-superstructure supporting air/surface search and navigation radar aerials.

Displacement full load, tons: 1950.0
Length, feet (metres): 321.5 (98.0)
Beam, feet (metres): 36.4 (11.1)
Draught, feet (metres): 9.2 (2.8)
Speed, knots: 18.0

Mines: Can lay mines through stern doors.
Radars:
　Air/surface search – Strut Curve.
　Navigation – TSR 333.

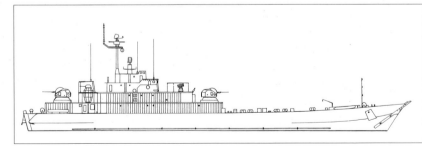

Frosch I Class

TELUK PELENG

van Ginderen Collection

Country: ITALY
Ship type: AMPHIBIOUS FORCES
Class: SAN GIORGIO (LPDs)
Active: 3

Name (Pennant Number): SAN GIORGIO (L 9892), SAN MARCO (L 9893), SAN GIUSTO (L 9894)

Recognition Features:
● Short forecastle with break up to aircraft carrier type flight deck, which continues to stern.
● Clean profile, high freeboard.
● 3 in mounting (B position).
● High, angular, square profile island superstructure sited starboard side, midships.
● Pole mainmast atop central island superstructure.
● Three LCVPs carried in davits, two port side opposite island superstructure, third starboard side forward of island superstructure.
● Small, square profile, raked funnel atop island superstructure.
● Note 1 – Bow ramp for amphibious landings. Stern docking well 20.5 x 7 m. Fitted with a 30 ton lift and two 40 ton travelling cranes for LCMs.
● Note 2 – *San Giusto* is 335 tons heavier, of similar design except for a slightly longer island and different LCVP davit arrangement. Also no bow doors and therefore no beaching capability.

Displacement full load, tons: 7665.0 (8000.0 *San Giusto*)
Length, feet (metres): 437.2 (133.3)
Beam, feet (metres): 67.3 (20.5)
Draught, feet (metres): 17.4 (5.3)
Flight deck, feet (metres): 328.1 x 67.3 (100 x 20.5)
Speed, knots: 21.0
Range, miles: 7500 at 16 kts

Guns: 1 OTO Melara 3 in *(76 mm)*/62, (/62 compact *San Giusto*).
2 Oerlikon 20 mm.
2 – 12.7 mm MGs.
Radars:
    Surface search – SMA SPS 702.
    Navigation – SMA SPN 748.
    Fire control – Selenia SPG 70 (RTN 10X).

Helicopters: 3 SH-3D Sea King or 5 AB 212.

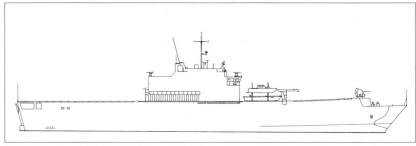

San Giorgio Class

SAN GIORGIO

Milpress

Ivan Rogov Class

Country: RUSSIA AND ASSOCIATED STATES
Ship type: AMPHIBIOUS FORCES
Class: IVAN ROGOV (LPDs)
Active: 3

Name (Pennant Number): IVAN ROGOV, ALEKSANDR NIKOLAEV, MITROFAN MOSKALENKO

Recognition Features:
● Raised forecastle with 3 in mounting (A position).
● Long tank deck aft to very large superstructure, well aft of midships.
● Curved leading edge to high main superstructure with large pyramid mainmast atop supporting air/surface search radar aerial.
● Lattice mast atop after end of superstructure.
● Four 30 mm/65 mountings, two port two starboard, outboard of mainmast and one deck down.
● SAM launcher at after end of superstructure.
● Short helicopter landing platform right aft with open quarterdeck below.
● Note 1 – Has bow ramp with beaching capability leading from a tank deck. Stern doors open into a docking bay.
● Note 2 – Helicopters can enter the hangar from both front and rear.

Displacement full load, tons: 12,600.0
Length, feet (metres): 518.2 (158.0)
Beam, feet (metres): 80.2 (80.2)
Draught, feet (metres): 21.2 (21.2)
Speed, knots: 25.0
Range, miles: 4000 at 18 kts

Missiles:
SAM – SA-N-4 Gecko twin launcher.
2 SA-N-5 Grail quad launchers.
Guns: 2 – 3 in *(76 mm)*/60 (twin).

1 – 122 mm BM-21 (naval).
2 x 20-barrelled rocket launcher.
4 – 30 mm/65 AK 630.
Decoys: 4 – 10-barrelled launchers.
Radars:
Air/surface search – Head Net C (first two); Half Plate (third).
Navigation – 2 Don Kay or 2 Palm Frond.
Fire control – Owl Screech.
Two Bass Tilt.
Pop Group.

Helicopters: 4 Ka-29 Helix B.

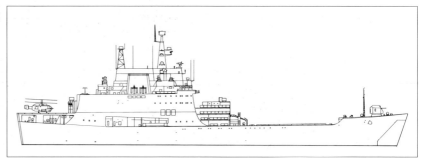

Ivan Rogov Class

MITROFAN MOSKALENKO

Polnochny Class

Country: RUSSIA AND ASSOCIATED STATES
Ship type: AMPHIBIOUS FORCES
Class: POLNOCHNY GROUP A (TYPE 770) (LSMs)
Active: 10
Class: POLNOCHNY GROUP B (TYPE 771) (LSMs)
Active: 16
Class: POLNOCHNY GROUP C (TYPE 773) (LSMs)
Active: 3

Name (Pennant Number): (Not available)

Recognition Features:
- This class varies in appearance to quite a large degree between groups and countries. Below are general common features.
- High bow with long deck aft to superstructure well aft of midships.
- Squared profile lower superstructure with bridge superstructure atop.
- Mainmast (lattice or tripod) at central superstructure.
- Low profile funnel aft of mainmast.
- Step down at after end of superstructure to short afterdeck.
- Note 1 – Have bow ramps only.
- Note 2 – Group D have a helicopter landing platform amidships.
- Note 3 – Also operated by, (Group A) – Bulgaria (active 2), Egypt (active 3), Yemen (active 1); (Group B) – Algeria (active 1), Angola (active 3), Cuba (active 2), Ethiopia (active 2), Syria (active 3), Vietnam (active 3); (Group C) – India (active 4), Poland (active 1); (Group D) – India (active 4), Libya (active 3).

Displacement full load, tons: 800.0 (Group A), 834 (Group B), 1150 (Group C)
Length, feet (metres): 239.5 (73.0) (A), 246.1 (75.0) (B), 266.7 (81.3) (C)

Beam, feet (metres): 27.9 (8.5) (A), 31.5 (9.6) (B), 31.8 (9.7) (C)
Draught, feet (metres): 5.8 (1.8) (A), 7.5 (2.3) (B), 7.9 (2.4) (C)
Speed, knots: 19.0; 18.0 (C).
Range, miles: 1000 at 18 kts (Groups A and B); 2000 at 12 kts (Group C)

Missiles:
    SAM – 2 SA-N-5 Grail quad launchers (A).
           4 SA-N-5 Grail quad launchers (B and C).
Guns: 2 – 30 mm (twin) (in one ship) (A).
2 or 4 – 30 mm (1 or 2 twin) (B).
4 – 30 mm (2 twin) (C).
2 – 140 mm rocket launchers (A, B and C).
Radars:
    Surface search – Spin Trough.
    Fire control – Drum Tilt.

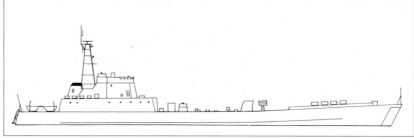

Polnochny Class

POLNOCHNY C

Ropucha Class

Country: RUSSIA AND ASSOCIATED STATES
Ship type: AMPHIBIOUS FORCES
Class: ROPUCHA I (TYPE B 23) (LSTs)
Active: 25
Class: ROPUCHA II (TYPE B 23) (LSTs)
Active: 3

Name (Pennant Number): (Only 4 ships show names), ALEKSANDR SHABALIN, KONSTANTIN OLSHANSKIY, TSESAR KUNIKOV, BOBRUISK

Recognition Features:

● Unusual squared-off forward end to forecastle.
● 57 mm/80 or 76 mm/60 mounting at forward end of superstructure.
● Large superstructure centred aft of midships.
● Pole mast atop bridge roof.
● Large lattice mainmast atop mid-superstructure.
● Very wide square section funnels aft of mainmast.
● Note 1 – A 'roll-on-roll-off' design with a tank deck running the whole length of the ship.
● Note 2 – All have very minor differences in appearance. (See Guns and Missiles section below).
● Note 3 – At least five of the class have rocket launchers at the after end of the forecastle.
● Note 4 – One Ropucha II has a masthead radar dome.
● Note 5 – Also operated by Yemen (active 1).

Displacement full load, tons: 4080.0
Length, feet (metres): 369.1 (112.5)
Beam, feet (metres): 49.2 (15.9)
Draught, feet (metres): 12.1 (3.7)
Speed, knots: 17.5
Range, miles: 6000 at 12 kts

Missiles:
SAM – 4 SA-N-5 Grail quad launchers (in at least two ships).
Guns: 4 – 57 mm/80 (2 twin) (Ropucha I).
1 – 76 mm/60 (Ropucha II).
2 – 30 mm/65 AK 630 (Ropucha II).
2 – 122 mm BM-21 (naval) (in some).
2 x 20-barrelled rocket launchers.
Mines: 92 contact type.
Radars:
Air/surface search – Strut Curve or Cross Dome (Ropucha II).
Navigation – Don 2 or Kivach.
Fire control – Muff Cob (Ropucha I).
Bass Tilt (Ropucha II).

ROPUCHA I

Country: UNITED KINGDOM
Ship type: AMPHIBIOUS FORCES
Class: FEARLESS (LPD)
Active: 2

Name (Pennant Number): FEARLESS (L 10), INTREPID (L 11)

Recognition Features:
● Blunt bow, long forecastle, high freeboard.
● Long, high superstructure centred forward of midships.
● SAM launchers (B mounting position)
● Short, enclosed foremast atop bridge roof.
● Large enclosed mainmast at mid-superstructure supporting surface search radar aerial.
● Two distinctive, tall, slim funnels at after end of superstructure, one port one starboard, staggered across the beam of the ship.
● CIWS mounting between funnels and mainmast.
● Long helicopter platform aft of superstructure.
● Small break down to quarterdeck which houses lattice crane jib.
● Note 1 – Landing craft are floated through the open stern by lowering ship through flooding compartments.
● Note 2 – Class are able to deploy tanks, vehicles and men.

Displacement full load, tons: 12,120.0
Length, feet (metres): 500.0 (152.4)
Beam, feet (metres): 80.0 (24.4)
Draught, feet (metres): 20.5 (6.2), 32.0 (9.8) (flooded)
Speed, knots: 21.0
Range, miles: 5000 at 20 kts

Missiles:
SAM – 2 Shorts Seacat GWS 20 launchers.
Guns: 2 GE/GD 20 mm Mk 15 Vulcan Phalanx (L10).
4 Oerlikon/BMARC 30 mm/75 GCM-AO3 (L 11).
2 Oerlikon/BMARC 20 mm GAM-BO1.
Decoys: 4 Sea Gnat launchers.
Radars:
Surface search – Plessey Type 994.
Navigation – Kelvin Hughes Type 1006.

Helicopters: Platform for up to 4 Westland Sea King HC 4.

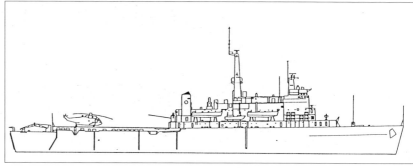

Fearless Class

FEARLESS

Walter Sartori

Austin Class

Country: UNITED STATES OF AMERICA
Ship type: AMPHIBIOUS FORCES
Class: AUSTIN (AMPHIBIOUS TRANSPORT DOCKS) (LPD)
Active: 11

Name (Pennant Number): AUSTIN (LPD 4), OGDEN (LPD 5), DULUTH (LPD 6), CLEVELAND (LPD 7), DUBUQUE (LPD 8), DENVER (LPD 9), JUNEAU (LPD 10), SHREVEPORT (LPD 12), NASHVILLE (LPD 13), TRENTON (LPD 14), PONCE (LPD 15)

Recognition Features:

- High bow with wire aerial structure on forecastle.
- Large superstructure forward of midships creating very high freeboard.
- Two CIWS mountings, one forward end of main superstructure, second atop superstructure immediately aft of mainmast.
- Two 3 in mountings, port and starboard, immediately forward of bridge (not usually carried).
- Large tripod mainmast atop mid-superstructure.
- Unusual tall, slim twin funnels. Starboard funnel well forward of port one.
- Crane derrick between funnels.
- Long flight deck aft.
- Note 1 – Enlarged version of Raleigh class (paid off).
- Note 2 – There are structural variations in the positions of guns and electronic equipment in different ships of the class.

Displacement full load, tons: 17,244.0
Length, feet (metres): 570.0 (173.8)
Beam, feet (metres): 100.0 (30.5)
Draught, feet (metres): 23.0 (7.0)
Speed, knots: 21.0
Range, miles: 7700 at 20 kts.

Guns: 2 or 4 USN 3 in *(76 mm)*/50 (1 or 2 twin) Mk 33.
2 GE/GD 20 mm/76 Vulcan Phalanx Mk 15.
Decoys: 4 Loral Hycor SRBOC 6-barrelled Mk 36.

Radars:
Air search – Lockheed SPS 40B/C.
Surface search – Raytheon SPS 10F or Norden SPS 67.
Navigation – Marconi LN 66.

Helicopters: Up to 6 CH-46D/E Sea Knight can be carried. Hangar for only 1 light (not in LPD 4).

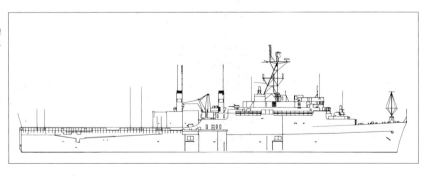

Austin Class

OGDEN

S Poynton, RAN

Country: UNITED STATES OF AMERICA
Ship type: AMPHIBIOUS FORCES
Class: BLUE RIDGE (AMPHIBIOUS COMMAND SHIPS) (LCC)
Active: 2

Name (Pennant Number): BLUE RIDGE (LCC 19), MOUNT WHITNEY (LCC 20)

Recognition Features:
● CIWS mountings at forward end of forecastle and right aft on specially built platform.
● Numerous communications aerials and masts along length of maindeck, including tall lattice mast mid-way between bows and superstructure.
● 3 in mounting between forward lattice mast and superstructure.
● Small superstructure amidships.
● Pole mainmast atop superstructure.
● Large, distinctive air search 3D radar aerial aft of mainmast atop superstructure (not usually carried).
● Two SAM launchers, one port one starboard, after end of superstructure at maindeck level.
● Twin, angled exhausts at top after end of superstructure.
● Very unusual flared hull midships section to protect stowages for LCPs and LCVPs.
● Large communications aerial mast mid-afterdeck
● Note – Hull design similar to Iwo Jima class.

Displacement full load, tons: 18,372.0 (LCC 19), 18,646 (LCC 20)
Length, feet (metres): 636.5 (194.0)
Beam, feet (metres): 107.9 (32.9)
Draught, feet (metres): 28.9 (8.8)
Speed, knots: 23.0
Range, miles: 13,000 at 16 kts

Missiles:
SAM – 2 Raytheon GMLS Mk 25 Mod 1.

Guns: 4 USN 3 in *(76 mm)*/50 (2 twin) Mk 33.
2 GE/GD 20 mm/76 Vulcan Phalanx Mk 15.
Decoys: 4 Loral Hycor SRBOC 6-barrelled Mk 36.
SLQ-25 Nixie; torpedo decoy.
Radars:
Air search – ITT SPS 48C, 3D.
　　　　　　　Lockheed SPS 40C.
　　　　　　　Hughes Mk 23 TAS.
Surface search – Raytheon SPS 65(V)1.
Navigation – Marconi LN 66.
　　　　　　Raytheon SPS 64(V)9.
Fire control – Two Mk 51.

Helicopters: 1 utility can be carried.

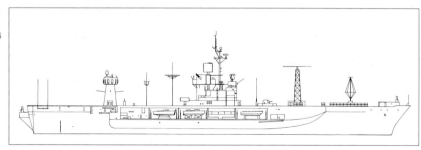

MOUNT WHITNEY

Maritime Photographic

Country: UNITED STATES OF AMERICA
Ship type: AMPHIBIOUS FORCES
Class: IWO JIMA (AMPHIBIOUS ASSAULT SHIPS) (LPH)
Active: 5

Name (Pennant Number): GUADALCANAL (LPH 7), GUAM (LPH 9), TRIPOLI (LPH 10), NEW ORLEANS (LPH 11), INCHON (LPH 12)

Recognition Features:

● Effectively aircraft carrier style with continuous flight deck and very high freeboard.
● Relatively small starboard side island amidships.
● Large single pole mainmast atop mid-island.
● 3 in mounting immediately forward of island and aft of SAM launcher.
● Small funnel aft of mainmast.
● SATCOM dome after end of island.
● SAM launcher on port quarter, and 3 in mounting right aft, below flight deck level.
● Two CIWS mountings, one outboard starboard side forward of island, second outboard port side aft.
● Two deck-edge lifts, one to port opposite the bridge and one to starboard aft of island.
● Note 1 – *Inchon* is planned to be converted to a mine warfare command and support ship by 1996 and will differ greatly in appearance.
● Note 2 – 3 in mountings not usually fitted.

Displacement full load, tons: 18,798.0
Length, feet (metres): 602.3 (183.7)
Beam, feet (metres): 104.0 (31.7)
Draught, feet (metres): 31.7 (9.7)
Flight deck, feet (metres):602.3 x 104 (183.7 x 31.7)
Speed, knots: 23.0
Range, miles: 10,000 at 20 kts

Missiles:
   SAM – 2 Raytheon GMLS Mk 25 launchers.
Guns: 4 USN 3 in *(76 mm)*/50 (2 twin) Mk 33.
2 GE/GD 20 mm Vulcan Phalanx Mk 15.
Up to 8 – 12.7 mm MGs.
Decoys: 4 Loral Hycor SRBOC 6-barrelled Mk 36.
Radars:
   Air search – Westinghouse SPS 58, 3D.
                      Lockheed SPS 40.
   Surface search – Raytheon SPS 10.
   Fire control – Two Mk 51.

Fixed wing aircraft: 4 AV-8B Harriers in place of helicopters.
Helicopters: Capacity for 20 CH-46D/E Sea Knight or 11 CH-53D Sea Stallion.

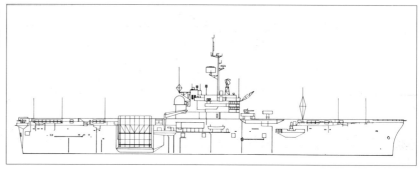

Iwo Jima Class

GUAM

Stefan Terzibaschitsch

Amphibious Forces – United States of America

Country: UNITED STATES OF AMERICA
Ship type: AMPHIBIOUS FORCES
Class: TARAWA (AMPHIBIOUS ASSAULT SHIPS) (multi-purpose) (LHA)
Active: 5

Name (Pennant Number): TARAWA (LHA 1), SAIPAN (LHA 2), BELLEAU WOOD (LHA 3), NASSAU (LHA 4), PELELIU (ex-*Da Nang*) (LHA 5)

Recognition Features:
● Similar outline to *Wasp* class but higher profile island.
● Two 5 in mountings set into recesses, port and starboard, below forward end of flight deck.
● CIWS mounting on platform at forward end of island.
● Two masts atop island, slightly taller lattice mast forward and pole mast aft.
● Air search 3D radar aerial atop after end of island, (forward end of island in *Wasp* class)
● Note 1 – Floodable docking well beneath the after elevator (268 ft long and 78 ft wide) capable of taking four LCUs.
● Note 2 n Class being fitted with rolling airframe missile (RAM) system to augment Vulcan Phalanx. RAM launchers sited above bridge offset to port and starboard side aft.

Displacement full load, tons: 39,967.0
Length, feet (metres): 834.0 (254.2)
Beam, feet (metres): 131.9 (40.2)
Draught, feet (metres): 25.9 (7.9)
Flight deck, feet (metres): 820 x 118.1 (250 x 36)
Speed, knots: 24.0
Range, miles: 10,000 at 20 kts

Missiles:
SAM – 2 GDC RAM.
Guns: 2 FMC 5 in *(127 mm)*/54 Mk 45 Mod 1.
6 Mk 242 25 mm automatic cannons.
2 GE/GD 20 mm/76 Vulcan Phalanx Mk 15.

Decoys: 4 Loral Hycor SRBOC 6-barrelled Mk 36.
SLQ 25 Nixie; torpedo decoy.
NATO Sea Gnat.
SLQ-49 buoys.
AEB SSQ-95.
Radars:
Air search – Hughes SPS 52C, 3D.
Lockheed SPS 40B/C/D.
Hughes Mk 23 TAS.
Surface search – Raytheon SPS 67.
Navigation – Raytheon SPS 64(V)9.
Fire control – Lockheed SPG 60.
Lockheed SPQ 9A.

Fixed wing aircraft: Harrier AV-8B VSTOL aircraft in place of helicopters as required.
Helicopters: 19 CH-53D Sea Stallion or 26 CH-46D/E Sea Knight.

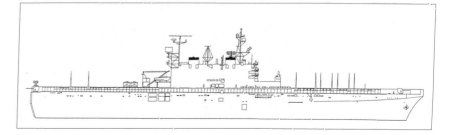

TARAWA

92 Wing RAAF

Wasp Class

Country: UNITED STATES OF AMERICA
Ship type: AMPHIBIOUS FORCES
Class: WASP (AMPHIBIOUS ASSAULT SHIP) (multi-purpose) (LHD)
Active: 3
Building: 3

Name (Pennant Number): WASP (LHD 1), ESSEX (LHD 2), KEARSARGE (LHD 3), BOXER (LHD 4), BATAAN (LHD 5), BONHOMME RICHARD (LHD 6)

Recognition Features:
● Effectively aircraft carrier style with continuous flight deck.
● Large starboard side island amidships.
● Two black-capped funnels, fore and aft atop island.
● Two SAM launchers, one at forward end of island second right aft on overhanging transom.
● Two similar pole masts atop island, after one slightly the taller of the two.
● Three CIWS mountings, one immediately forward of bridge other two on each quarter.
● Two aircraft elevators, one to starboard and aft of the island and one to port amidships.
● Note 1 – Stern doors with well deck of 267 x 50 ft to accommodate up to three LCACs.
● Note 2 – Vehicle storage is available for five M1 tanks, 25 LAVs, eight M198 guns, 68 trucks, 10 logistic vehicles and several service vehicles.

Displacement full load, tons: 40,532.0
Length, feet (metres): 844.0 (257.3)
Beam, feet (metres): 140.1 (42.7)
Draught, feet (metres): 26.6 (8.1)
Flight deck, feet (metres): 819 x 106 (249.6 x 32.3)
Speed, knots: 22.0
Range, miles: 9500 at 18 kts

Missiles:
SAM – 2 Raytheon GMLS Mk 29 launchers.
Guns: 3 GE/GD 20 mm Vulcan Phalanx Mk 15.
8 – 12.7 mm MGs.

Decoys: 4 or 6 Loral Hycor SRBOC 6-barrelled Mk 36.
SLQ 25 Nixie; torpedo decoy.
NATO Sea Gnat.
SLQ-49 buoys.
AEB SSQ-95.
Radars:
Air search – Hughes SPS 52C, 3D (LHD 1).
ITT SPS 48E, 3D (except LHD 1).
Raytheon SPS 49(V)9.
Hughes Mk 23 TAS.
Surface search – Norden SPS 67.
Navigation – SPS 64(V)9.

Fixed wing aircraft: 6-8 AV-8B Harriers or up to 20 in secondary role.
Helicopters: Capacity for 42 CH-46E Sea Knight. Capability to support AH-1W Super Cobra, CH-53E Super Stallion, CH-53D Sea Stallion, UH-1N Twin Huey, AH-1T Sea Cobra, and SH-60B Seahawk.

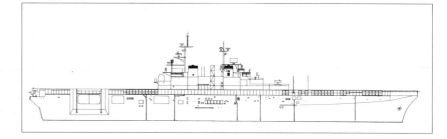

ESSEX

Ingalls

Whidbey Island and Harpers Ferry Class

Country: UNITED STATES OF AMERICA
Ship type: AMPHIBIOUS FORCES
Class: WHIDBEY ISLAND (DOCK LANDING SHIPS) (LSD and LSD-CV)
Active: 8
Class: HARPERS FERRY (DOCK LANDING SHIPS) (LSD and LSD-CV)
Building: 4

Name (Pennant Number): WHIDBEY ISLAND (LSD 41), GERMANTOWN (LSD 42), FORT McHENRY (LSD 43), GUNSTON HALL (LSD 44), COMSTOCK (LSD 45), TORTUGA (LSD 46), RUSHMORE (LSD 47), ASHLAND (LSD 48), HARPERS FERRY (LSD 49), CARTER HALL (LSD 50), OAK HILL (LSD 51), PEARL HARBOR (LSD 52)

Recognition Features:
● Short forecastle with wire aerial structure on forecastle.
● High superstructure well forward of midships.
● Large lattice mainmast atop mid-superstructure.
● Two CIWS mountings atop main superstructure, one on bridge roof, second immediately forward of funnel.
● Large funnel with sloping after profile at after end of superstructure.
● Large crane aft of funnel.
● Long afterdeck.
● Note 1 – Based on the earlier Anchorage class.
● Note 2 – Well deck measures 440 x 50 ft (134.1 x 15.2 m) in the LSD but is shorter in the Cargo Variant (CV).
● Note 3 – There is approximately 90% commonality between the two variants.

Displacement full load, tons: 15,726.0 (LSD 41-48), 16,740 (LSD 49 onwards)
Length, feet (metres): 609.0 (185.6)
Beam, feet (metres): 84.0 (25.6)
Draught, feet (metres): 20.5 (6.3)

Speed, knots: 22.0
Range, miles: 8000 at 18 kts

Guns: 2 GE/GD 20 mm/76 Vulcan Phalanx Mk 15.
2 Mk 68 Mod 1 20 mm.
8 – 12.7 mm MGs.
2 Mk 88 25 mm Bushmaster (LSD 47 and 48 vice the 20 mm guns).
Decoys: 4 Loral Hycor SRBOC 6-barrelled Mk 36.
Radars:
　Air search – Raytheon SPS 49V.
　Surface search – Norden SPS 67V.
　Navigation – Raytheon SPS 64(V)9.

Helicopters: Platform only for 2 CH-53 series Stallion.

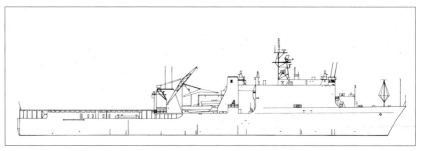

TORTUGA

H M Steele

Flower Class

Country: BELGIUM
Ship type: MINE WARFARE FORCES
Class: FLOWER (TRIPARTITE) (MINEHUNTERS – COASTAL)
Active: 7

Name (Pennant Number): ASTER (M 915), BELLIS (M 916), CROCUS (M 917), LOBELIA (M 921), MYOSOTIS (M 922), NARCIS (M 923), PRIMULA (M 924)

Recognition Features:
- High bow and high freeboard.
- Continuous maindeck aft to break down to low freeboard quarterdeck.
- 20 mm/20 mounting (A position).
- Low superstructure from forecastle aft to quarterdeck.
- Bridge set atop forward end of superstructure.
- Pole mainmast atop after end of bridge.
- Squat, tapered, black-capped funnel with sloping top, atop superstructure.
- Small crane on quarterdeck.
- Note – Also operated by France (active 9), Indonesia (active 2), Netherlands (active 15).

Displacement full load, tons: 595.0
Length, feet (metres): 168.9 (51.5)
Beam, feet (metres): 29.2 (8.9)
Draught, feet (metres): 8.2 (2.5)
Speed, knots: 15.0
Range, miles: 3000 at 12 kts

Guns: 1 DCN 20 mm/20.
1 – 12.7 mm MG.
Countermeasures: MCM – 2 PAP 104 remote-controlled mine locators. Mechanical sweep gear (medium depth).

Radars:
Navigation – Racal Decca 1229.
Sonars: Thomson Sintra DUBM 21A; hull-mounted; minehunting.

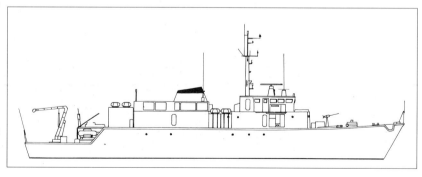

Flower Class

NARCIS

Harald Carstens

Wosao Class

Country: CHINA
Ship type: MINE WARFARE FORCES
Class: WOSAO (MINESWEEPER – COASTAL)
Active: 6
Building: 2

Name (Pennant Number): (4422) + 5

Recognition Features:
● Low freeboard with continuous maindeck from stem to stern.
● Sweeping forecastle with 25 mm/60 mounting (A position).
● Relatively high superstructure just forward of midships. Superstructure stepped down at after end.
● Short lattice mainmast atop superstructure just aft of bridge.
● 25 mm/60 mounting aft of superstructure.
● Sweep winches and davits right aft.

Displacement full load, tons: 310.0
Length, feet (metres): 147.0 (44.8)
Beam, feet (metres): 20.3 (6.2)
Draught, feet (metres): 7.5 (2.3)
Speed, knots: 15.5
Range, miles: 500 at 15 kts

Guns: 4 China 25 mm/60 (2 twin).
Countermeasures: Acoustic, magnetic and mechanical sweeps.

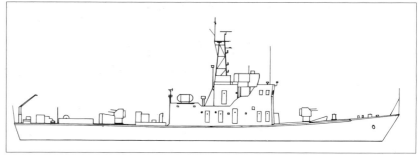

Wosao Class

WOSAO

US Navy

Frankenthal Class

Country: GERMANY
Ship type: MINE WARFARE FORCES
Class: FRANKENTHAL (TYPE 332) (MINEHUNTERS – COASTAL)
Active: 5
Building: 5

Name (Pennant Number): FRANKENTHAL (M 1066), WEIDEN (M 1060), ROTTWEIL (M 1061), BAD BEVENSEN (M 1063), BAD RAPPENAU (M 1067), GRÖMITZ (M 1064), DATTELN (M 1068), DILLINGEN (M 1065), HOMBURG (M 1069), SULZBACH-ROSENBERG (M 1062)

Recognition Features:
● High freeboard forward with break down to maindeck level amidships.
● 40 mm/70 mounting (A position).
● Tall, substantial superstructure stepped down aft of midships.
● Small lattice foremast atop bridge.
● Slim, tripod mainmast amidships.
● Small crane on quarterdeck.
● Note 1 – Same hull, similar superstructure as Type 343.
● Note 2 – Two Pinguin-B3 drones with sonar and TV cameras.

Displacement full load, tons: 650.0
Length, feet (metres): 178.8 (54.5)
Beam, feet (metres): 30.2 (9.2)
Draught, feet (metres): 8.5 (2.6)
Speed, knots: 18.0

Missiles:
  SAM – 2 Stinger quad launchers.
Guns: 1 Bofors 40 mm/70.
Radars:
  Navigation – Raytheon.
Sonars: Atlas Elektronik DSQS-11M; hull-mounted.

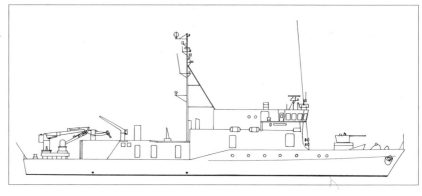

Frankenthal Class

FRANKENTHAL

STN SystemTechnik Nord

Hameln Class

Country: GERMANY
Ship type: MINE WARFARE FORCES
Class: HAMELN (TYPE 343) (MINESWEEPERS – COASTAL)
Active: 10

Name (Pennant Number): HAMELN (M 1092), ÜBERHERRN (M 1095), LABOE (M 1097), PEGNITZ (M 1090), KULMBACH (M 1091), SIEGBURG (M 1098), ENSDORF (M 1094), PASSAU (M 1096), HERTEN (M 1099), AUERBACH (M 1093)

Recognition Features:
● Very similar profile to Frankenthal class with main distinguishing differences as follows.
● Lattice, pyramid shaped mainmast atop bridge roof supporting surface search/fire control radar dome.
● 40 mm/70 mounting aft (X position).
● Long sweep deck aft of superstructure.
● Sweep gear gantries right aft.

Displacement full load, tons: 635.0
Length, feet (metres): 178.5 (54.4)
Beam, feet (metres): 30.2 (9.2)
Draught, feet (metres): 8.2 (2.5)
Speed, knots: 18.0

Missiles:
    SAM – 2 Stinger quad launchers.
Guns: 2 Bofors 40 mm/70.
Mines: 60.
Decoys: 2 Silver Dog rocket launchers.
Radars:
    Surface Search/fire control – Signaal WM 20/2.
    Navigation – Raytheon SPS 64.
Sonars: Atlas Elektronik DSQS-11M; hull-mounted.

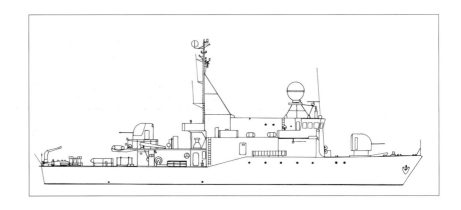

Hameln Class

PASSAU

Harald Carstens

Country: GERMANY
Ship type: MINE WARFARE FORCES
Class: LINDAU (TYPE 331, MINEHUNTERS)
Active: 10
Class: LINDAU (TYPE 351, TROIKA) (MINESWEEPERS – COASTAL and MINEHUNTERS)
Active: 6

Name (Pennant Number): GÖTTINGEN (M 1070), KOBLENZ (M 1071), LINDAU (M 1072), SCHLESWIG * (M 1073), TÜBINGEN (M 1074), WETZLAR (M 1075), PADERBORN * (M 1076), WEILHEIM (M 1077), CUXHAVEN (M 1078), DÜREN * (M 1079), MARBURG (M 1080), KONSTANZ * (M 1081), WOLFSBURG * (M 1082), ULM * (M 1083), MINDEN (M 1085), VOLKLINGEN (M 1087) * Troika control ships

Recognition Features:
- High freeboard forward with break down to maindeck level amidships.
- 40 mm/70 mounting (A position).
- Superstructure extending from after end of forecastle to forward end of sweep deck.
- Lattice framework supporting navigation radar aerial atop mid- superstructure.
- Squat, sloping-topped, funnel aft of midships.
- Pole mainmast immediately forward of funnel (lattice in some).
- Small derrick at after end of superstructure.
- Sweep gear gantries right aft.

Displacement full load, tons: 463.0 (Hunters), 465.0 (Troika)
Length, feet (metres): 154.5 (47.1)
Beam, feet (metres): 27.2 (8.3)
Draught, feet (metres): 9.8 (3.0 Hunters), 9.2 (2.8 Troika)
Speed, knots: 16.5
Range, miles: 850 at 16.5 kts

Guns: 1 Bofors 40 mm/70.
Radars:
  Navigation – Kelvin Hughes 14/9 or Atlas Elektronik TRS N.
Sonars: Atlas Elektronik DSQS 11; minehunting or Plessey 193M; minehunting.

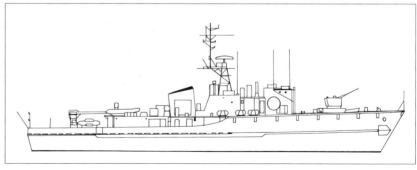

Lindau Class

PADERBORN

Kondor II Class

Country: INDONESIA
Ship type: MINE WARFARE FORCES
Class: KONDOR II (TYPE 89) (MINESWEEPERS – COASTAL)
Active: 9

Name (Pennant Number): PULAU ROTE (ex-*Wolgast* V 811) (721), PULAU RAAS (ex-*Hettstedt* 353) (722), PULAU ROMANG (ex-*Pritzwalk* 325) (723), PULAU RIMAU (ex-*Bitterfeld* 332, M 2672) (724), PULAU RONDO (ex-*Zerbst* 335) (725), PULAU RUSO (ex-*Oranienburg* 341) (726), PULAU RANGSANG (ex-*Jüterbog* 342) (727), PULAU RAIBU (ex-*Sömmerda* 311, M 2670) (728), PULAU REMPANG (ex-*Grimma* 336) (729)

Recognition Features:
● Low freeboard with continuous maindeck from stem to stern.
● High, stepped, smooth contoured superstructure centred well forward of midships.
● Sturdy pole mainmast immediately aft of bridge, supporting radar aerials.
● Squat, square sectioned funnel with sloping top sited midships.
● Small square structure on afterdeck.
● Sweep gear right aft.
● Note 1 – Also operated by Latvia (active 2) and Uruguay (active 4). Kondor I operated by Germany (active 3), Guinea (active 1), Lithuania (active 1), Malta (active 2) and Tunisia (active 4).
● Note 2 – Very similar in appearance to Kondor I class. Kondor II some 16ft longer, than Kondor I. Kondor I has square profile funnel with sloping top, Kondor II has rounded funnel with wedge shaped smoke deflector at its after edge.

Displacement standard, tons: 414.0
Length, feet (metres): 186.0 (56.7)
Beam, feet (metres): 24.6 (7.5)
Draught, feet (metres): 7.9 (2.4)
Speed, knots: 21.0

Guns: 6 – 25 mm (3 twin).
Radars:
   Navigation – TSR 333.
Sonars: Bendix AQS 17(V) VDS.

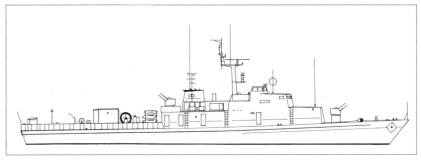

Kondor II Class

KONDOR II

Hartmut Ehlers

Country: ITALY
Ship type: MINE WARFARE FORCES
Class: LERICI (MINEHUNTERS/SWEEPERS)
Active: 4
Class: GAETA (MINEHUNTERS/SWEEPERS)
Active: 6
Building: 2

Name (Pennant Number): LERICI (M 5550), SAPRI (M 5551), MILAZZO (M 5552), VIESTE (M 5553), GAETA (M 5554), TERMOLI (M 5555), ALGHERO (M 5556), NUMANA (M 5557), CROTONE (M 5558), VIAREGGIO (M 5559), CHIOGGIA (M 5560), RIMINI (M 5561)

Recognition Features:
- High bow, high freeboard. Sloping break, aft of funnel, down to sweep deck.
- 20 mm/70 mounting (A position).
- High bridge superstructure with forward sloping bridge windows.
- Tapered funnel with unusual, wedge shaped, smoke deflector atop.
- Note 1 – Two types easily distinguished by large pole mainmast sited immediately aft of bridge (Lerici) and immediately forward of funnel (Gaeta).
- Note 2 – Lerici operated by Malaysia (active 4), Nigeria (active 2). 12 of modified design being built by the USA. Six of class to be built by Australia as Osprey class.
- Note 3 – From No 5 onwards ships are 1 m longer. Fitted with telescopic crane for launching Callegari boats.

Displacement full load, tons: 502.0, (672 *Gaeta* on)
Length, feet (metres): 164.0 (50.0), (172.1 (52.5) *Gaeta* on)
Beam, feet (metres): 31.5 (9.6)
Draught, feet (metres): 8.6 (2.6)
Speed, knots: 15.0

Range, miles: 2500 at 12 kts

Guns: 1 Oerlikon 20 mm/70 or 2 Oerlikon 20 mm/70 (twin) (*Gaeta* onwards).
Countermeasures: Minehunting – 1 MIN 77 Mk 2 ROV or MIN Mk 2 (*Gaeta* on).
1 Pluto mine destruction system.
Minesweeping – Oropesa Mk 4 wire sweep.
Radars:
  Navigation – SMA SPN 728V(3).
Sonars: FIAR SQQ 14(IT) VDS (lowered from keel fwd of bridge).

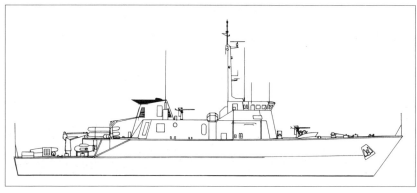

LERICI

Country: JAPAN
Ship type: MINE WARFARE FORCES
Class: HATSUSHIMA (MINEHUNTERS/SWEEPERS – COASTAL)
Active: 23
Class: UWAJIMA (MINEHUNTERS/SWEEPERS – COASTAL)
Active: 4
Building: 3

Name (Pennant Number): HATSUSHIMA (MSC 649), NINOSHIMA (MSC 650), MIYAJIMA (MSC 651), ENOSHIMA (MSC 652), UKISHIMA (MSC 653), OOSHIMA (MSC 654), NIIJIMA (MSC 655), YAKUSHIMA (MSC 656), NARUSHIMA (MSC 657), CHICHIJIMA (MSC 658), TORISHIMA (MSC 659), HAHAJIMA (MSC 660), TAKASHIMA (MSC 661), NUWAJIMA (MSC 662), ETAJIMA (MSC 663), KAMISHIMA (MSC 664), HIMESHIMA (MSC 665), OGISHIMA (MSC 666), MOROSHIMA (MSC 667), YURISHIMA (MSC 668), HIKOSHIMA (MSC 669), AWASHIMA (MSC 670), SAKUSHIMA (MSC 671), UWAJIMA (MSC 672), IESHIMA (MSC 673), TSUKISHIMA (MSC 674), MAEJIMA (MSC 675), KUMEJIMA (MSC 676), – (MSC 677), – (MSC 678), (UWAJIMA CLASS MSC 672 on)

Recognition Features:
- Continuous deck from bow aft to break, adjacent to funnel, down to lower deck level.
- Small bridge superstructure well forward of midships.
- Tall tripod mainmast midships.
- Tall, black-capped funnel aft of mainmast at deck break.
- Slender aftermast forward of sweep deck.
- Sweeping gantrys at after end of sweep deck.

Displacement full load, tons: 510.0
Length, feet (metres): 180.4 (55.0), (189.3 (57.7) MSC 670 on)
Beam, feet (metres): 30.8 (9.4)
Draught, feet (metres): 7.9 (2.4)
Speed, knots: 14.0

Guns: 1 JM-61 20 mm/76 Sea Vulcan 20.
Radars:
   Surface search – Fujitsu OPS 9.
Sonars: Nec/Hitachi ZQS 2B or ZQS 3 (MSC 672 onwards); hull-mounted; minehunting.

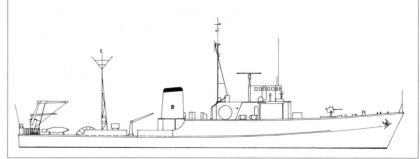

HATSUSHIMA

Country: JAPAN
Ship type: MINE WARFARE FORCES
Class: YAEYAMA (MINEHUNTER/SWEEPER – OCEAN)
Active: 3

Name (Pennant Number): YAEYAMA (MSO 301), TSUSHIMA (MSO 302), HACHIJYO (MSO 303)

Recognition Features:
- Continuous maindeck with break down to sweep deck.
- High central superstructure with wide bridge at forward end.
- Small radar dome atop bridge roof.
- Tall, slightly tapered black-capped funnel at after end of main superstructure.
- Lattice mainmast atop after end of superstructure.
- Minesweeping gantry and small crane on sweep deck.
- Note – Appears to be a derivative of the USN Avenger class.

Displacement full load, tons: 1275.0
Length, feet (metres): 219.8 (67.0)
Beam, feet (metres): 38.7 (11.8)
Draught, feet (metres): 10.2 (3.1)
Speed, knots: 14.0

Guns: 1 GE 20 mm/76 Sea Vulcan.
Radars:
  Surface search – Fujitsu OPS 9.
Sonars: Raytheon SQQ 32 VDS.

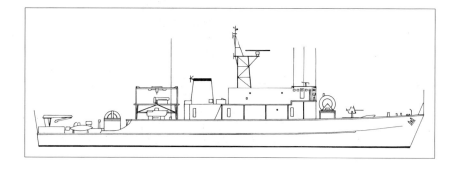

Yaeyama Class

TSUSHIMA

Hachiro Nakai

Country: NORWAY
Ship type: MINE WARFARE FORCES
Class: OKSØY/ALTA (MINEHUNTERS/SWEEPERS)
Building: 9

Name (Pennant Number): OKSØY * (M 340), KARMØY * (M 341), MALØY * (M 342), HINNØY * (M 343), ALTA (M 350), OTRA (M 351), RAUMA (M 352), ORKLA (M 353), GLOMMA (M 354), (* OKSØY CLASS).

Recognition Features:
● Unusual blunt, flat-fronted bow.
● Twin-hulled.
● Flat, uncluttered forecastle forward of stepped, substantial superstructure.
● Bridge just forward of midships set atop superstucture.
● Lattice mainmast atop after end of bridge.
● Unusual, square section twin funnels at after end of main superstructure.
● Deck aft of funnels drops down to small sweep deck.
● Note – This is a distinctive, modern design ship with clean, smooth lines and high freeboard.

Displacement full load, tons: 367.0
Length, feet (metres): 181.1 (55.2)
Beam, feet (metres): 44.6 (13.6)
Draught, feet (metres): 7.5 (2.3)
Speed, knots: 25.0
Range, miles: 1200 at 22 kts

Guns: 2 Rheinmetall 20 mm.
2 – 12.7 mm MGs.
Countermeasures: Minehunters – 2 Pluto submersibles. Minesweepers – Mechanical and influence sweeping equipment.

Radars:
Navigation – 2 Racal Decca.
Sonars: Thomson Sintra/Simrad TSM 2023N; hull-mounted (minehunters).
Simrad Subsea SA 950; hull-mounted (minesweepers).

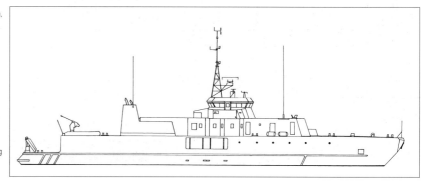

OKSØY

H M Steele

Country: RUSSIA AND ASSOCIATED STATES
Ship type: MINE WARFARE FORCES
Class: NATYA I (TYPE 266M) (MINER) (MINESWEEPERS – OCEAN)
Active: 30
Class: NATYA II (TYPE 266ME) (MINER) (MINESWEEPERS – OCEAN)
Active: 1

Name (Pennant Number): DIZELIST, ELEKTRIK, POLEMETCHIK, RADIST, NAVODCHIK, MINER, MOTORIST, RULEVOY, DOBROTAY, PARAVAN, STARSHKIY, SIGNALSHIK, ZAPAL, ZARYAD, TRAL, SNAYPR, TURBINIST, ZENITCHIK, ARTILLERIST, +12

Recognition Features:
● High bow, short forecastle with slender mast at forward end.
● 30 mm/65 mounting (A position).
● Continuous maindeck aft to break down to sweep deck.
● Main superstructure well forward of midships.
● Large lattice mainmast atop after end of superstructure supporting distinctive radar aerial.
● Black-capped funnel with sloping top aft of midships.
● Ship's boat in davits, starboard side just forward of funnel.
● 30 mm/65 mounting (X position).
● Distinctive hydraulic gantries right aft (in some).
● Note 1 – Also operated by Ethiopia (active 1), India (active 12), Libya (active 8), Syria (active 1) and Yemen (active 1).
● Note 2 – Natya II was built without minesweeping gear to make way for a lengthened superstructure.
● Note 3 – Some have Gatling 30 mm guns.

Displacement full load, tons: 770.0
Length, feet (metres): 200.1 (61.0)
Beam, feet (metres): 31.8 (9.7)
Draught, feet (metres): 8.9 (2.7)
Speed, knots: 19.0

Range, miles: 4000 at 10 kts

Missiles:
SAM – 2 SA-N-5 Grail quad launchers (in some).
Guns: 4 – 30 mm/65 (2 twin) or 2 – 30 mm/65 AK 630.
4 – 25 mm/80 (2 twin) (Natya I).
A/S mortars: 2 RBU 1200 5-tubed (Natya I).
Countermeasures: MCM – Capable of magnetic, acoustic and mechanical sweeping.
Radars:
Surface search – Don 2 or Low Trough.
Fire control – Drum Tilt (not in all).
Sonars: Hull-mounted; minehunting.

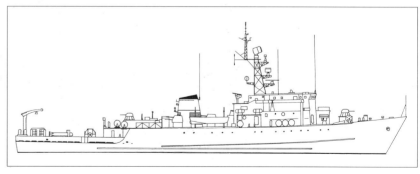

Natya Class

NATYA I

Country: SWEDEN
Ship type: MINE WARFARE FORCES
Class: LANDSORT (MINEHUNTERS)
Active: 7

Radars:
 Navigation – Thomson-CSF Terma.
Sonars: Thomson-CSF TSM-2022; hull-mounted; minehunting.

Name (Pennant Number): LANDSORT (M 71), ARHOLMA (M 72), KOSTER (M 73), KULLEN (M 74), VINGA (M 75), VEN (M 76), ULVÖN (M 77)

Recognition Features:
- High freeboard with continuous maindeck from stem to stern.
- Main superstructure forward of midships.
- Bridge set atop mid-superstructure.
- 40 mm/70 mounting (B position).
- Sturdy pole mainmast at after end of main superstructure with twin funnels at its base.
- Note – Also operated by Singapore (building 4).

Displacement full load, tons: 360.0
Length, feet (metres): 155.8 (47.5)
Beam, feet (metres): 31.5 (9.6)
Draught, feet (metres): 7.3 (2.2)
Speed, knots: 15.0
Range, miles: 2000 at 12 kts

Guns: 1 Bofors 40 mm/70 Mod 48.
2 – 7.62 mm MGs.
A/S mortars: 4 Saab Elma 9-tubed launchers.
Decoys: 2 Philips Philax launchers can be carried.
Countermeasures: MCM – Fitted for mechanical sweeps for moored mines, magnetic and acoustic sweeps.
Possible to operate 2 – unmanned magnetic and acoustic sweepers.

Landsort Class

ARHOLMA

Per Kornefeldt

Country: THAILAND
Ship type: MINE WARFARE FORCES
Class: BANG RACHAN (MINEHUNTERS/SWEEPERS)
Active: 2

Name (Pennant Number): BANG RACHAN (2), NONGSARAI (3)

Recognition Features:

- High freeboard maindeck from bows aft to sloping break down to sweep deck.
- Low profile superstructure forward of midships.
- Unusual, all-round bridge atop after end of superstructure.
- Tripod mainmast atop bridge roof.
- Large twin funnels immediately aft of superstructure with black exhausts protruding from top.
- Gantry at after end of sweep deck and small crane derrick at forward end.

Displacement full load, tons: 444.0
Length, feet (metres): 161.1 (49.1)
Beam, feet (metres): 30.5 (9.3)
Draught, feet (metres): 8.2 (2.5)
Speed, knots: 17.0
Range, miles: 3100 at 12 kts

Guns: 3 Oerlikon GAM-BO1 20 mm.
Countermeasures: MCM – MWS 80R minehunting system.
Acoustic, magnetic and mechanical sweeps.
2 Gaymarine Pluto 15 submersibles.
Radars:
  Navigation – 2 Atlas Elektronik 8600 ARPA.
Sonars: Atlas Elektronik DSQS-11H; hull-mounted; minehunting.

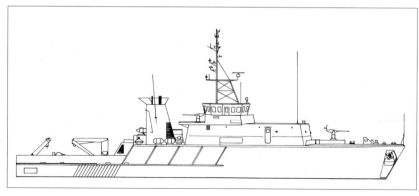

Bang Rachan Class

BANG RACHAN

Royal Thai Navy

Hunt Class

Country: UNITED KINGDOM
Ship type: MINE WARFARE FORCES
Class: HUNT (MINESWEEPERS/MINEHUNTERS – COASTAL)
Active: 13

Name (Pennant Number): BRECON (M 29), LEDBURY (M 30), CATTISTOCK (M 31), COTTESMORE (M 32), BROCKLESBY (M 33), MIDDLETON (M 34), DULVERTON (M 35), BICESTER (M 36), CHIDDINGFOLD (M 37), ATHERSTONE (M 38), HURWORTH (M 39), BERKELEY (M 40), QUORN (M 41)

Radars:
   Navigation – Kelvin Hughes Type 1006.
Sonars: Plessey Type 193M Mod 1; hull-mounted; minehunting.
Mil Cross mine avoidance sonar; hull-mounted.
Type 2059 addition to track PAP 104/105.

Recognition Features:
● High freeboard maindeck.
● Continuous maindeck aft to sloping break down to sweep deck.
● 30 mm/75 mounting mid-forecastle.
● Midships superstructure has high bridge at forward end.
● Tapered, enclosed mainmast amidships.
● Navigation radar aerial atop bridge roof.
● Large, black-capped funnel aft of mainmast.
● Large structure on afterdeck housing various minehunting and minesweeping equipment.

Displacement full load, tons: 750.0
Length, feet (metres): 197.0 (60.0)
Beam, feet (metres): 32.8 (10.0)
Draught, feet (metres): 9.5 (2.9)
Speed, knots: 15.0
Range, miles: 1500 at 12 kts

Guns: 1 Oerlikon/BMARC 30 mm/75 DS 30B.
2 Oerlikon/BMARC 20 mm GAM-CO1.
2 – 7.62 mm MGs.
Decoys: 2 Wallop Barricade (enhancement).
2 Irvin Replica RF; passive decoys.

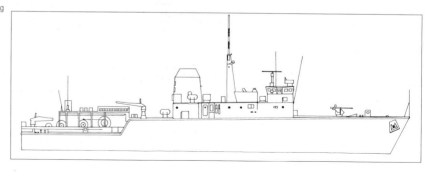

Hunt Class

BROCKLESBY

Country: UNITED KINGDOM
Ship type: MINE WARFARE FORCES
Class: SANDOWN (MINEHUNTERS)
Active: 5
Building: 4
Proposed: 3

Name (Pennant Number): SANDOWN (M 101), INVERNESS (M 102), CROMER (M 103), WALNEY (M 104), BRIDPORT (M 105)

Recognition Features:
● Short, sloping forecastle with 30 mm/75 mounting (A position).
● Long superstructure extending from forecastle to small quarterdeck.
● Most of superstructure is flush with ships side giving a slab-sided effect.
● Bridge sited atop superstructure just forward of midships.
● Navigation radar aerial atop bridge roof.
● Tapered, enclosed mainmast amidships, with short pole mast atop.
● Square profile, black-capped funnel with sloping top, aft of mainmast.
● Note – Also operated by Saudi Arabia (active 2, building 1, proposed 3).

Displacement full load, tons: 484.0
Length, feet (metres): 172.2 (52.5)
Beam, feet (metres): 34.4 (10.5)
Draught, feet (metres): 7.5 (2.3)
Speed, knots: 13.0
Range, miles: 3000 at 12 kts

Guns: 1 Oerlikon/DES 30 mm/75 DS 30B.

Radars:
  Navigation – Kelvin Hughes Type 1007.
Sonars: Marconi Type 2093 VDS, mine search and classification.

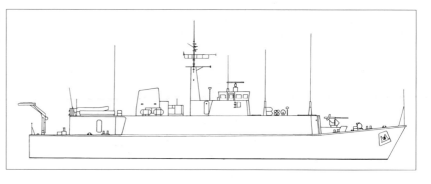

CROMER

Wright & Logan

Country: UNITED STATES OF AMERICA
Ship type: MINE WARFARE FORCES
Class: AVENGER (MINE COUNTERMEASURES VESSELS) (MCM)
Active: 13
Building: 1

Name (Pennant Number): AVENGER (MCM 1), DEFENDER (MCM 2), SENTRY (MCM 3), CHAMPION (MCM 4), GUARDIAN (MCM 5), DEVASTATOR (MCM 6), PATRIOT (MCM 7), SCOUT (MCM 8), PIONEER (MCM 9), WARRIOR (MCM 10), GLADIATOR (MCM 11), ARDENT (MCM 12), DEXTROUS (MCM 13), CHIEF (MCM 14)

Recognition Features:
● High bow, sloping forecastle.
● Continuous maindeck profile from bow aft, with two breaks down aft of main superstructure.
● High superstructure extending from forecastle to sweep deck.
● Large, distinctive tripod mainmast on bridge roof with short pole mast atop.
● Very large tapered funnel aft of midships with sloping top and flat, sloping after end.
● Sweep cable reels and floats on sweepdeck.
● Note – Easily identifiable ships. Unusually large for MCM craft.

Displacement full load, tons: 1312.0
Length, feet (metres): 224.0 (68.3)
Beam, feet (metres): 39.0 (11.9)
Draught, feet (metres): 12.2 (3.7)
Speed, knots: 13.5

Guns: 2 – 12.7 mm Mk 26 MGs.

Countermeasures: MCM – 2 SLQ-48; ROV mine neutralisation system. SLQ 37(V)2; magnetic/acoustic influence sweep. Oropesa Type O Size 1; mechanical sweep.
Radars:
    Surface search – ISC Cardion SPS 55.
Sonars: General Electric SQQ 30 (Raytheon/Thomson Sintra SQQ 32 (MCM 10 on) VDS, minehunting.

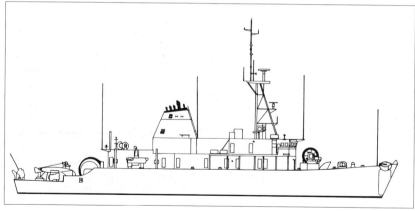

AVENGER

H M Steele

Country: UNITED STATES OF AMERICA
Ship type: MINE WARFARE FORCES
Class: OSPREY (MINEHUNTERS COASTAL) (MHC)
Active: 1
Building: 11

Name (Pennant Number): OSPREY (MHC 51), HERON (MHC 52), PELICAN (MHC 53), ROBIN (MHC 54), ORIOLE (MHC 55), KINGFISHER (MHC 56), CORMORANT (MHC 57), BLACK HAWK (MHC 58), FALCON (MHC 59), CARDINAL (MHC 60), RAVEN (MHC 61), SHRIKE (MHC 62)

Recognition Features:
● Continuous maindeck from bow, aft to break down to low freeboard afterdeck.
● Main superstructure extending from forecastle to break.
● High bridge at forward end of superstructure with unusual outward- sloping bridge windows.
● Bulky, square section, tapered funnel at after end of superstructure with wedge shaped smoke deflector Rad-Haz screen atop.
● Narrow, square section enclosed mainmast immediately forward of funnel.
● Large crane derrick on afterdeck.
● Note – Design based on Lerici class.

Displacement full load, tons: 889.0
Length, feet (metres): 188.0 (57.3)
Beam, feet (metres): 35.9 (11.0)
Draught, feet (metres): 9.5 (2.9)
Speed, knots: 12.0
Range, miles: 1500 at 12 kts

Guns: 2 – 12.7 mm MGs.
Countermeasures: MCM – SLQ-48 ROV mine neutralisation system.

Radars:
Navigation – Raytheon SPS 64.
Sonars: Raytheon/Thomson Sintra SQQ 32 VDS, minehunting.

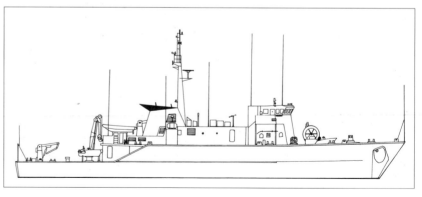

Osprey Class

OSPREY

Intermarine

Collins Class

Country: AUSTRALIA
Ship type: SUBMARINES
Class: COLLINS (SSK)
Building: 6

Name (Pennant Number): COLLINS (71), FARNCOMB (72), WALLER (73), DECHAINEUX (74), SHEEAN (75), RANKIN (76)

Recognition Features:
- Blunt bow.
- Low, slim fin with forward edge sloping slightly aft.
- Unusual, flat extension to the top after end of the fin.
- Conventional diving planes low down on fin.
- Rounded top to casing.
- X rudders visible above waterline, aft.

Displacement surfaced, tons: 3051.0
Displacement dived, tons: 3353.0
Length, feet (metres): 254.0 (77.5)
Beam, feet (metres): 25.6 (7.8)
Draught, feet (metres): 23.0 (7.0)
Speed, knots: 10 surfaced; 10 snorting; 20 dived
Range, miles: 9000 at 10 kts

Missiles:
    SSM – McDonnell Douglas Sub-Harpoon.
Torpedoes: 6 – 21 in *(533 mm)* fwd tubes.
Decoys: 2 SSDE.
Radars:
    Navigation – GEC Marconi.
Sonars: Thomson Sintra Scylla bow and flank arrays. Kariwara or Thomson Sintra passive towed array.

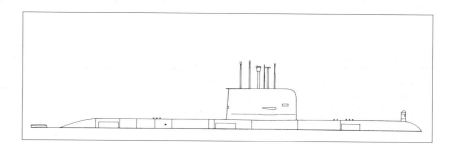

Collins Class

COLLINS

Han Class

Country: CHINA
Ship type: SUBMARINES
Class: HAN (SSN)
Active: 5

Name (Pennant Number): (401), (402), (403), (404), (405)
Names not available.

Recognition Features:
● Fin sited well forward of midships, with diving planes at its forward edge, just above mid-height.
● Fin has vertical forward edge, top sloping down towards after end and sloping after edge, curved at the bottom.
● Tall rudder with sloping forward edge and vertical after edge.
● Note – Ying Ji SSM tubes fitted aft of the fin.

Displacement dived, tons: 5000.0
Length, feet (metres): 330.0 (100.0), 356.0 (108.0) (403 on)
Beam, feet (metres): 36.0 (11.0)
Draught, feet (metres): 27.9 (8.5)
Speed, knots: 25 dived

Missiles:
  SSM (403 onwards); Ying Ji (Eagle Strike) (C-801).
Torpedoes: 6 – 21 in *(533 mm)* bow tubes.
Sonars: May include French DUUX-5.

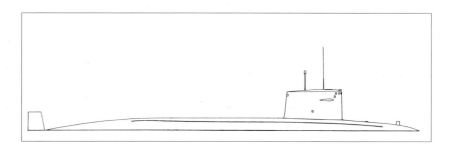

Han Class

HAN 402

Country: CHINA
Ship type: SUBMARINES
Class: XIA (TYPE 092) (SSBN)
Active: 1

Name (Pennant Number): XIA (406)

Recognition Features:
- Large submarine with low bow.
- Small, slim sonar transducer dome atop forward end of casing.
- Low, streamlined fin well forward of midships.
- Large-span diving planes near forward end of fin at mid-height.
- Large, distinctive structure atop main casing running aft from fin housing the 12 vertical launch SLBMs.
- Missile housing is flat-topped and drops down steeply at its after end.
- Large rudder.

Displacement dived, tons: 8000.0
Length, feet (metres): 393.6 (120.0)
Beam, feet (metres): 33.0 (10.0)
Draught, feet (metres): 26.2 (8.0)
Speed, knots: 22 dived

Missiles:
  SLBM – 12 CSS-N-3.
Torpedoes: 6 – 21 in *(533 mm)* bow tubes.

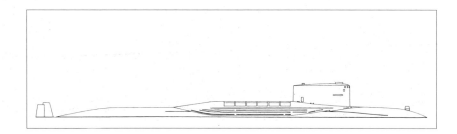

Xia Class

XIA

Country: FRANCE
Ship type: SUBMARINES
Class: AGOSTA (SSK)
Active: 4

Name (Pennant Number): AGOSTA (S 620), BÉVÉZIERS (S 621), LA PRAYA (S 622), OUESSANT (S 623)

Recognition Features:

- Blunt, bull-nose bow with sonar pod atop forward end of casing.
- Wide fin with rounded surfaces. Fin has vertical leading edge with straight, sloping after edge. Distinctive protrusion at top after end of fin.
- Bow-mounted diving planes.
- Flat top to casing.
- Rudder has steeply sloping forward edge.
- Note – Also operated by Pakistan (active 2), Spain (active 4).

Displacement standard, tons: 1230.0
Displacement surfaced, tons: 1510.0
Displacement dived, tons: 1760.0
Length, feet (metres): 221.7 (67.7)
Beam, feet (metres): 22.3 (6.8)
Draught, feet (metres): 17.7 (5.4)
Speed, knots: 12 surfaced; 20 dived
Range, miles: 8500 at 9 kts snorting; 350 at 3.5 kts dived

Missiles:

SSM – Aerospatiale SM 39 Exocet; launched from 21 in *(533 mm)* tubes.
Torpedoes: 4 – 21 in *(533 mm)* bow tubes. ECAN L5 Mod 3 and ECAN F17 Mod 2.

Radars:
Search – Thomson-CSF DRUA 33.
Sonars: Thomson Sintra DSUV 22; DUUA 2D; DUUA 1D; DUUX 2; DSUV 62A towed array.

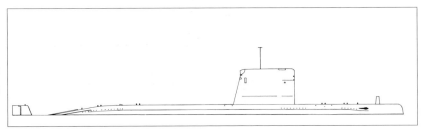

Agosta Class

LA PRAYA

D & B Teague

Country: FRANCE
Ship type: SUBMARINES
Class: DAPHNÉ (SSK)
Active: 3

Name (Pennant Number): JUNON (S 648), PSYCHÉ (S 650), SIRÈNE (S 651)

Recognition Features:
● Pointed bow, flat fronted in profile.
● Large, distinctive sonar dome atop casing at bow.
● Slim fin with vertical leading edge and sloping after edge.
● Flat top to casing.
● Bow-mounted diving planes and rudder are not visible.
● Also operated by Pakistan (active 4), Portugal (active 3), South Africa (active 3),
  Spain (active 4).

Displacement surfaced, tons: 860.0
Displacement dived, tons: 1038.0
Length, feet (metres): 189.6 (57.8)
Beam, feet (metres): 22.3 (6.8)
Draught, feet (metres): 15.1 (4.6)
Speed, knots: 13.5 surfaced; 16 dived
Range, miles: 10,000 at 7 kts surfaced; 3000 at 7 kts snorting;
2700 at 12.5 kts dived

Torpedoes: 12 – 21.7 in *(550 mm)* (8 bow, 4 stern) tubes.
ECAN E15.
Radars:
  Search – Thomson-CSF Calypso.
Sonars: Thomson Sintra DSUV 2; DUUA 2; DUUX 2.

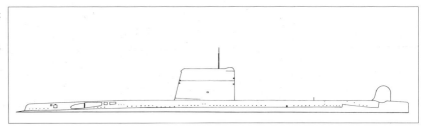

Daphné Class

JUNON

H M Steele

Rubis Class

Country: FRANCE
Ship type: SUBMARINES
Class: RUBIS (SNA 72)
Active: 6

Name (Pennant Number): RUBIS (S 601), SAPHIR (S 602), CASABIANCA (S 603), EMERAUDE (S 604), AMETHYSTE (S 605), PERLE (S 606)

Recognition Features:
- Rounded, smooth lined hull.
- Small, prominent pod atop casing forward of fin.
- Rounded top to casing.
- Slim fin forward of midships with vertical leading edge and sloping after edge. Top of the fin is slightly rounded in profile and slopes down at the after end.
- Diving planes sited near the top of the fin at its leading edge.
- Rudder, right aft, has sloping forward edge.
- Note – S 605 and onwards have had their length increased to 241.5 ft (73.6 m) and are being built to a modified design. This includes a new bow form, a new DSUV 62C towed array sonar, and further streamlining of the superstructure.

Displacement surfaced, tons: 2385.0 (2410.0, S 605 on)
Displacement dived, tons: 2670.0
Length, feet (metres): 236.5 (72.1), (241.5 (73.6) (S 605 on))
Beam, feet (metres): 24.9
Draught, feet (metres): 21.0
Speed, knots: 25

Missiles:
SSM – Aerospatiale SM 39 Exocet; launched from 21 in *(533 mm)* torpedo tubes.
Torpedoes: 4 – 21 in *(533 mm)* tubes. ECAN L5 Mod 3 and ECAN F17 Mod 2.

Radars:
Search – Thomson-CSF DRUA 33.
Sonars: Thomson Sintra DMUX 20 multi-function.
DUUA 2B.
DUUX 5.
DSUV 62C; towed array.

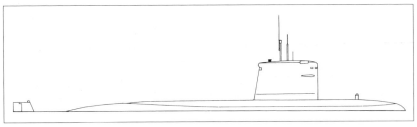

Rubis Class

EMERAUDE

Walter Sartori

Country: FRANCE
Ship type: SUBMARINES
Class: L'INFLEXIBLE (SNLE)
Active: 5

Name (Pennant Number): LE FOUDROYANT (S 610), LE TERRIBLE (S 612), L'INDOMPTABLE (S 613), LE TONNANT (S 614), L'INFLEXIBLE (S 615)

Recognition Features:
● Streamlined fin with diving planes at forward end towards its top.
● Large, flat-topped casing atop main pressure hull housing the SLBM tubes.
● The casing extends well aft of the fin and slopes down more steeply at its after end.
● Square-topped rudder with slightly sloping forward edge, right aft.
● Note – Improved streamlining of the M4 conversion submarines changes the silhouette so that they resemble *L'Inflexible*.

Displacement surfaced, tons: 8080.0
Displacement dived, tons: 8920.0
Length, feet (metres): 422.1 (128.7)
Beam, feet (metres): 34.8 (10.6)
Draught, feet (metres): 32.8 (10.0)
Speed, knots: 20 surfaced; 25 dived
Range, miles: 5000 at 4 kts on auxiliary propulsion only

Missiles:
  SLBM – 16 Aerospatiale M4.
  SSM – Aerospatiale SM 39 Exocet; launched from 21 in *(533 mm)* torpedo tubes.
Torpedoes: 4 – 21 in *(533 mm)* tubes. ECAN L5 Mod 3 and ECAN F17 Mod 2.
Radars:
  Navigation – Thomson-CSF DRUA 33.

Sonars: Thomson Sintra DSUX 21, passive bow and flank arrays.
DUUX 5.
DSUV 61; towed array.

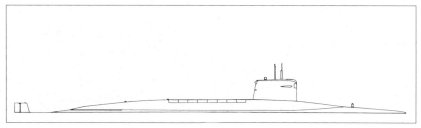

L'Inflexible Class

LE TERRIBLE   *SIRPA/ECPA*

LE FOUDROYANT   *SIRPA/ECPA*

Type 206 Class

Country: GERMANY
Ship type: SUBMARINES
Class: TYPE 206 (SSK)
Active: 6
Class: TYPE 206A
Active: 12

Name (Pennant Number): U 13 (S 192), U 14 (S 193), U 15 * (S 194), U 16 * (S 195), U 17 * (S 196), U 18 * (S 197), U 19 (S 198), U 20 (S 199), U 21 * (S 170), U 22 * (S 171), U 23 * (S 172), U 24 * (S 173), U 25 * (S 174), U 26 * (S 175), U 27 (S 1-76), U 28 * (S 177), U 29 * (S 178), U 30 * (S 179)
* Type 206A

Recognition Features:
- Distinctive, bulbous bow narrowing down to slim casing.
- Large, bulky, irregular shaped fin with vertical forward edge, rounded at top. Fin is stepped at its after end with sloping after edge down to casing.
- Round top to casing of which very little is visible aft of the fin.
- Bow-mounted diving planes not visible.
- Note 1 – Modernised Type 206A submarines have a slight difference in superstructure shape.
- Note 2 – Unusual GRP mine containers are secured either side of the hull forward of the fin.

Displacement surfaced, tons: 450.0
Displacement dived, tons: 498.0
Length, feet (metres): 159.4 (48.6)
Beam, feet (metres): 15.1 (4.6)
Draught, feet (metres): 14.8 (4.5)
Speed, knots: 10 surfaced; 17 dived
Range, miles: 4500 at 5 kts surfaced

Torpedoes: 8 – 21 in *(533 mm)* bow tubes. AEG Seeschlenge (Type 206) and DMT (ex-AEG) Seeal 3 (Type 206A).
Radars:
Surface search – Thomson-CSF Calypso II.
Sonars: Thomson Sintra DUUX 2; Atlas Elektronik 410 A4 (Type 206); Atlas Elektronik DBQS-21D (Type 206A).

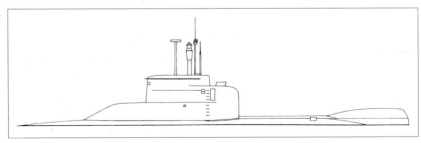

U 24

Maritime Photographic

Country: GREECE
Ship type: SUBMARINES
Class: GLAVKOS (209 TYPES 1100 and 1200) (SSK)
Active: 8

Name (Pennant Number): GLAVKOS (S 110), NEREUS (S 111), TRITON (S 112), PROTEUS (S 113), POSYDON (S 116), AMPHITRITE (S 117), OKEANOS (S 118), PONTOS (S 119)

Recognition Features:

● Blunt bow profile with bow mounted diving planes not visible.
● Round top to casing.
● Low, long fin mounted on raised part of the casing, (Type 1200), with blunt profile forward and sloping profile aft.
● Fin has vertical leading and after edges.
● Rudder just visible right aft.
● Note 1 – These are a single-hull design with two ballast tanks and forward and after trim tanks.
● Note 2 – This class has several types and is operated by many countries and there are slight variations in appearance.
● Note 3 – Also operated by Argentina (active 2), Brazil (active 1), Chile (active 2), Colombia (active 2), Ecuador (active 2), India (active 4), Indonesia (active 2), South Korea (active 3), Peru (active 6), Turkey (active 6), Venezuela (active 2).

Displacement surfaced, tons: 1100.0
Displacement dived, tons: 1210.0; (1285, S 112, 116-119)
Length, feet (metres): 178.4 (54.4); (183.4 (55.9) (S 112, 116-119)
Beam, feet (metres): 20.3 (6.2)
Draught, feet (metres): 17.9 (5.5)
Speed, knots: 11 surfaced; 21.5 dived

Missiles:

McDonnell Douglas Sub-Harpoon (after modernisation). Can be discharged from 4 tubes only.

Torpedoes: 8 – 21 in *(533 mm)* bow tubes. Probably AEG SST 4.
Radars:
   Surface search – Thomson-CSF Calypso II.
Sonars: Atlas Elektronik CSU 3-2 (unmodernised); hull-mounted.
Atlas Elektronik PRS-3-4; passive ranging.
Atlas Elektronik CSU 83-90 (DBQS-21) (modernisation).
Atlas Elektronik CSU-3-4 (S 112, 116-119); hull-mounted.
Thomson Sintra DUUX 2.

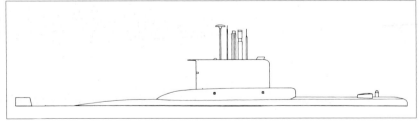

Glavkos Class

AMPHITRITE

van Ginderen Collection

Sauro Class

Country: ITALY
Ship type: SUBMARINES
Class: SAURO (1081 TYPE) (SSK)
Active: 4

Name (Pennant Number): NAZARIO SAURO (S 518), FECIA DI COSSATO (S 519), LEONARDO DA VINCI (S 520), GUGLIELMO MARCONI (S 521)

Recognition Features:
● Blunt, rounded bow.
● Three sets of diving planes, one at bow, one on fin and one aft.
● Bow-mounted planes can be stowed vertically.
● Flat top to casing.
● Low profile, slim fin with vertical forward edge and sloping after edge.
● Rudder visible right aft with vertical leading edge and sloping after edge.

Displacement surfaced, tons: 1456.0
Displacement dived, tons: 1631.0
Length, feet (metres): 210.0 (63.9)
Beam, feet (metres): 22.5 (6.8)
Draught, feet (metres): 18.9 (5.7)
Speed, knots: 11 surfaced; 12 snorting; 19 dived
Range, miles: 11,000 surfaced at 11 kts; 250 dived at 4 kts

Torpedoes: 6 - 21 in *(533 mm)* bow tubes. 12 Whitehead A184.
Radars:
    Search/navigation – SMA BPS 704.
Sonars: Selenia Elsag IPD 70/S.
Selenia Elsag MD 100.

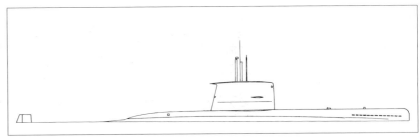

Sauro Class

LEONARDO DA VINCI

Marina Fraccaroli

Country: JAPAN
Ship type: SUBMARINES
Class: HARUSHIO (SSK)
Active: 5
Building: 2

Name (Pennant Number): HARUSHIO (SS 583), NATSUSHIO (SS 584), HAYASHIO (SS 585), ARASHIO (SS 586), WAKASHIO (SS 587), FUYUSHIO (SS 588), – (SS 589)

Recognition Features:
- Low profile bow.
- Rounded top to casing.
- Only short amount of casing visible forward of fin which is sited well forward of midships.
- Tall fin, tapered from forward to aft with vertical leading and after edges.
- Diving planes on fin at leading edge, just below mid-height.
- Curved, hump-back profile to hull.
- Rudder visible right aft with sloping forward edge.
- Note 1 – The slight growth in all dimensions and same basic shape suggests a natural progression from the Yuushio class (active 10).
- Note 2 – The Yuushio class is an enlarged version of the older Uzushio class (active 2).

Displacement standard, tons: 2450.0
Displacement dived, tons: 2750.0
Length, feet (metres): 262.5 (80.0)
Beam, feet (metres): 35.4 (10.8)
Draught, feet (metres): 25.6 (7.8)
Speed, knots: 12 surfaced; 20+ dived

Missiles:
   SSM – McDonnell Douglas Sub-Harpoon, fired from torpedo tubes.

Torpedoes: 6 – 21 in *(533 mm)* tubes. Japanese Type 89.
Radars:
   Surface search – JRC ZPS 6.
Sonars: Hughes/Oki ZQQ 5B; hull-mounted.
ZQR 1 towed array similar to BQR 15.

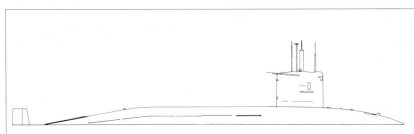

ARASHIO

Hachiro Nakai

Country: NETHERLANDS
Ship type: SUBMARINES
Class: WALRUS (SSK)
Active: 4

Name (Pennant Number): WALRUS (S 802), ZEELEEUW (S 803), DOLFIJN (S 808), BRUINVIS (S 810)

Sonars: Thomson Sintra TSM 2272 Eledone Octopus; hull-mounted. GEC Avionics Type 2026; towed array. Thomson Sintra DUUX 5.

Recognition Features:

- Low bow with small pod at forward end of casing.
- Flat top to casing.
- Large slender fin with leading edge sloping slightly aft and vertical after end.
- Diving planes at extreme forward edge of fin and just above mid-height.
- X rudders just visible right aft.
- Note – These are improved Zwaardvis class (active 2) with similar dimensions and silhouettes except for X stern.

Displacement standard, tons: 1900.0
Displacement surfaced, tons: 2465.0
Displacement dived, tons: 2800.0
Length, feet (metres): 223.1 (67.7)
Beam, feet (metres): 27.6 (8.4)
Draught, feet (metres): 21.6 (6.6)
Speed, knots: 13 surfaced; 20 dived
Range, miles: 10,000 at 9 kts snorting

Missiles:
SSM – McDonnell Douglas Sub-Harpoon.
Torpedoes: 4 – 21 in *(533 mm)* tubes. Honeywell Mk 48 Mod 4 and Honeywell NT 37D.
Radars:
Surface search – Signaal/Racal ZW 07.

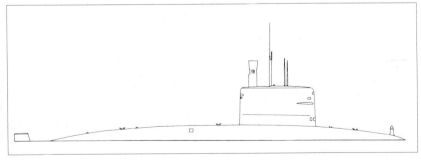

Walrus Class

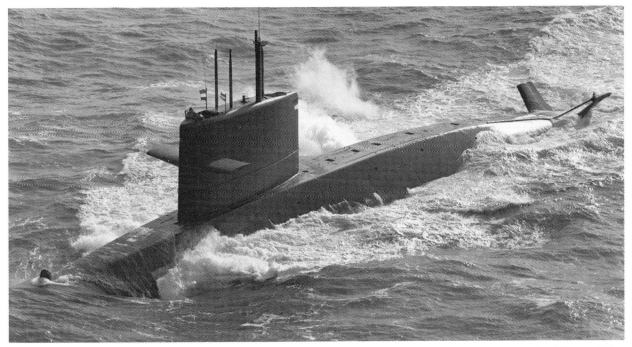

ZEELEEUW

Royal Netherlands Navy

Country: NORWAY
Ship type: SUBMARINES
Class: MODERNISED KOBBEN (TYPE 207) (SSK)
Active: 6

Name (Pennant Number): SKLINNA (S 314 (ex-S 305)), SKOLPEN (S 306), STORD (S 308), SVENNER (S 309), KOBBEN (S 318), KUNNA (S 319)

Recognition Features:
- Small submarine with low bow.
- Sonar pod atop forward end of casing.
- Rounded top to casing.
- Diving planes sited at bow, not visible.
- Fin set well aft from bows.
- Very distinctive shape to fin with sloping leading edge and stepped after end. Very little of the casing shows above water aft of the fin.
- Note – This class is a development of IKL Type 205 (German U4-U8).

Displacement standard, tons: 459.0
Displacement dived, tons: 524.0
Length, feet (metres): 155.5 (47.4)
Beam, feet (metres): 15.0 (4.6)
Draught, feet (metres): 14.0 (4.3)
Speed, knots: 12 surfaced; 18 dived.
Range, miles: 5000 at 8 kts (snorting)

Torpedoes: 8 – 21 in *(533 mm)* bow tubes. FFV Type 61 and Honeywell NT37C.
Radars:
Surface search – Kelvin Hughes 1007.
Sonars: Atlas Elektronik or Simrad.

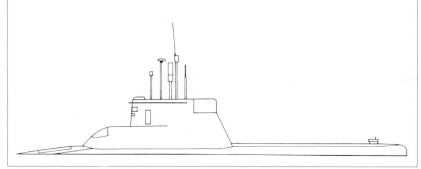

Modernised Kobben Class

KOBBEN

Walter Sartori

Ula Class

Country: NORWAY
Ship type: SUBMARINES
Class: ULA (TYPE P 6071 (Ex-210)) (SSK)
Active: 6

Name (Pennant Number): ULA (S 300), UREDD (S 305), UTVAER (S 303), UTHAUG (S 304), UTSTEIN (S 302), UTSIRA (S 301)

Recognition Features:
● Blunt, high bow. Flat-topped casing slopes down from bow to water level right aft.
● Diving planes sited at bow, not visible.
● Fin sited just aft of midships.
● Fin is unusually low in profile with vertical leading edge and sharp, sloping after edge with notch cut out at mid-point.
● X rudders just visible right aft.

Displacement surfaced, tons: 1040.0
Displacement dived, tons: 1150.0
Length, feet (metres): 193.6 (59.0)
Beam, feet (metres): 17.7 (5.4)
Draught, feet (metres): 15.1 (4.6)
Speed, knots: 11 surfaced; 23 dived
Range, miles: 5000 at 8 kts

Torpedoes: 8 – 21 in *(533 mm)* bow tubes. AEG DM 2A3 Seeal.
Radars:
    Surface search – Kelvin Hughes 1007.
Sonars: Atlas Elektronik CSU83.
Thomson Sintra flank array.

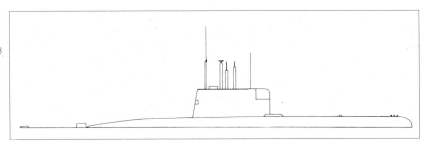

Ula Class

UTHAUG

Stefan Terzibaschitsch

Country: RUSSIA AND ASSOCIATED STATES
Ship type: SUBMARINES
Class: KILO (GRANAY) (TYPE 877/877K/877M) (SSK)
Active: 23
Building: 1

Name (Pennant Number): (Not available).

Recognition Features:
● Blunt, rounded bow.
● Flat-topped casing, tapering towards after end.
● Long, low fin with vertical leading and after edges and flat top.
● Two windows either side at top, leading edge of fin.
● Hull-mounted diving planes not visible.
● Rudder just visible.
● Note 1 – Has a better hull form than the Foxtrot or Tango.
● Note 2 – Also operated by Algeria (active 2), India (active 8), Iran (active 2), Poland (active 1), Romania (active 1).

Displacement surfaced, tons: 2325.0
Displacement dived, tons: 3076.0
Length, feet (metres): 242.1 (73.8)
Beam, feet (metres): 32.5 (9.9)
Draught, feet (metres): 21.7 (6.6)
Speed, knots: 10 surfaced; 17 dived
Range, miles: 6000 at 7 kts surfaced; 400 at 3 kts dived.

Torpedoes: 6 – 21 in *(533 mm)* tubes. Type 53.
Radars:
Surface search – Snoop Tray.
Sonars: Shark Teeth; hull-mounted.
Mouse Roar; hull-mounted.

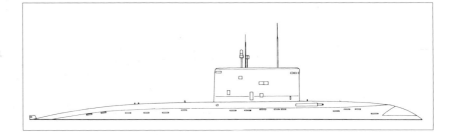

Kilo Class

KILO

Country: RUSSIA AND ASSOCIATED STATES
Ship type: SUBMARINES
Class: TANGO (TYPE 641B) (SSK)
Active: 18

Name (Pennant Number): (Not available).

Recognition Features:
● Long, slender submarine with slightly tapered bow, flat-fronted in profile.
● Hull-mounted diving planes retracted when surfaced.
● Flat top to casing.
● Very slender fin, of almost square profile, with raised section at after end.
● Fin sited just forward of midships.
● Rudder not visible.
● Note 1 – One of class is fitted with a visible towed array stern tube.
● Note 2 – There is a large array mounted above the torpedo tubes as well as a bow-mounted dome.

Displacement surfaced, tons: 3000.0
Displacement dived, tons: 3800.0
Length, feet (metres): 298.6 (91.0)
Beam, feet (metres): 29.9 (9.1)
Draught, feet (metres): 23.6 (7.2)
Speed, knots: 13 surfaced; 16 dived

Torpedoes: 6 – 21 in *(533 mm)* tubes. Type 53.
Radars:
   Surface search – Snoop Tray.
Sonars: Shark Teeth; hull-mounted.

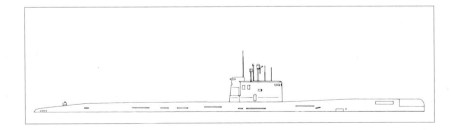

TANGO

Country: RUSSIA AND ASSOCIATED STATES
Ship type: SUBMARINES
Class: AKULA (BARS) (TYPE 971) (SSN)
Active: 11
Building: 5

Name (Pennant Number): BARS, LEOPARD, PANTERA, PUMA, VOLK, TIGR +5

Recognition Features:
- Blunt, bull-nosed bow.
- Large diameter hull, flat-topped aft of fin.
- Very distinctive, low profile fin, unusually long and has smoothly rounded hydrodynamic lines moulded into the casing.
- Retractable diving planes not visible.
- Large stern pod (towed array dispenser) on rudder.
- Note 1 – Has the same broad hull as Sierra.
- Note 2 – A number of prominent water environment sensors have begun to appear on the fin leading edge and on the forward casing.

Displacement surfaced, tons: 7500.0
Displacement dived, tons: 9100.0
Length, feet (metres): 360.1 (110.0)
Beam, feet (metres): 45.9 (14.0)
Draught, feet (metres): 34.1 (10.4)
Speed, knots: 18 surfaced; 32 dived

Missiles:
  SLCM – SS-N-21 Sampson fired from 21 in *(533 mm)* tubes.
  A/S – SS-N-15 fired from 21 in *(533 mm)* tubes.
    SS-N-16 fired from 25.6 in *(650 mm)* tubes; payload Type 45 torpedo.

Torpedoes: 4 – 21 in *(533 mm)* and 4 – 25.6 in *(650 mm)* tubes. Type 53 and Type 65.
Radars:
  Surface search – Snoop Pair with back-to-back aerials on same mast as ESM.
Sonars: Shark Gill; hull-mounted.
Mouse Roar; hull-mounted.

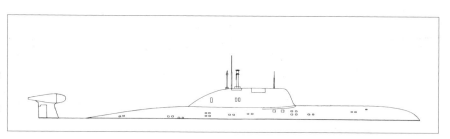

Akula Class

AKULA

Sierra II Class

Country: RUSSIA AND ASSOCIATED STATES
Ship type: SUBMARINES
Class: SIERRA II (BARACUDA II) (TYPE 945B) (SSN)
Active: 2

Name (Pennant Number): OREL, KASATKA

Recognition Features:
- Low, blunt bow.
- Retractable, hull-mounted diving planes.
- Large diameter hull with rounded top.
- Very unusual fin of slightly rounded box-like construction. Forward end is flat and little attempt seems to have been made at streamlining.
- Two windows each side at top of leading edge of fin. Outboard windows slightly lower.
- Large stern pod, (housing a towed array dispenser), mounted atop rudder.
- Note – A follow-on class to the Sierra I. Main differences are that the Sierra II has larger overall dimensions, a longer fin by some 16.5 ft which is of a different profile. In addition, the towed communications buoy has been recessed and a 10 point environmental sensor is fitted at the front end of the fin.

Displacement surfaced, tons: 7200.0
Displacement dived, tons: 8200.0
Length, feet (metres): 364.2 (111.0)
Beam, feet (metres): 46.6 (14.2)
Draught, feet (metres): 28.9 (8.8)
Speed, knots: 18 surfaced; 32 dived

Missiles:
   SLCM – SS-N-21 Sampson fired from 21 in *(533 mm)* tubes.
   A/S – SS-N-15 fired from 21 in *(533 mm)* tubes.
      SS-N-16 fired from 25.6 in *(650 mm)* tubes; payload Type 45 torpedo.
Torpedoes: 8 – 25.6 in *(650 mm)* tubes. Type 53 and Type 65.

Radars:
   Surface search – Snoop Pair with back-to-back ESM aerial.
Sonars: Shark Gill; hull-mounted.
Mouse Roar; hull-mounted.

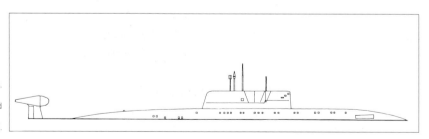

Sierra II Class

SIERRA II

Country: RUSSIA AND ASSOCIATED STATES
Ship type: SUBMARINES
Class: VICTOR III (KEFAL III) (TYPE 671RTM) (SSN)
Active: 26

Name (Pennant Number): (Not available).

Recognition Features:
- Low, blunt bow.
- Retractable, hull-mounted diving planes.
- Large diameter, bulbous hull with a low profile.
- Rounded top to casing.
- Relatively small, rounded fin with slightly sloping leading edge and shallow sloping after edge.
- Distinctive, large, streamlined pod, housing towed array dispenser, mounted on rudder.
- Note 1 – All Victors present a very similar profile.
- Note 2 – Victor III is heavier and longer than Victor I, but of similar lines. Most obvious difference is the pod mounted on the rudder in Victor III.
- Note 3 – Victor II is an enlarged Victor I design, 9 m longer to provide more space for torpedo stowage.

Displacement surfaced, tons: 4850.0
Displacement dived, tons: 6300.0
Length, feet (metres): 351.1 (107.0)
Beam, feet (metres): 34.8 (10.6)
Draught, feet (metres): 24.3 (7.4)
Speed, knots: 18 surfaced; 30 dived

Missiles:
    SLCM – SS-N-21 Sampson fired from 21 in *(533 mm)* tubes.
    A/S – SS-N-15 fired from 21 in *(533 mm)* tubes.
        SS-N-16 A/B fired from 25.6 in *(650 mm)* tubes;
        payload Type 45 torpedo.

Torpedoes: 2 – 21 in *(533 mm)* and 4 – 25.6 in *(650 mm)* tubes. Type 53 and Type 65.
Radars:
    Surface search – Snoop Tray.
Sonars: Shark Gill; hull-mounted.
Mouse Roar; hull-mounted.

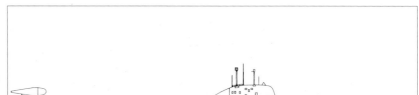

VICTOR III

Delta IV Class

Country: RUSSIA AND ASSOCIATED STATES
Ship type: SUBMARINES
Class: DELTA IV (DELFIN) (TYPE 667BDRM) (SSBN)
Active: /

Name (Pennant Number): (Not available).

Recognition Features:
- Blunt, rounded, low bow.
- Flat top to casing aft of fin.
- Low profile fin sited well forward.
- Large diving planes on fin at leading edge, about mid-height.
- Very large and distinctive missile casing aft of the fin with its forward end moulded round after edge of fin. Missile casing runs straight for approximately half the distance to the stern where it smoothly tapers away.
- Rudder, with sloping forward edge, just visible right aft.
- Note 1 – Delta II, III and IV are of similar size and similar profiles.
- Note 2 – Delta IV differs from III by being about 29 ft longer, has a pressure-tight fitting on the after end of the missile tube housing and has two 650 mm torpedo tubes.
- Note 3 – Delta III differs from II by the missile casing being higher to accommodate SS-N-18 missiles which are longer than the SS-N-8s.
- Note 4 – Delta II is a larger edition of Delta I designed to carry four extra missile tubes and has a straight run on the after part of the missile casing.

Displacement surfaced, tons: 10,750.0
Displacement dived, tons: 12,150.0
Length, feet (metres): 544.6 (166.0)
Beam, feet (metres): 39.4 (12.0)
Draught, feet (metres): 28.5 (8.7)
Speed, knots: 19 surfaced; 24 dived

Missiles:
  SLBM – SS-N-23 Skiff.
Torpedoes: 21 in *(533 mm)* and 25.6 in *(650 mm)* tubes. Type 53 and Type 65.
Radars:
  Surface search – Snoop Tray.
Sonars: Shark Gill; hull-mounted.
Mouse Roar; hull-mounted.

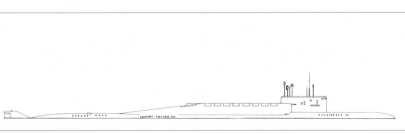

DELTA IV

Typhoon Class

Country: RUSSIA AND ASSOCIATED STATES
Ship type: SUBMARINES
Class: TYPHOON (TYPE 941) (SSBN)
Active: 6

Name (Pennant Number): (Not available).

Recognition Features:
- Easily identified, the largest submarine ever built.
- Blunt, bull-nosed bows with huge cylindrical hull.
- Flat top to casing.
- Streamlined fin, with windows at the top forward edge, sited well aft of midships.
- The fin has a relatively low profile with the lower part being larger and rounded where it moulds onto the main casing.
- In profile the leading edge to the fin is vertical and the after edge has a slight slope.
- Retractable diving planes are not visible.
- The very large rudder at the after end gives this class an unmistakable profile.
- Note – An unusual feature of Typhoon is that the missile tubes are mounted forward of the fin.

Displacement surfaced, tons: 21,500.0
Displacement dived, tons: 26,500.0
Length, feet (metres): 562.7 (171.5)
Beam, feet (metres): 80.7 (24.6)
Draught, feet (metres): 42.7 (13.0)
Speed, knots: 19 surfaced; 26 dived

Missiles:
SLBM – SS-N-20 Sturgeon.
SAM – There are suggestions that this class may have a SAM capability.

A/S – SS-N-15 fired from 21 in *(533 mm)* tubes.
SS-N-16 fired from 25.6 in *(650 mm)* tubes; payload Type 45 torpedo. There is also a 16B version with a nuclear warhead.
Torpedoes: 21 in *(533 mm)* and 25.6 in *(650 mm)* tubes. Type 53 and Type 65.
Radars:
Surface search – Snoop Pair.
Sonars: Shark Gill; hull-mounted.
Mouse Roar; hull-mounted.

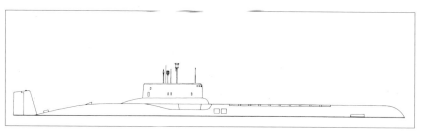

TYPHOON

Country: RUSSIA AND ASSOCIATED STATES
Ship type: SUBMARINES
Class: OSCAR II (ANTYEY) (TYPE 949A) (SSGN)
Active: 9
Building: 1
Proposed: 1
Class: OSCAR I (GRANIT) (TYPE 949) (SSGN)
Active: 2

Name (Pennant Number): (Not available).

Recognition Features:
- Blunt, rounded, low bow.
- Exceptionally large diameter hull with rounded top.
- Low, smooth profile fin forward of midships.
- Fin is tapered at the leading and after edges.
- Three windows at either side of top leading edge of fin.
- Retractable diving planes, not visible.
- Large rudder right aft.
- Note 1 – Of similar displacement to the Delta class but much shorter and much larger diameter.
- Note 2 – SSM missile tubes are in banks of 12 either side and external to the 8.5 m diameter pressure hull.
- Note 3 – All but the first of class have a tube on the rudder fin as in Delta IV which may be used for dispensing a VLF floating aerial.

Displacement surfaced, tons: 10,200.0 (I), 10,700.0 (II)
Displacement dived, tons : 12,500.0 (I), 13,500.0 (II)
Length, feet (metres): 469.2 (143.0) (I); 505.2 (154.0) (II)
Beam, feet (metres): 59.7 (18.2)
Draught, feet (metres): 29.5 (9.0)
Speed, knots: 19 surfaced; 30; 28 (II) dived

Missiles:
SSM – 24 SS-N-19 Shipwreck.
A/S – SS-N-15 fired from 21 in *(533 mm)* tubes.
SS-N-16 fired from 25.6 in *(650 mm)* tubes; payload Type 45 torpedo.
Torpedoes: 4 – 21 in *(533 mm)* and 4 – 25.6 in *(650 mm)* tubes. Type 53 and Type 65.
Radars:
Surface search – Snoop Head/Pair.
Sonars: Shark Gill; hull-mounted.
Mouse Roar; hull-mounted.

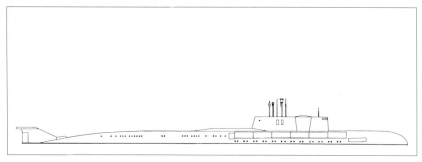

OSCAR

Country: SWEDEN
Ship type: SUBMARINES
Class: NÄCKEN (A 14) (SSK)
Active: 3

Name (Pennant Number): NÄCKEN, NAJAD, NEPTUN

Recognition Features:
- Distinctive, unusually blunt bow.
- Long, slim, constant-sized hull.
- Large, very slim fin with vertical leading and after edges.
- Slightly curved top to fin profile.
- Fin-mounted diving planes, well aft from leading edge and below mid- height.
- Note 1 – *Näcken* was installed with a closed-circuit Tillma Stirling diesel which involved the boat being lengthened by 6 m. The other two of the class will not be similarly modified.
- Note 2 – The very high beam to length ratio is notable in this hull design. Has large bow-mounted sonar. Single periscope.

Displacement surfaced, tons: 1015.0
Displacement dived, tons: 1085.0
Length, feet (metres): 162.4 (49.5); 182.1 (55.5) (*Näcken*)
Beam, feet (metres): 18.7 (5.7)
Draught, feet (metres): 18.0 (5.5)
Speed, knots: 12 surfaced; 20 dived

Torpedoes: 6 – 21 in *(533 mm)* tubes. FFV Type 613.
2 – 15.75 in *(400 mm)* tubes. FFV Type 431.
Radars:
    Navigation – Terma.
Sonars: Thomson Sintra; hull-mounted.

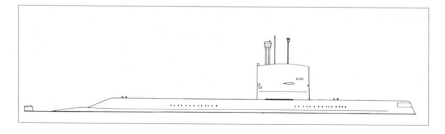

Näcken Class

NÄCKEN

Erik Laursen

Sjöormen Class

Country: SWEDEN
Ship type: SUBMARINES
Class: SJÖORMEN (A 12) (SSK)
Active: 5

Name (Pennant Number): SJÖORMEN, SJÖLEJONET, SJÖHUNDEN, SJÖBJÖRNEN, SJÖHÄSTEN

Recognition Features:
- Low, blunt bow.
- Low profile hull with smooth, sloping forward and after ends.
- Rounded top to casing.
- Bulky fin with unusual curves to leading edge. Vertical after edge, slightly flared at bottom.
- Fin-mounted diving planes sited at centre of fin and well below mid- height.
- Note – Albacore hull. Twin-decked.

Displacement surfaced, tons: 1130.0
Displacement dived, tons: 1210.0
Length, feet (metres): 167.3 (51.0)
Beam, feet (metres): 20.0 (6.1)
Draught, feet (metres): 19.0 (5.8)
Speed, knots: 12 surfaced; 20 dived

Torpedoes: 4 – 21 in *(533 mm)* bow tubes. FFV Type 613.
2 – 15.75 in *(400 mm)* tubes. FFV Type 431.
Radars:
    Navigation – Terma.
Sonars: Plessey Hydra; hull-mounted.

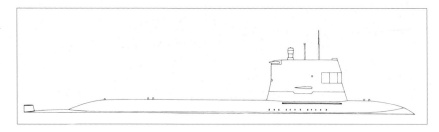

SJÖHÄSTEN

Erik Laursen

Country: SWEDEN
Ship type: SUBMARINES
Class: VÄSTERGÖTLAND (A 17) (SSK)
Active: 4

Name (Pennant Number): VÄSTERGÖTLAND, HÄLSINGLAND, SÖDERMANLAND, ÖSTERGÖTLAND

Recognition Features:
- Rounded bow, small pod atop forward casing.
- Smooth, symmetrical casing with rounded top.
- Large, distinctive fin with sloping top at forward edge.
- Fin is slightly flared out (in profile) for the lower one third of its height.
- Fin-mounted diving planes, aft from forward edge below mid-height.
- Note – Single hulled, with an X type rudder/after hydroplane design.

Displacement surfaced, tons: 1070.0
Displacement dived, tons: 1143.0
Length, feet (metres): 159.1 (48.5)
Beam, feet (metres): 20.0 (6.1)
Draught, feet (metres): 18.4 (5.6)
Speed, knots: 11 surfaced; 20 dived

Torpedoes: 6 – 21 in *(533 mm)* tubes. FFV Type 613.
3 – 15.75 in *(400 mm)* tubes. FFV Type 431.
Radars:
  Navigation – Terma.
Sonars: Atlas Elektronik CSU83; hull-mounted.

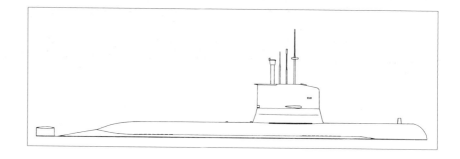

Västergötland Class

VÄSTERGÖTLAND

Maritime Photographic

Swiftsure Class

Country: UNITED KINGDOM
Ship type: SUBMARINES
Class: SWIFTSURE (SSN)
Active: 5

Name (Pennant Number): SOVEREIGN (S 108), SUPERB (S 109), SCEPTRE (S 104), SPARTAN (S 105), SPLENDID (S 106)

Recognition Features:

- Submarine has hump-backed appearance in profile.
- The pressure hull maintains its diameter for most of the hull length.
- Retractable, hull-mounted diving planes.
- Prominent, slender sonar pod atop casing forward of fin.
- Fin mounted just forward of midships. Fin has vertical leading and after edges and is tapered to point at after end.
- Slopes steeply down at after end of hull compared with shallow slope at forward end.
- Large, flat-topped rudder with sloping forward edge at after end of casing.

Displacement standard, tons: 4400.0
Displacement dived, tons: 4900.0
Length, feet (metres): 272.0 (82.9)
Beam, feet (metres): 32.3 (9.8)
Draught, feet (metres): 28.0 (8.5)
Speed, knots: 30+ dived

Missiles:
  SSM – McDonnell Douglas UGM-84B Sub Harpoon.
Torpedoes: 5 – 21 in *(533 mm)* bow tubes. Marconi Tigerfish Mk 24 Mod 2.
Decoys: 2 SSE Mk 6 launchers.
Radars:
  Navigation – Kelvin Hughes Type 1006.

Sonars: AUWE Type 2001 or Plessey Type 2020 or Marconi/Plessey Type 2074; hull-mounted.
BAC Type 2007; hull-mounted; flank array.
Ferranti Type 2046; towed array.
Thomson Sintra Type 2019 PARIS.

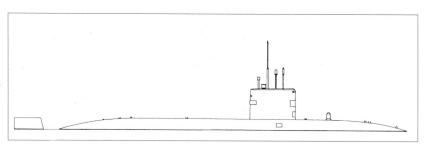

Swiftsure Class

SPLENDID

Trafalgar Class

Country: UNITED KINGDOM
Ship type: SUBMARINES
Class: TRAFALGAR (BATCHES 1 and 2) (SSN)
Active: 7
Proposed: 5

Name (Pennant Number): TRAFALGAR (S 107), TURBULENT (S 87), TIRELESS (S 88), TORBAY (S 90), TRENCHANT (S 91), TALENT (S 92), TRIUMPH (S 93)

Recognition Features:
● Long, low hull with almost identical sloping profiles at the forward and after ends of the pressure hull.
● Rounded top to casing.
● Retractable, forward, hull-mounted diving planes.
● Prominent, slender sonar pod atop casing forward of fin.
● Fin is mounted just forward of midships. Fin has vertical leading and after edges and is tapered to point at after end.
● Large, flat-topped rudder at after end of casing.
● Note 1 – *Turbulent* has a hump on the after casing housing a small winch.
● Note 2 – The pressure hull and outer surfaces are covered with conformal anechoic noise reduction coatings.
● Note 3 – Strengthened fins for under ice operations.

Displacement surfaced, tons: 4700.0; 5400.0 (Batch 2)
Displacement dived, tons: 5208.0; 5900.0 (Batch 2)
Length, feet (metres): 280.1 (85.4); 293.3 (89.4) (Batch 2)
Beam, feet (metres): 32.1 (9.8)
Draught, feet (metres): 31.2 (9.5)
Speed, knots: 32 dived

Missiles:
   SSM – McDonnell Douglas UGM-84B Sub-Harpoon.
Torpedoes: 5 – 21 in *(533 mm)* bow tubes. Marconi Spearfish and Marconi Tigerfish Mk 24 Mod 2.
Decoys: 2 SSE Mk 8 launchers.
Radars:
   Navigation – Kelvin Hughes Type 1006 or Type 1007.
Sonars: BAe Type 2007 AC or Marconi 2072; hull-mounted.
Plessey Type 2020 or Marconi/Plessey 2074; hull-mounted.
GEC Avionics Type 2026 or Ferranti Type 2046 or Marconi/Plessey 2057; towed array.
Thomson Sintra Type 2019 PARIS or THORN EMI 2082.
Marconi Type 2077.

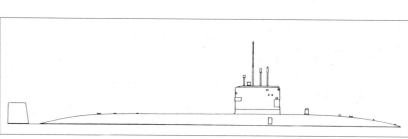

Trafalgar Class

TRIUMPH

Giorgio Arra

Country: UNITED KINGDOM
Ship type: SUBMARINES
Class: RESOLUTION (SSBN)
Active: 2

Name (Pennant Number): REPULSE (S 23), RENOWN (S 26)

Recognition Features:
- Low, blunt bow.
- Long, tapered, hull-mounted diving planes level with top of casing and set well aft from bows.
- Very slim fin, with slightly sloping leading and after edges, forward of midships.
- Prominent, slender sonar pod atop casing just aft of diving planes.
- Large, raised casing aft of fin, dropping down steeply at its after end. SLBM doors clearly visible atop casing.
- Tall, slim rudder right aft. Clear water between after end of casing and rudder.

Displacement surfaced, tons: 7600.0
Displacemen dived, tons: 8500.0
Length, feet (metres): 425.0 (129.5)
Beam, feet (metres): 33.0 (10.1)
Draught, feet (metres): 30.0 (9.1)
Speed, knots: 20 surfaced; 25 dived

Missiles:
   SLBM – Lockheed Polaris A3.
Torpedoes: 6 – 21 in *(533 mm)* bow tubes. Marconi Tigerfish Mk 24 Mod 2.
Decoys: 2 SSDE launchers.
Radars:
   Navigation – Kelvin Hughes Type 1006.

Sonars: Plessey Type 2001; hull-mounted.
BAe Type 2007; hull-mounted.
Ferranti Type 2046; towed array.
Thomson Sintra Type 2019 PARIS or THORN EMI Type 2082.

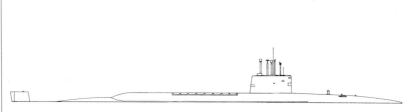

Resolution Class

REPULSE

Vanguard Class

Country: UNITED KINGDOM
Ship type: SUBMARINES
Class: VANGUARD (SSBN)
Active: 1
Building: 3

Name (Pennant Number): VANGUARD (S 28), VICTORIOUS (S 29), VIGILANT (S 30), VENGEANCE (S 31)

Recognition Features:
● Casing slopes down forward of fin to water line.
● Slim, tapered fin well forward of midships.
● Hull-mounted diving planes approximately midway between fin and bow.
● Large, distinctive, flat-topped casing aft of fin, dropping down steeply at its after end. Casing houses SLBMs.
● Large rudder with curved top.
● Note – The outer surface of the submarine is covered with conformal anechoic noise reduction coatings.

Displacement dived, tons: 15,900.0
Length, feet (metres): 491.8 (149.9)
Beam, feet (metres): 42.0 (12.8)
Draught, feet (metres): 39.4 (12.0)
Speed, knots: 25 dived

Missiles:
SLBM – Lockheed Trident 2 (D5).
Torpedoes: 4 – 21 in *(533 mm)* tubes. Marconi Spearfish and Marconi Tigerfish Mk 24 Mod 2.
Decoys: 2 SSE Mk 10 launchers.
Radars:
Navigation – Kelvin Hughes Type 1007.

Sonars: Marconi/Plessey Type 2054, hull-mounted. Marconi/Ferranti Type 2046 towed array.

VANGUARD

G Davies

Los Angeles Class

Country: UNITED STATES OF AMERICA
Ship type: SUBMARINES
Class: LOS ANGELES (SSN)
Active: 54
Building: 7

Name (Pennant Number): LOS ANGELES (SSN 688), PHILADELPHIA (SSN 690), MEMPHIS (SSN 691), OMAHA (SSN 692), CINCINNATI (SSN 693), GROTON (SSN 694), BIRMINGHAM (SSN 695), NEW YORK CITY (SSN 696), INDIANAPOLIS (SSN 697), BREMERTON (SSN 698), JACKSONVILLE (SSN 699), DALLAS (SSN 700), LA JOLLA (SSN 701), PHOENIX (SSN 702), BOSTON (SSN 703), BALTIMORE (SSN 704), CITY OF CORPUS CHRISTI (SSN 705), ALBUQUERQUE (SSN 706), PORTSMOUTH (SSN 707), MINNEAPOLIS–SAINT PAUL (SSN 708), HYMAN G RICKOVER (SSN 709), AUGUSTA (SSN 710), SAN FRANCISCO (SSN 711), ATLANTA (SSN 712), HOUSTON (SSN 713), NORFOLK (SSN 714), BUFFALO (SSN 715), SALT LAKE CITY (SSN 716), OLYMPIA (SSN 717), HONOLULU (SSN 718), PROVIDENCE (SSN 719), PITTSBURGH (SSN 720), CHICAGO (SSN 721), KEY WEST (SSN 722), OKLAHOMA CITY (SSN 723), LOUISVILLE (SSN 724), HELENA (SSN 725), NEWPORT NEWS (SSN 750), SAN JUAN (SSN 751), PASADENA (SSN 752), ALBANY (SSN 753), TOPEKA (SSN 754), MIAMI (SSN 755), SCRANTON (SSN 756), ALEXANDRIA (SSN 757), ASHEVILLE (SSN 758), JEFFERSON CITY (SSN 759), ANNAPOLIS (SSN 760), SPRINGFIELD (SSN 761), COLUMBUS (SSN 762), SANTA FE (SSN 763), BOISE (SSN 764), MONTPELIER (SSN 765), CHARLOTTE (SSN 766), HAMPTON (SSN 767), HARTFORD (SSN 768), TOLEDO (SSN 769), TUCSON (SSN 770), COLUMBIA (SSN 771), GREENEVILLE (SSN 772), CHEYENNE (SSN 773).

Recognition Features:
- Blunt bow, very low profile pressure hull.
- Hull profile tapers gently and consistently down to water level from bow to stern.
- Slender fin, with vertical leading and after edges, is sited well forward of midships.
- Fin-mounted diving planes at mid-height. Diving planes have distinct swept wing appearance.

- Tall rudder right aft with sloping forward edge.
- Note 1 – From SSN 719 onwards all are equipped with the Vertical Launch System.
- Note 2 – From SSN 751 onwards the class have acoustic tile cladding to augment the 'mammalian' skin which up to then had been the standard USN outer casing coating.
- Note 3 – From SSN 751 onwards the forward diving planes are hull- fitted forward instead of on the fin.
- Note 4 – The towed sonar array is stowed in a blister on the side of the casing.

Displacement standard, tons: 6080.0
Displacement dived, tons: 6927.0
Length, feet (metres): 362.0 (110.3)
Beam, feet (metres): 33.0 (10.1)
Draught, feet (metres): 32.3 (9.9)
Speed, knots: 32 dived

Missiles:
SLCM – GDC Tomahawk (TLAM-N).
SSM – GDC Tomahawk (TASM).
McDonnell Douglas Harpoon.
Torpedoes: 4 – 21 in *(533 mm)* tubes midships. Gould Mk 48.
Decoys: Emerson Electric Mk 2; torpedo decoy.

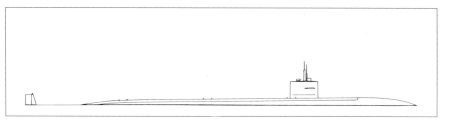

Los Angeles Class

BALTIMORE (Fin-mounted Diving Planes)   *Giorgio Arra*

ALBANY (Hull-mounted Diving Planes)   *Giorgio Arra*

Radars:
Surface search/nav/fire control – Sperry BPS 15 A.
Sonars: IBM BQQ 5A(V)1 (being updated to BQQ 5D/E).

BQR 23/25 (being replaced by TB-23/29); towed array.
Ametek BQS 15. MIDAS (mine and ice avoidance system) (SSN 751 on).

Country: UNITED STATES OF AMERICA
Ship type: SUBMARINES
Class: STURGEON (SSN)
Active: 29

Name (Pennant Number): WHALE (SSN 638), TAUTOG (SSN 639), GRAYLING (SSN 646), POGY (SSN 647), ASPRO (SSN 648), SUNFISH (SSN 649), PARGO (SSN 650), PUFFER (SSN 652), SAND LANCE (SSN 660), GURNARD (SSN 662), HAMMERHEAD (SSN 663), HAWKBILL (SSN 666), BERGALL (SSN 667), SPADEFISH (SSN 668), SEAHORSE (SSN 669), FINBACK (SSN 670), PINTADO (SSN 672), FLYING FISH (SSN 673), TREPANG (SSN 674), BLUEFISH (SSN 675), BILLFISH (SSN 676), DRUM (SSN 677), ARCHERFISH (SSN 678), WILLIAM H BATES *(ex-Redfish)* (SSN 680), BATFISH (SSN 681), TUNNY (SSN 682), PARCHE (SSN 683), CAVALLA (SSN 684), L MENDEL RIVERS (SSN 686)

Recognition Features:
● Bulbous pressure hull with unusually tall fin set well forward.
● Fin has vertical leading and after edges and is tapered at the forward and aft ends.
● Slender, fin-mounted diving planes at approximately mid-height. Diving planes have distinct swept wing appearance.
● Hull does not slope away until well aft of the fin.
● Large rudder right aft with slightly sloping forward edge.
● Note 1 – Fin height is 20 ft 6 in above deck.
● Note 2 – Fin-mounted diving planes rotate to vertical for breaking through ice when surfacing.
● Note 3 – SSN 678-684 and 686 are 10 ft longer than remainder of class.

Displacement standard, tons: 4250.0; 4460.0 (SSN 678-684, 686)
Displacement dived, tons: 4780.0; 4960.0 (SSN 678-684, 686)
Length, feet (metres): 302.2 (92.1) (SSN 678-684, 687); 292.0 (89.0)

Beam, feet (metres): 31.8 (9.7)
Draught, feet (metres): 28.9 (8.8)
Speed, knots: 15 surfaced; 30 dived

Missiles:
SLCM – GDC Tomahawk (TLAM-N).
SSM – GDC Tomahawk (TASM).
McDonnell Douglas Harpoon.
Torpedoes: 4 – 21 in *(533 mm)* Mk 63 tubes midships. Gould Mk 8.
Decoys: Emerson Electric Mk 2; torpedo decoy.
Radars:
Surface search/navigation/fire control – Sperry BPS 15 or Raytheon BPS 14.
Sonars: IBM BQQ 5 (SSN 678 onwards) or Raytheon BQQ 2.
EDO BQS 8 or Raytheon BQS 14A.
Raytheon BQS 13.
BQR 15; towed array.

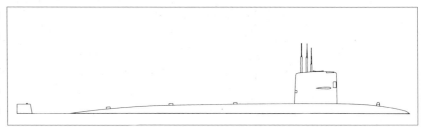

Sturgeon Class

STURGEON

Giorgio Arra

Country: UNITED STATES OF AMERICA
Ship type: SUBMARINES
Class: OHIO (SSBN)
Active: 14
Building: 4

Name (Pennant Number): OHIO (SSBN 726), MICHIGAN (SSBN 727), FLORIDA (SSBN 728), GEORGIA (SSBN 729), HENRY M JACKSON (SSBN 730), ALABAMA (SSBN 731), ALASKA (SSBN 732), NEVADA (SSBN 733), TENNESSEE (SSBN 734), PENNSYLVANIA (SSBN 735), WEST VIRGINIA (SSBN 736), KENTUCKY (SSBN 737), MARYLAND (SSBN 738), NEBRASKA (SSBN 739), RHODE ISLAND (SSBN 740), MAINE (SSBN 741), WYOMING (SSBN 742), LOUISIANA (SSBN 743)

Recognition Features:

● Very long, low profile pressure hull.
● Hull steeply sloped at the forward end with a long shallow slope down to the rudder aft.
● Comparatively small, slim fin sited well forward with vertical leading and after edges. After end of fin is tapered.
● Long, slender fin-mounted diving planes at mid-height.
● Note – The size of Trident submarines is dictated primarily by the 24 vertically launched Trident missiles and the larger reactor plant.

Displacement surfaced, tons: 16,600.0
Displacement dived, tons: 18,750.0
Length, feet (metres): 560.0 (170.7)
Beam, feet (metres): 42.0 (12.8)
Draught, feet (metres): 36.4 (11.1)
Speed, knots: 20+ dived

Missiles:

SLBM – Lockheed Trident I (C4) (726-733).
Lockheed Trident II (D5) (734 onwards).

Torpedoes: 4 – 21 in *(533 mm)* Mk 68 bow tubes. Gould Mk 48.
Decoys: 8 launchers for Emerson Electric Mk 2; torpedo decoy.
Radars:
Surface search/navigation/fire control – BPS 15A.
Sonars: IBM BQQ 6.
Raytheon BQS 13; spherical array for BQQ 6.
Ametek BQS 15.
Western Electric BQR 15 (with BQQ 9 signal processor). Raytheon BQR 19.

Ohio Class

WEST VIRGINIA

Giorgio Arra